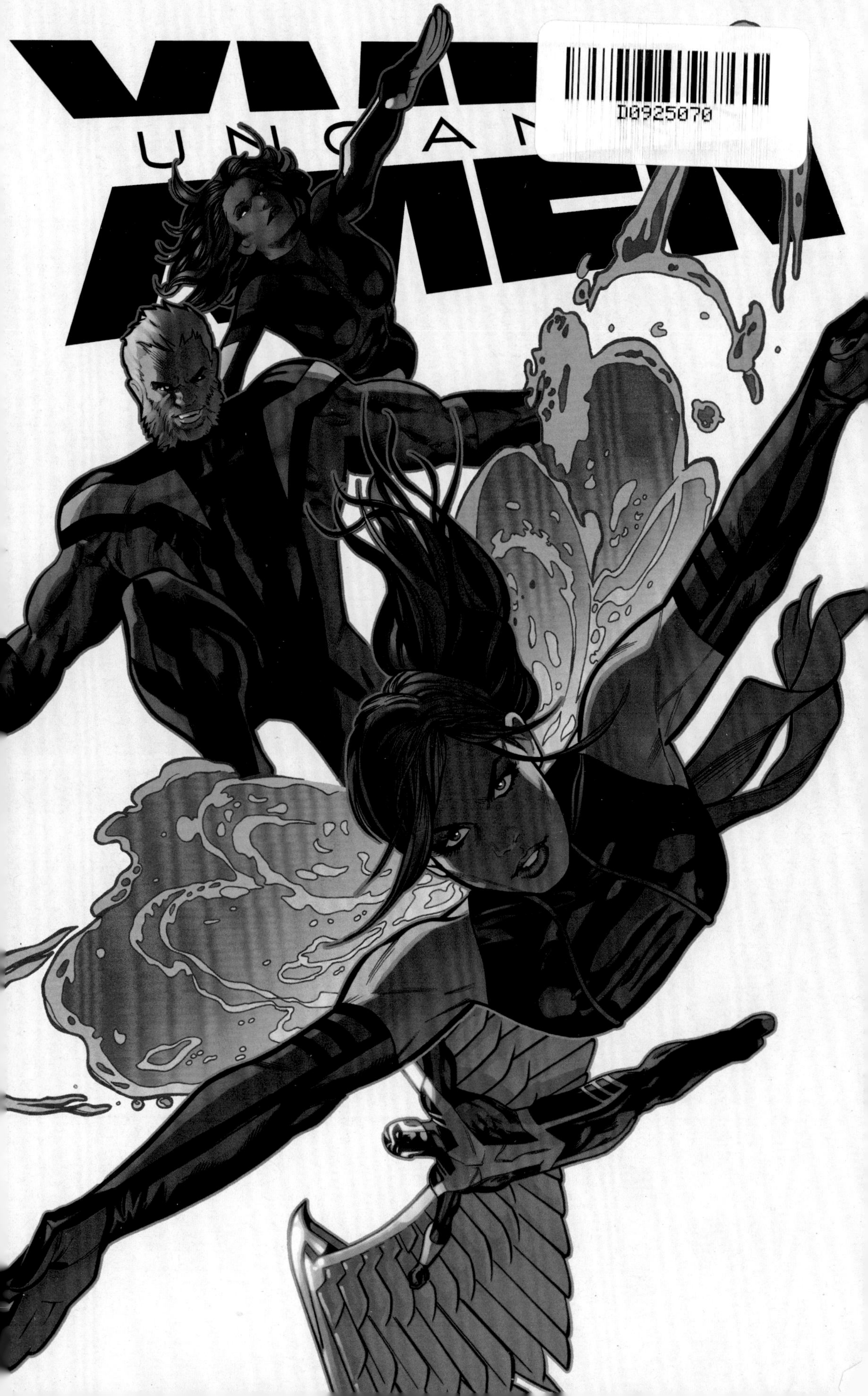

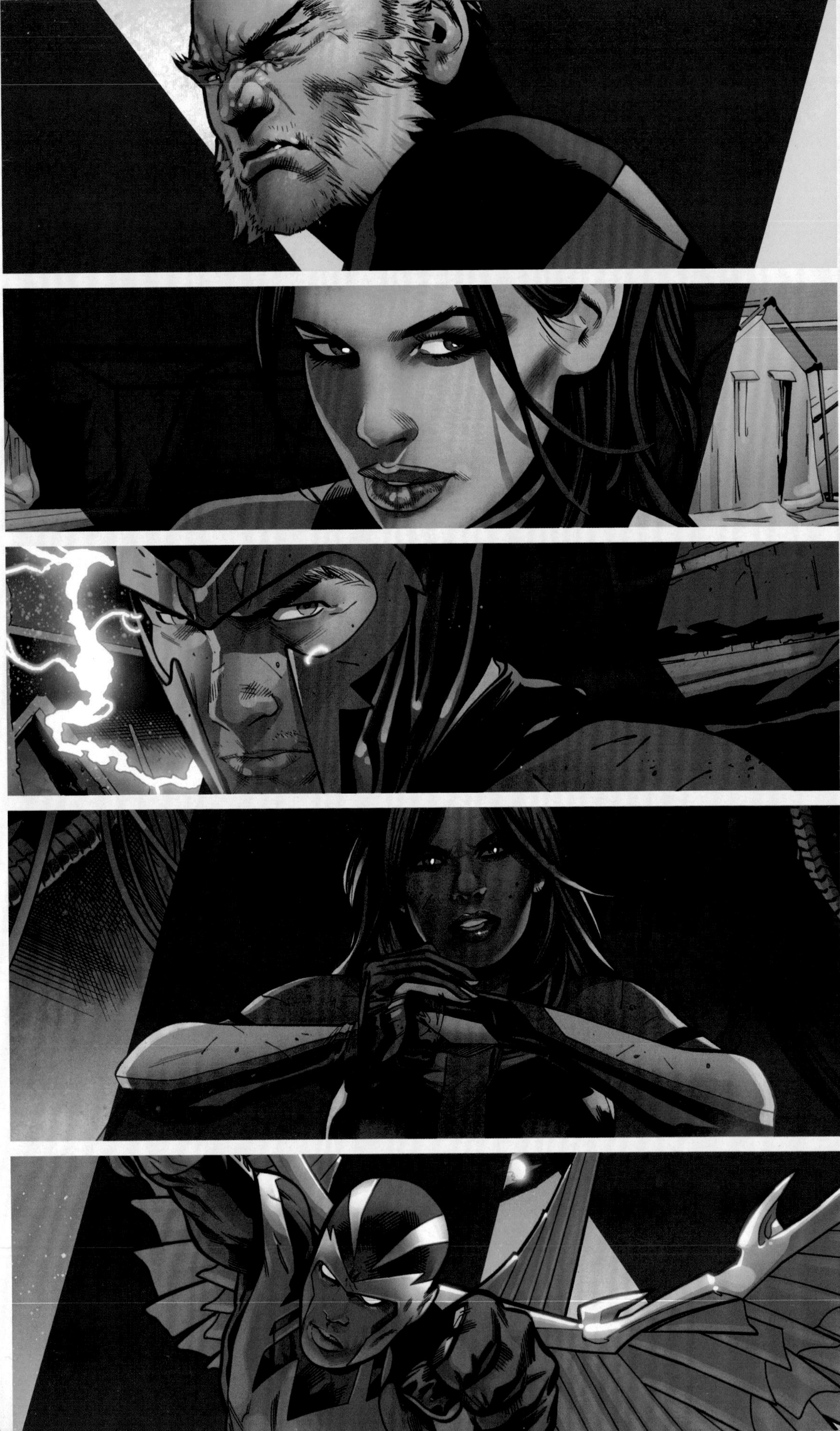

...TED A WORLD THAT HATES AND FEARS
...TIMENT REACHES A FEVER PITCH, THE
...ND THEMSELVES NOT JUST FIGHTING
...R LIVES. AS THE SITUATION BECOMES
...ECOMES EVIDENT: BIGGER THREATS
REQUIRE MORE THREATENING X-MEN...

UNCANNY X-MEN

SURVIVAL OF THE FITTEST

CULLEN BUNN
WRITER

GREG LAND
PENCILER

JAY LEISTEN
INKER

NOLAN WOODARD
COLORIST

VC'S JOE CARAMAGNA
LETTERER

GREG LAND, JAY LEISTEN & NOLAN WOODARD
COVER ART

CHRISTINA HARRINGTON
ASSISTANT EDITOR

DANIEL KETCHUM
EDITOR

MARK PANICCIA
X-MEN GROUP EDITOR

X-MEN CREATED BY *STAN LEE & JACK KIRBY*

COLLECTION EDITOR: ***JENNIFER GRÜNWALD***
ASSOCIATE EDITOR: ***SARAH BRUNSTAD***
ASSOCIATE MANAGING EDITOR: ***ALEX STARBUCK***
EDITOR, SPECIAL PROJECTS: ***MARK D. BEAZLEY***
VP, PRODUCTION & SPECIAL PROJECTS: ***JEFF YOUNGQUIST***
SVP PRINT, SALES & MARKETING: ***DAVID GABRIEL***
BOOK DESIGNER: ***JAY BOWEN***

EDITOR IN CHIEF: ***AXEL ALONSO***
CHIEF CREATIVE OFFICER: ***JOE QUESADA***
PUBLISHER: ***DAN BUCKLEY***
EXECUTIVE PRODUCER: ***ALAN FINE***

NCANNY X-MEN: SUPERIOR VOL. 1 — SURVIVAL OF THE FITTEST. Contains material originally published in magazine form as UNCANNY X-MEN #1-5. First printing 2016. ISBN# 978-0-7851-9607-5. Published by ARVEL WORLDWIDE, INC., a subsidiary of MARVEL ENTERTAINMENT, LLC. OFFICE OF PUBLICATION: 135 West 50th Street, New York, NY 10020. **Printed in Canada.** ALAN FINE, resident, Marvel Entertainment; DAN BUCKLEY, President, TV, Publishing & Brand Management; JOE QUESADA, Chief Creative Officer; TOM BREVOORT, SVP of Publishing; DAVID BOGART, SVP of Business Affairs & perations, Publishing & Partnership; C.B. CEBULSKI, VP of Brand Management & Development, Asia; DAVID GABRIEL, SVP of Sales & Marketing, Publishing; JEFF YOUNGQUIST, VP of Production & Special Projects; DAN ARR, Executive Director of Publishing Technology; ALEX MORALES, Director of Publishing Operations; SUSAN CRESPI, Production Manager; STAN LEE, Chairman Emeritus. For information regarding advertising in Marvel omics or on Marvel.com, please contact Vit DeBellis, Integrated Sales Manager, at vdebellis@marvel.com. For Marvel subscription inquiries, please call 888-511-5480. **Manufactured between 5/6/2016 and 6/13/2016 y SOLISCO PRINTERS, SCOTT, QC, CANADA.**

0987654321

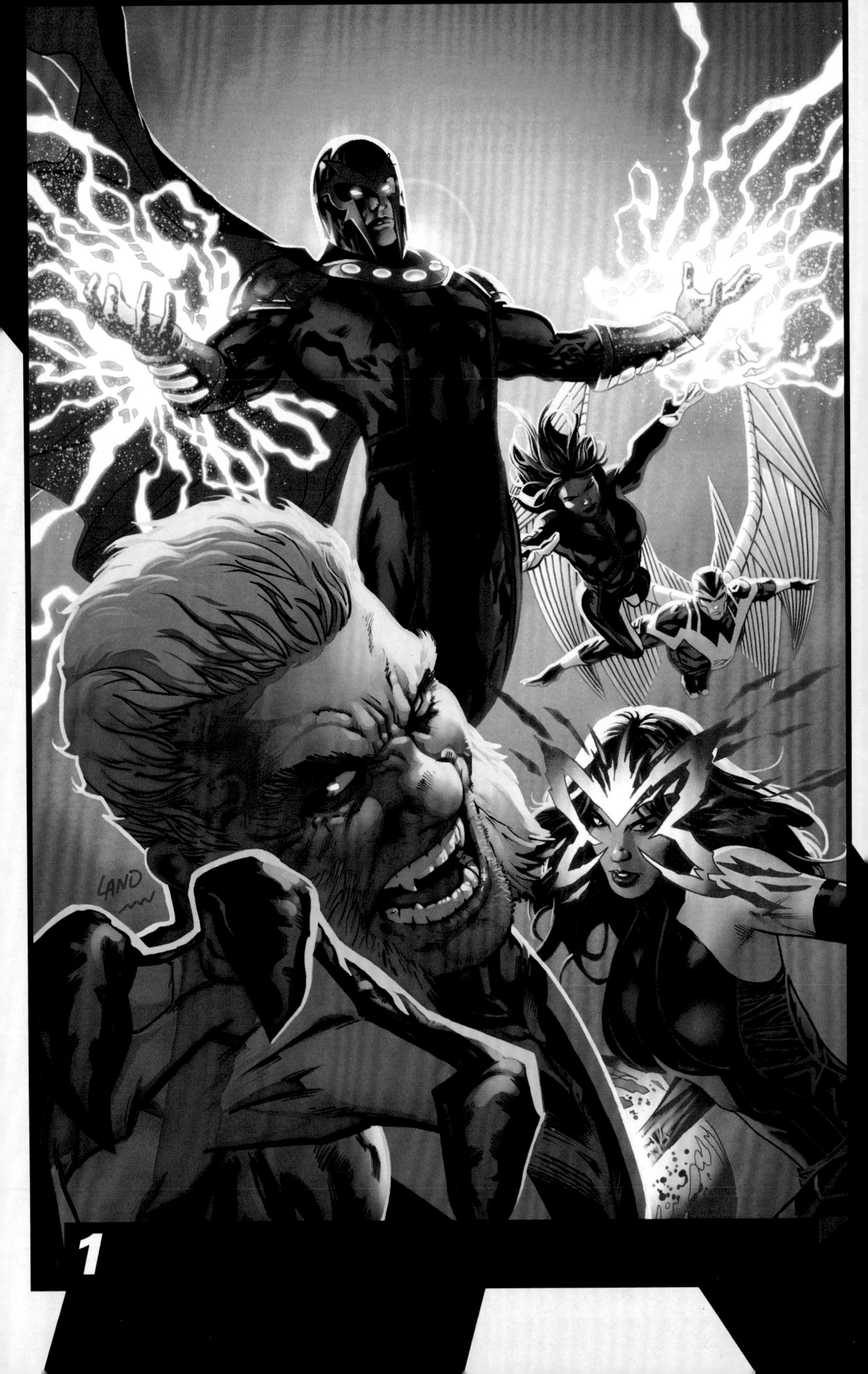
LAND

1

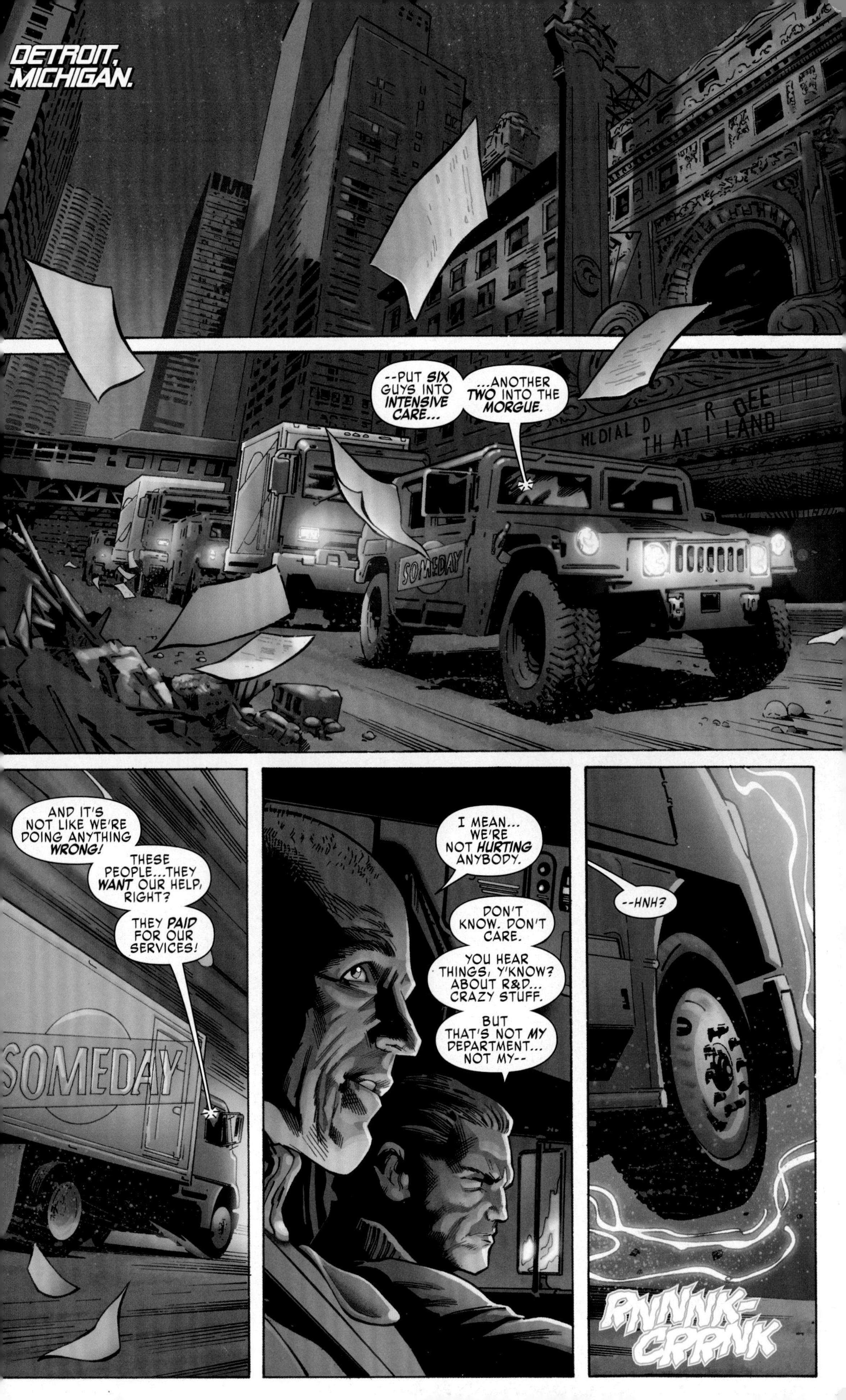

DETROIT, MICHIGAN.
--PUT SIX GUYS INTO INTENSIVE CARE...
...ANOTHER TWO INTO THE MORGUE.
SOMEDAY
AND IT'S NOT LIKE WE'RE DOING ANYTHING WRONG!
THESE PEOPLE...THEY WANT OUR HELP, RIGHT?
THEY PAID FOR OUR SERVICES!
SOMEDAY
I MEAN... WE'RE NOT HURTING ANYBODY.
DON'T KNOW. DON'T CARE.
YOU HEAR THINGS, Y'KNOW? ABOUT R&D... CRAZY STUFF.
BUT THAT'S NOT MY DEPARTMENT... NOT MY--
--HNH?
RNNNK-CRRNK

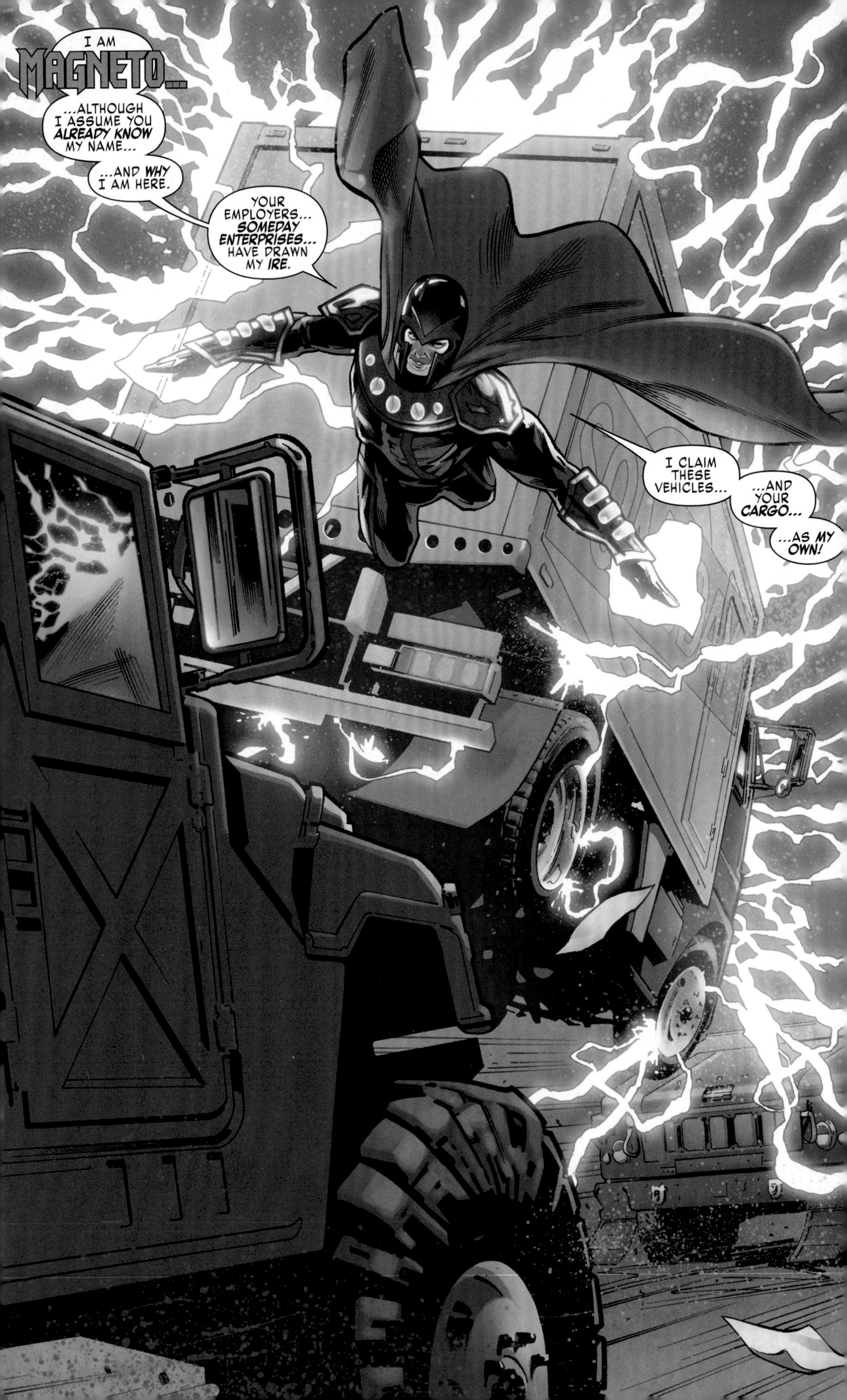
I AM MAGNETO...
...ALTHOUGH I ASSUME YOU ALREADY KNOW MY NAME...
...AND WHY I AM HERE.
YOUR EMPLOYERS... SOMEDAY ENTERPRISES... HAVE DRAWN MY IRE.
I CLAIM THESE VEHICLES...
...AND YOUR CARGO...
...AS MY OWN!

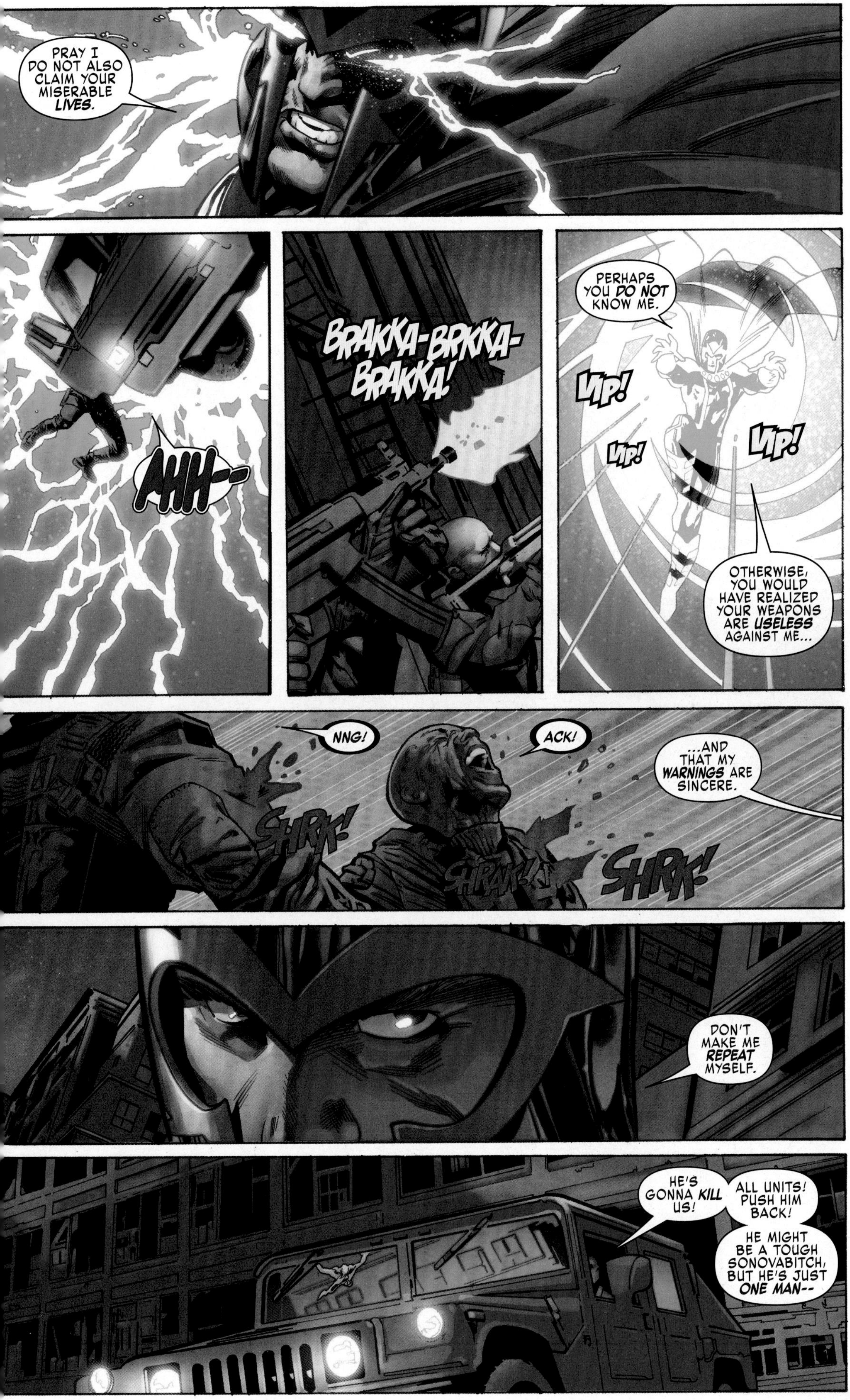
PRAY I DO NOT ALSO CLAIM YOUR MISERABLE LIVES.
AHH--
BRAKKA-BRKKA-BRAKKA!
PERHAPS YOU DO NOT KNOW ME.
VIP!
VIP!
VIP!
OTHERWISE, YOU WOULD HAVE REALIZED YOUR WEAPONS ARE USELESS AGAINST ME...
NNG!
ACK!
...AND THAT MY WARNINGS ARE SINCERE.
SHRK!
SHRAK!
SHRK!
DON'T MAKE ME REPEAT MYSELF.
HE'S GONNA KILL US!
ALL UNITS! PUSH HIM BACK!
HE MIGHT BE A TOUGH SONOVABITCH, BUT HE'S JUST ONE MAN--

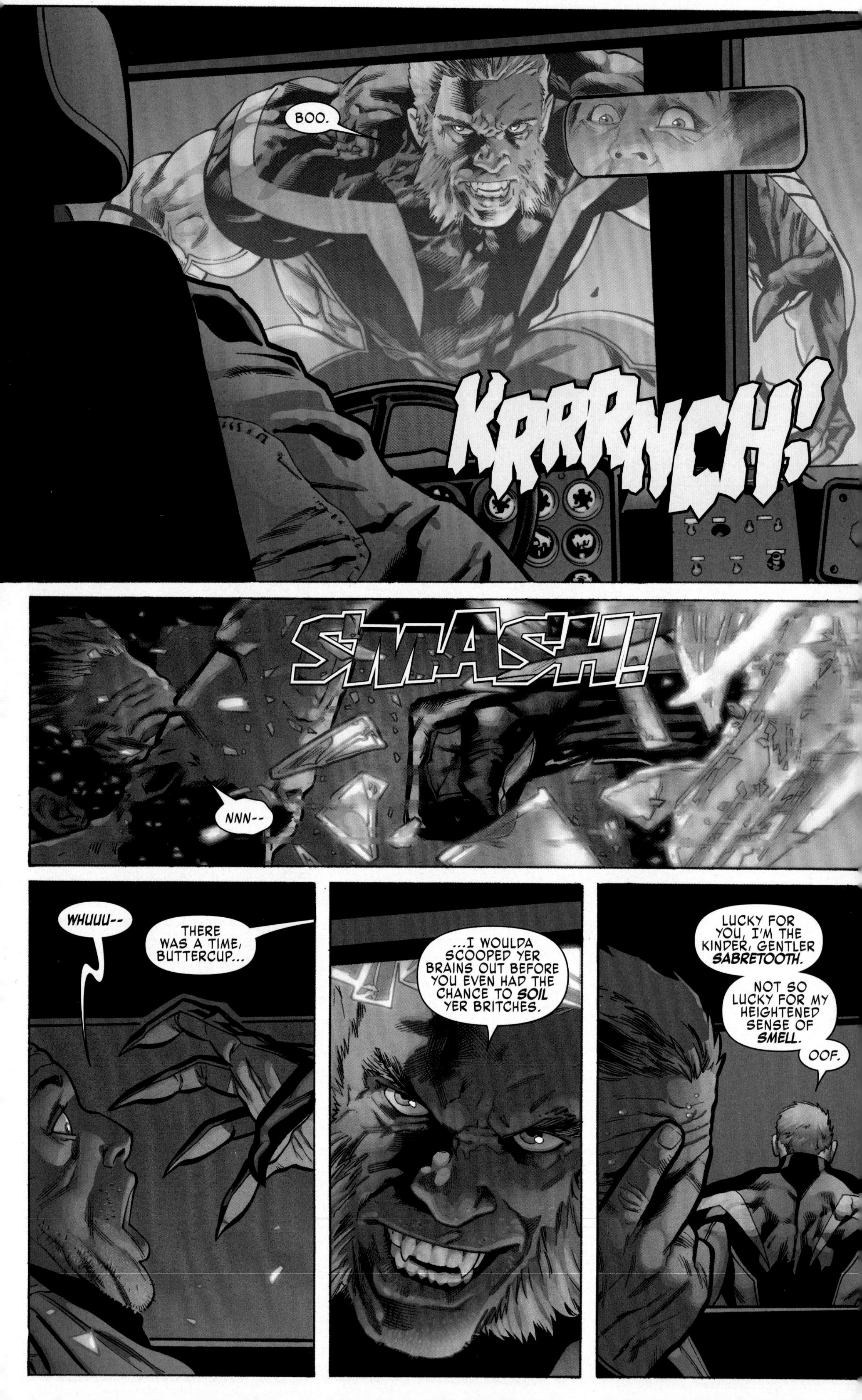
BOO.
KRRRNCH!
SMASH!
NNN--
WHUUU--
THERE WAS A TIME, BUTTERCUP...
...I WOULDA SCOOPED YER BRAINS OUT BEFORE YOU EVEN HAD THE CHANCE TO SOIL YER BRITCHES.
LUCKY FOR YOU, I'M THE KINDER, GENTLER SABRETOOTH.
NOT SO LUCKY FOR MY HEIGHTENED SENSE OF SMELL.
OOF.

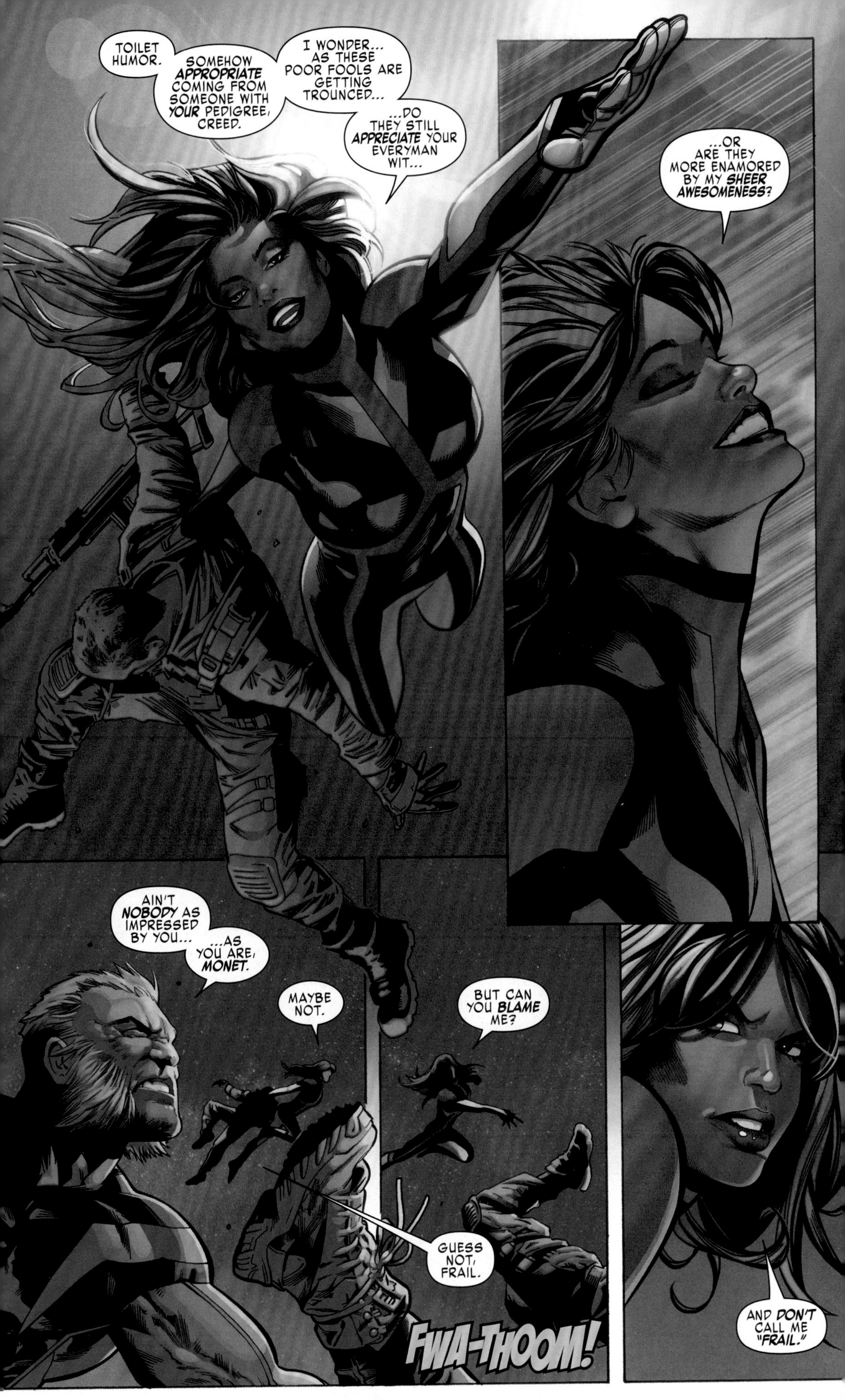
TOILET HUMOR.
SOMEHOW APPROPRIATE COMING FROM SOMEONE WITH YOUR PEDIGREE, CREED.
I WONDER... AS THESE POOR FOOLS ARE GETTING TROUNCED...
...DO THEY STILL APPRECIATE YOUR EVERYMAN WIT...
...OR ARE THEY MORE ENAMORED BY MY SHEER AWESOMENESS?
AIN'T NOBODY AS IMPRESSED BY YOU...
...AS YOU ARE, MONET.
MAYBE NOT.
BUT CAN YOU BLAME ME?
GUESS NOT, FRAIL.
FWA-THOOM!
AND DON'T CALL ME "FRAIL."

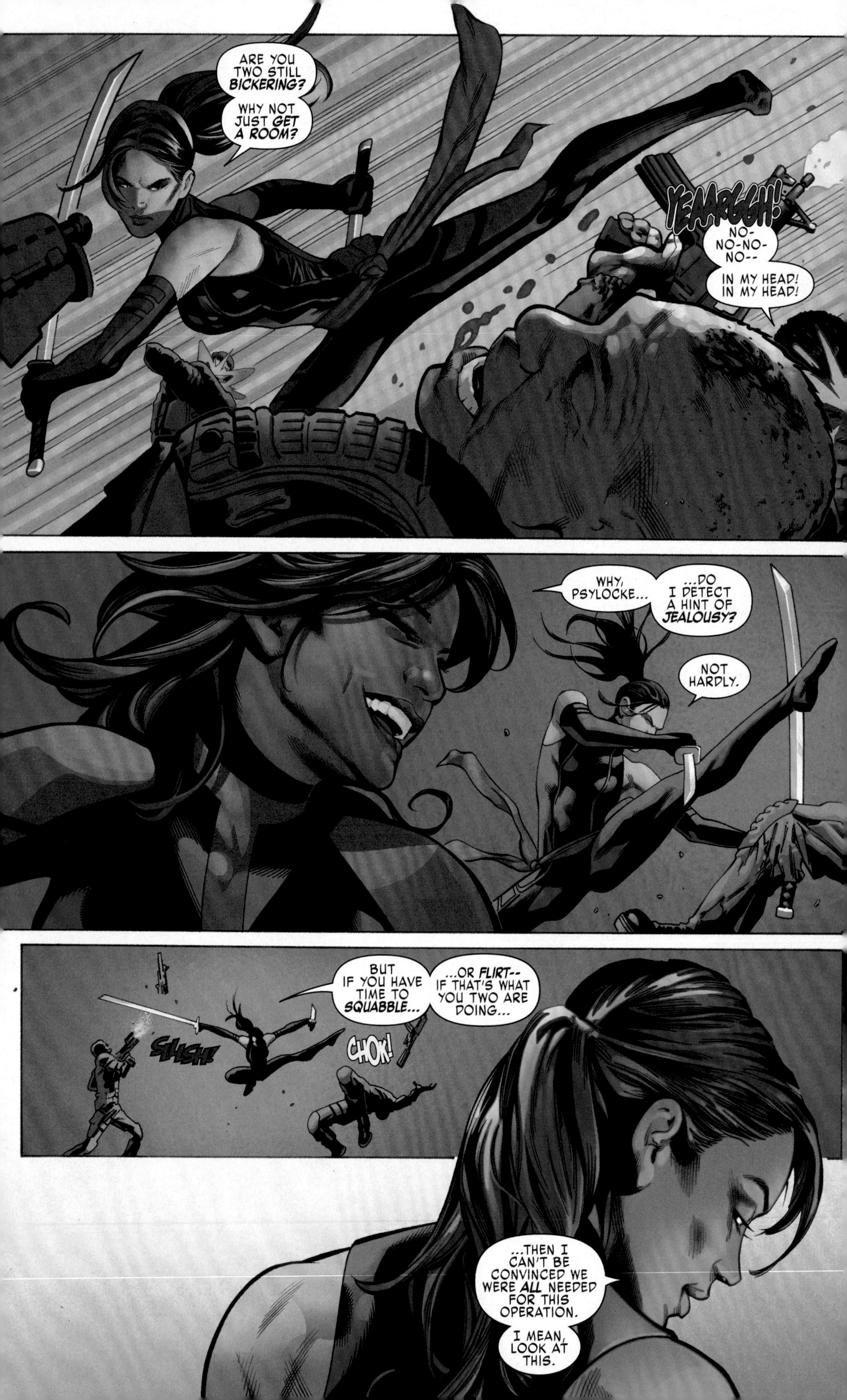
ARE YOU TWO STILL BICKERING?
WHY NOT JUST GET A ROOM?
YEAARGGH!
NO- NO-NO-NO--
IN MY HEAD! IN MY HEAD!
WHY, PSYLOCKE...
...DO I DETECT A HINT OF JEALOUSY?
NOT HARDLY.
BUT IF YOU HAVE TIME TO SQUABBLE...
...OR FLIRT-- IF THAT'S WHAT YOU TWO ARE DOING...
SHUSH!
CHOK!
...THEN I CAN'T BE CONVINCED WE WERE ALL NEEDED FOR THIS OPERATION.
I MEAN, LOOK AT THIS.

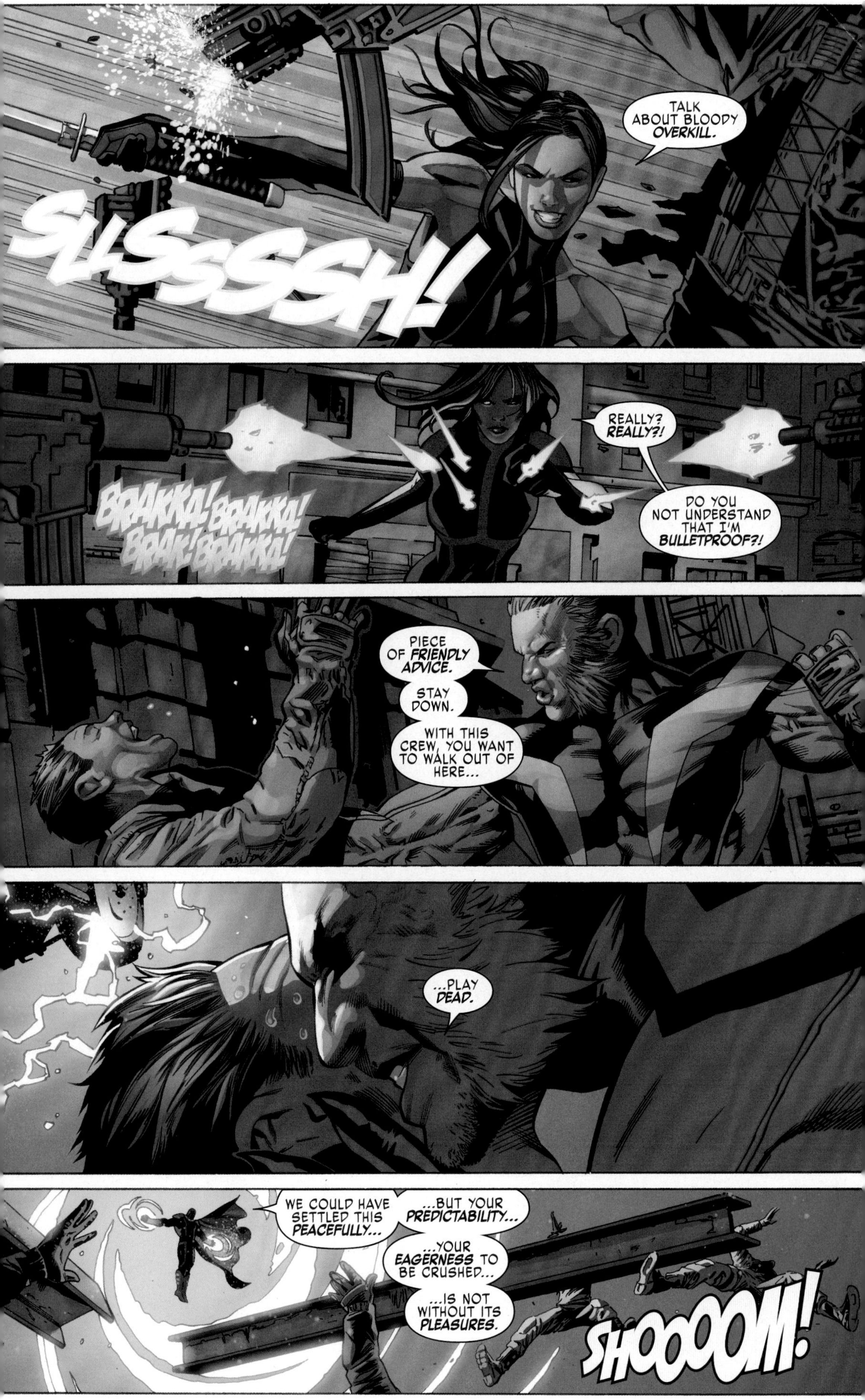
TALK ABOUT BLOODY OVERKILL.
SLISSSSH!
BRAKKA! BRAKKA! BRAK! BRAKKA!
REALLY? REALLY?!
DO YOU NOT UNDERSTAND THAT I'M BULLETPROOF?!
PIECE OF FRIENDLY ADVICE.
STAY DOWN.
WITH THIS CREW, YOU WANT TO WALK OUT OF HERE...
...PLAY DEAD.
WE COULD HAVE SETTLED THIS PEACEFULLY...
...BUT YOUR PREDICTABILITY...
...YOUR EAGERNESS TO BE CRUSHED...
...IS NOT WITHOUT ITS PLEASURES.
SHOOOOM!

KR- WHOOOM!

...PUSHED MYSELF TOO HARD...

...MY POWERS...

...OVERTAXED...

NNN

DEATH...

...STILL PULLING AT ME...

...TRYING TO DRAG ME BACK.

GO, MAN! *GO!* GET OUT OF HERE!

RUN 'EM DOWN IF YOU HAVE TO!

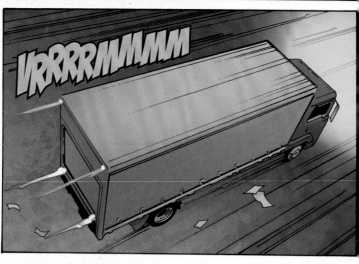

VRRRRMMMM

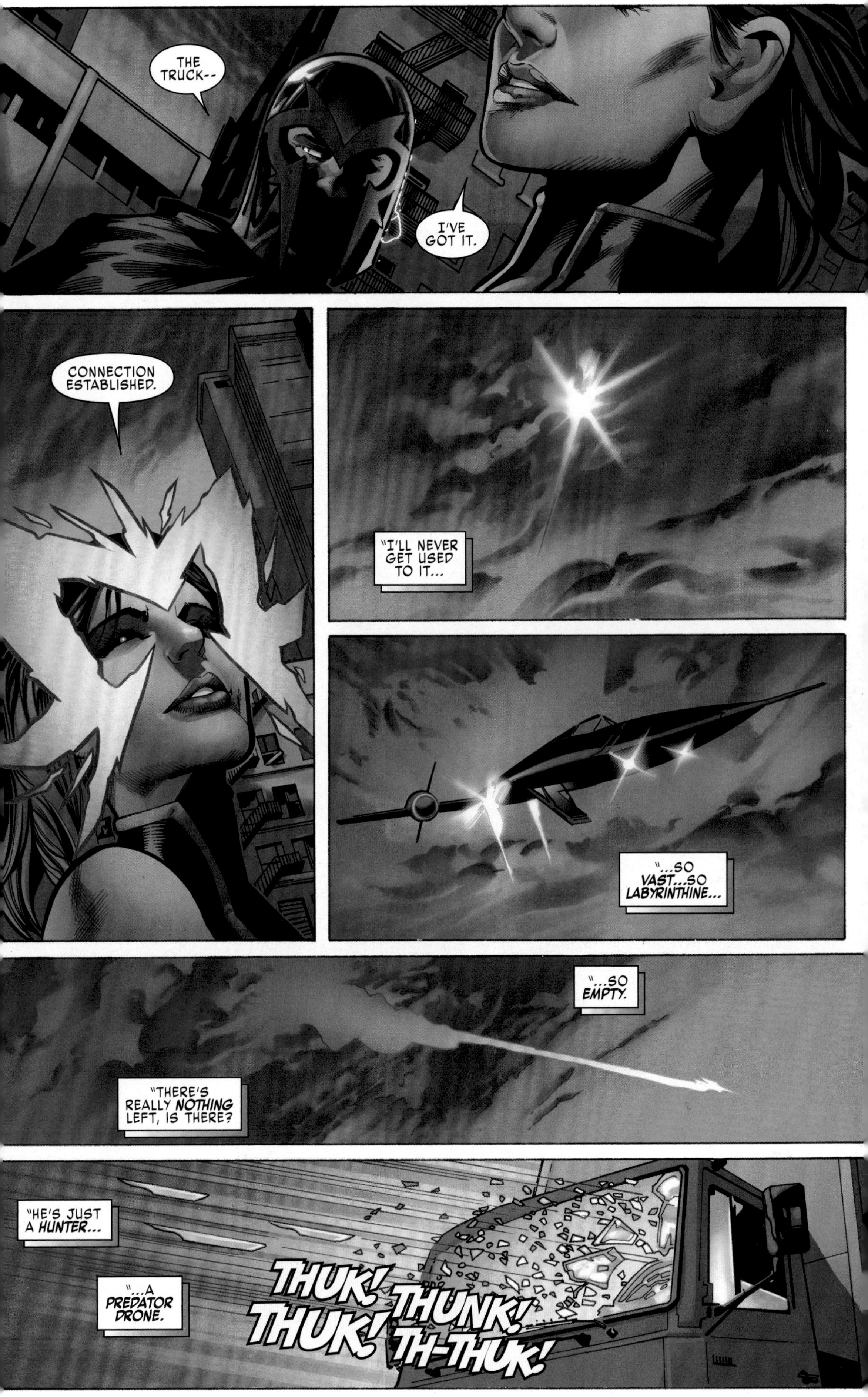
THE TRUCK--
I'VE GOT IT.
CONNECTION ESTABLISHED.
"I'LL NEVER GET USED TO IT...
"...SO VAST...SO LABYRINTHINE...
"...SO EMPTY.
"THERE'S REALLY NOTHING LEFT, IS THERE?
"HE'S JUST A HUNTER...
"...A PREDATOR DRONE.
THUK! THUK! THUNK! TH-THUK!

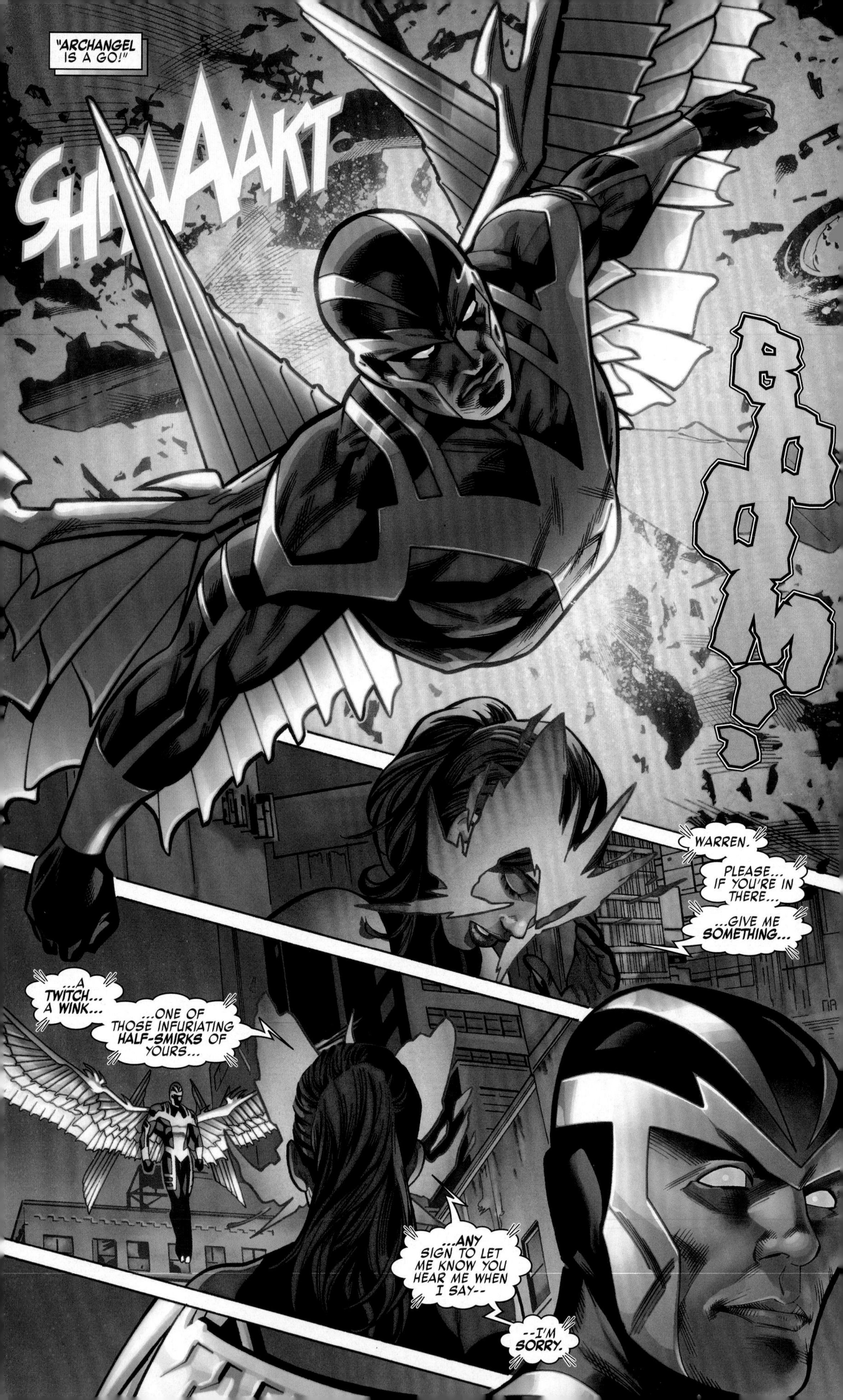
"ARCHANGEL IS A GO!"
SHRAAAKT
BOOM
WARREN.
PLEASE... IF YOU'RE IN THERE...
...GIVE ME SOMETHING...
...A TWITCH... A WINK...
...ONE OF THOSE INFURIATING HALF-SMIRKS OF YOURS...
...ANY SIGN TO LET ME KNOW YOU HEAR ME WHEN I SAY--
--I'M SORRY.

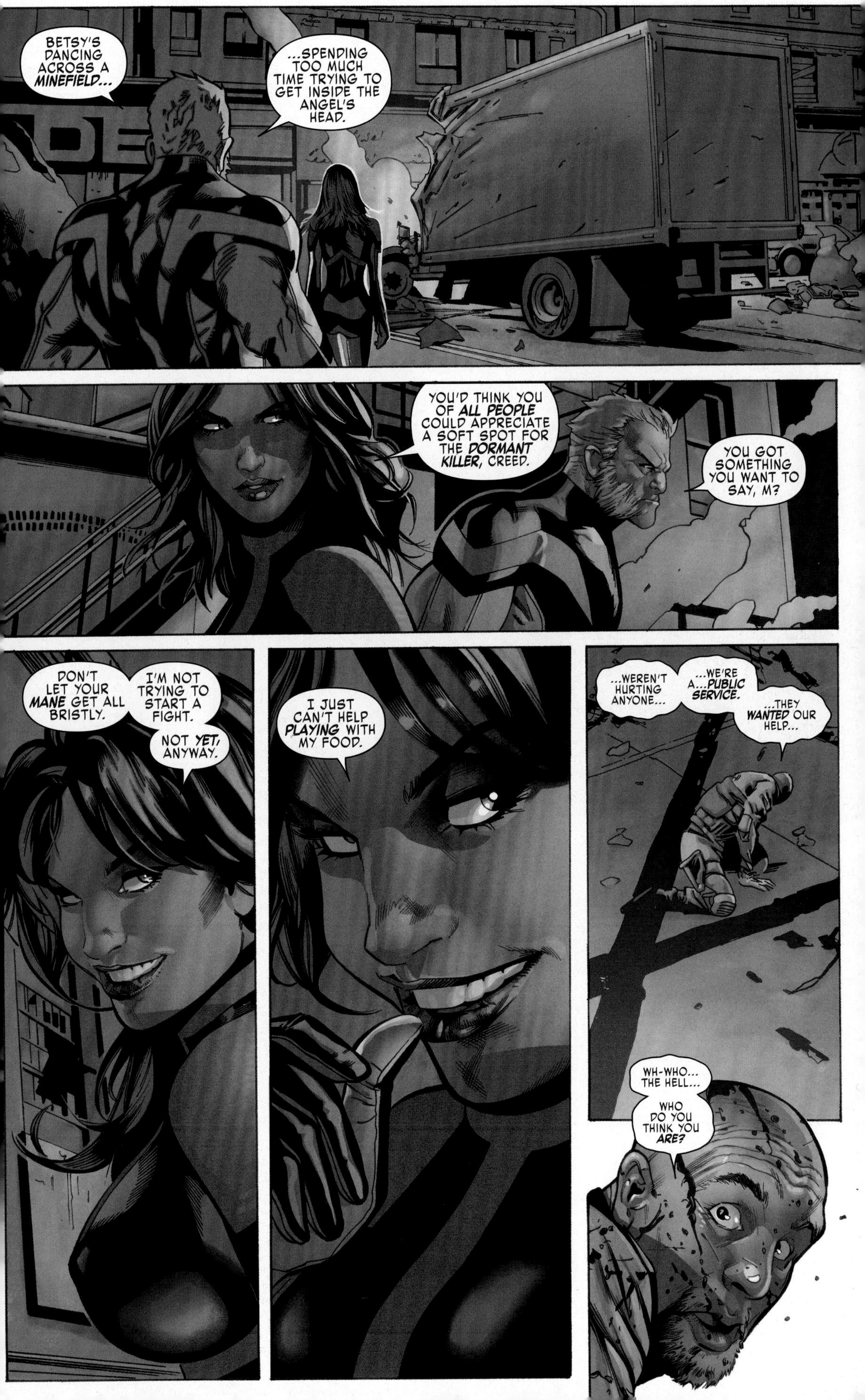

BETSY'S DANCING ACROSS A MINEFIELD...
...SPENDING TOO MUCH TIME TRYING TO GET INSIDE THE ANGEL'S HEAD.
YOU'D THINK YOU OF ALL PEOPLE COULD APPRECIATE A SOFT SPOT FOR THE DORMANT KILLER, CREED.
YOU GOT SOMETHING YOU WANT TO SAY, M?
DON'T LET YOUR MANE GET ALL BRISTLY.
I'M NOT TRYING TO START A FIGHT.
NOT YET, ANYWAY.
I JUST CAN'T HELP PLAYING WITH MY FOOD.
...WEREN'T HURTING ANYONE...
...WE'RE A...PUBLIC SERVICE.
...THEY WANTED OUR HELP...
WH-WHO... THE HELL...
WHO DO YOU THINK YOU ARE?

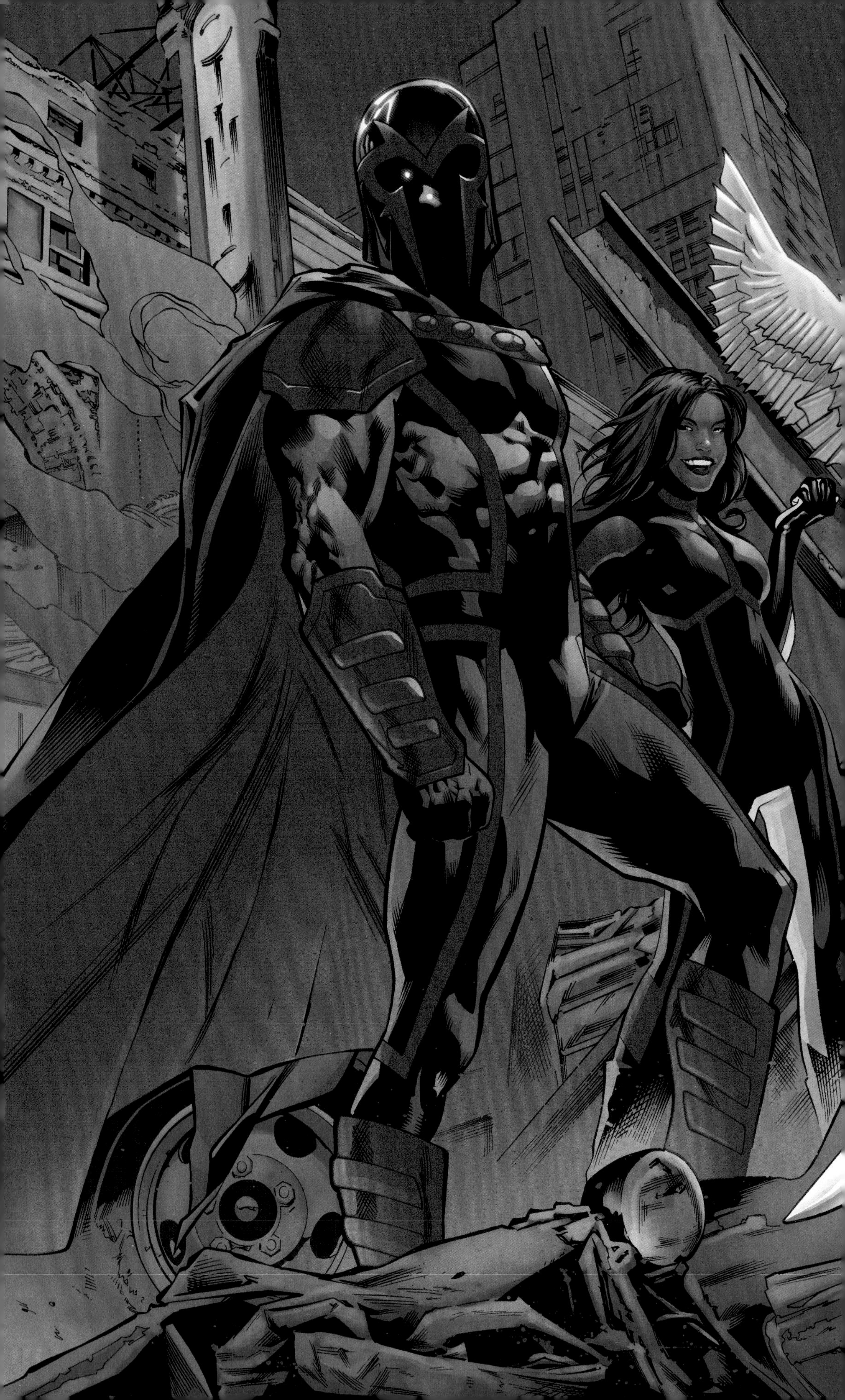

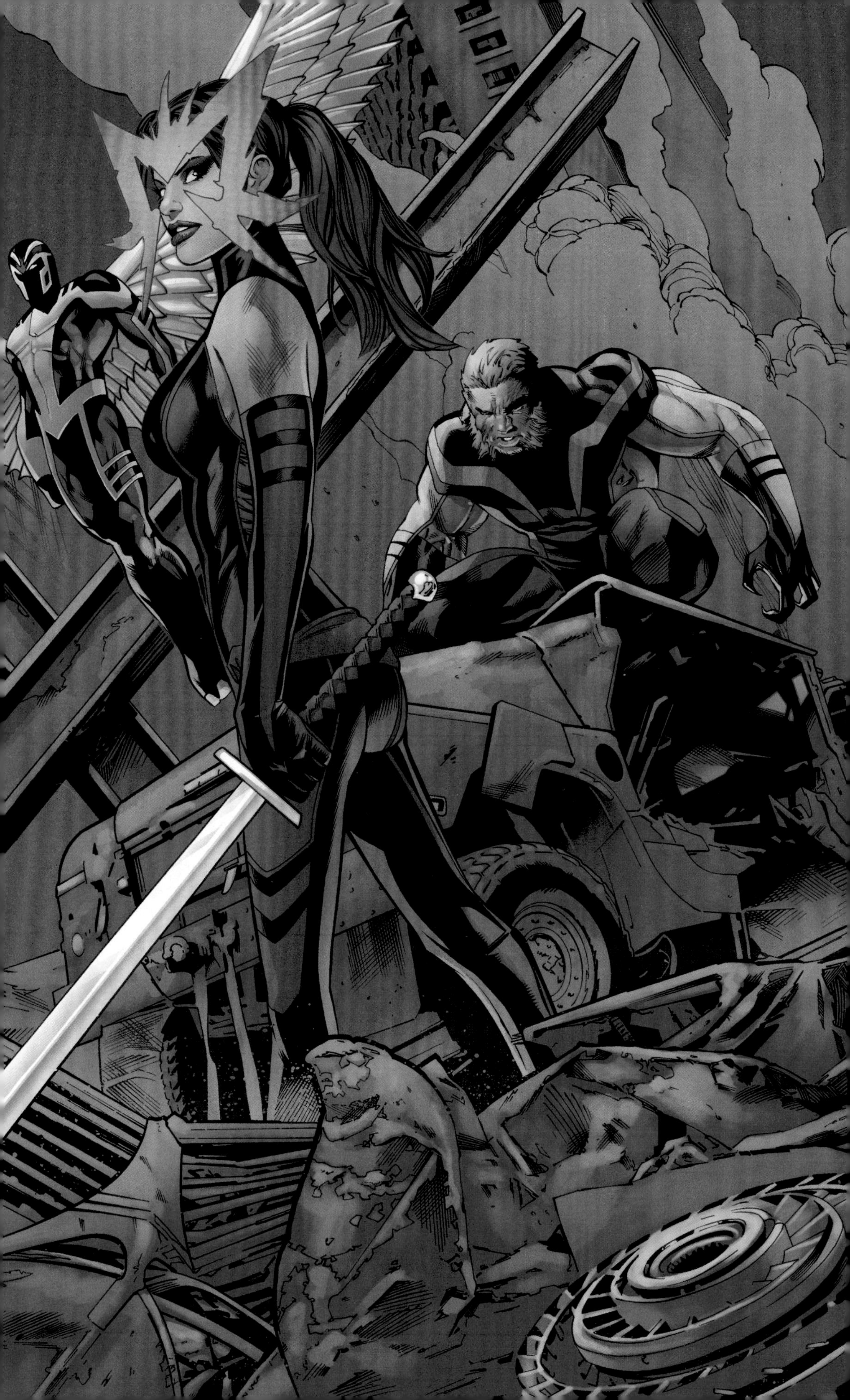

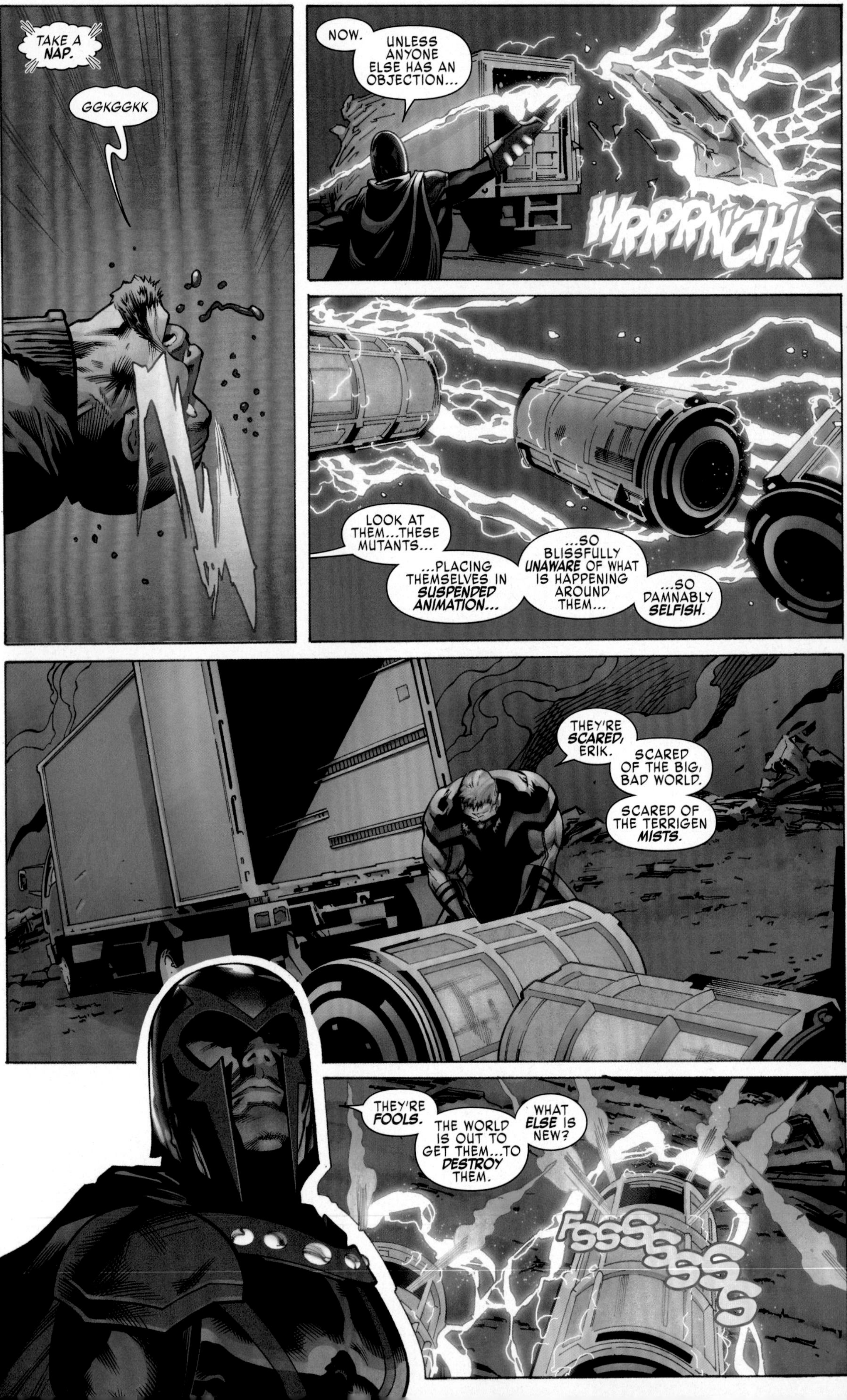
TAKE A NAP.
GGKGGKK
NOW.
UNLESS ANYONE ELSE HAS AN OBJECTION...
WRRRNCH!
LOOK AT THEM...THESE MUTANTS...
...PLACING THEMSELVES IN SUSPENDED ANIMATION...
...SO BLISSFULLY UNAWARE OF WHAT IS HAPPENING AROUND THEM...
...SO DAMNABLY SELFISH.
THEY'RE SCARED, ERIK.
SCARED OF THE BIG, BAD WORLD.
SCARED OF THE TERRIGEN MISTS.
THEY'RE FOOLS.
THE WORLD IS OUT TO GET THEM...TO DESTROY THEM.
WHAT ELSE IS NEW?
FSSSSSSS

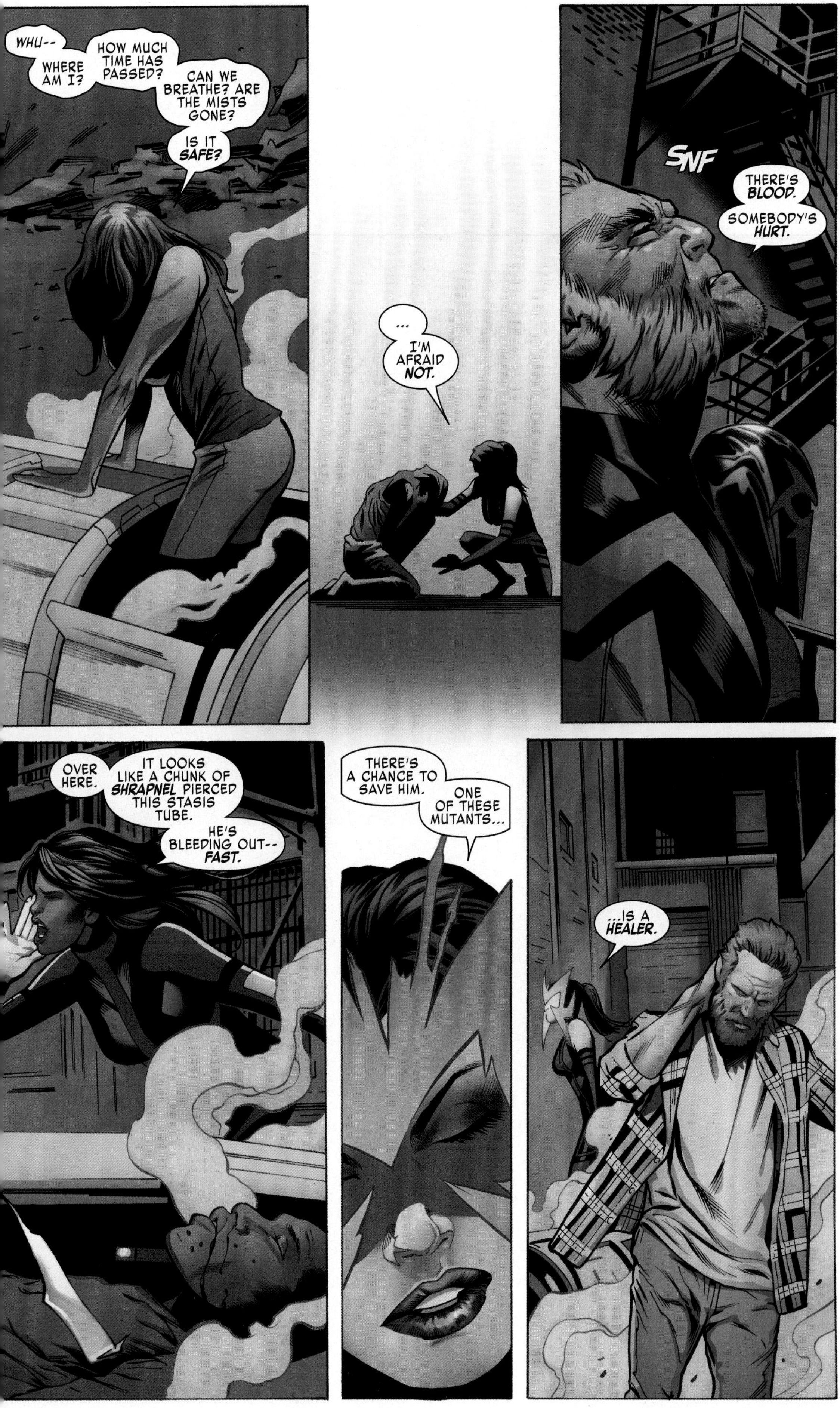
WHU--
WHERE AM I?
HOW MUCH TIME HAS PASSED?
CAN WE BREATHE? ARE THE MISTS GONE?
IS IT SAFE?
...
I'M AFRAID NOT.
SNF
THERE'S BLOOD.
SOMEBODY'S HURT.
OVER HERE.
IT LOOKS LIKE A CHUNK OF SHRAPNEL PIERCED THIS STASIS TUBE.
HE'S BLEEDING OUT-- FAST.
THERE'S A CHANCE TO SAVE HIM.
ONE OF THESE MUTANTS...
...IS A HEALER.

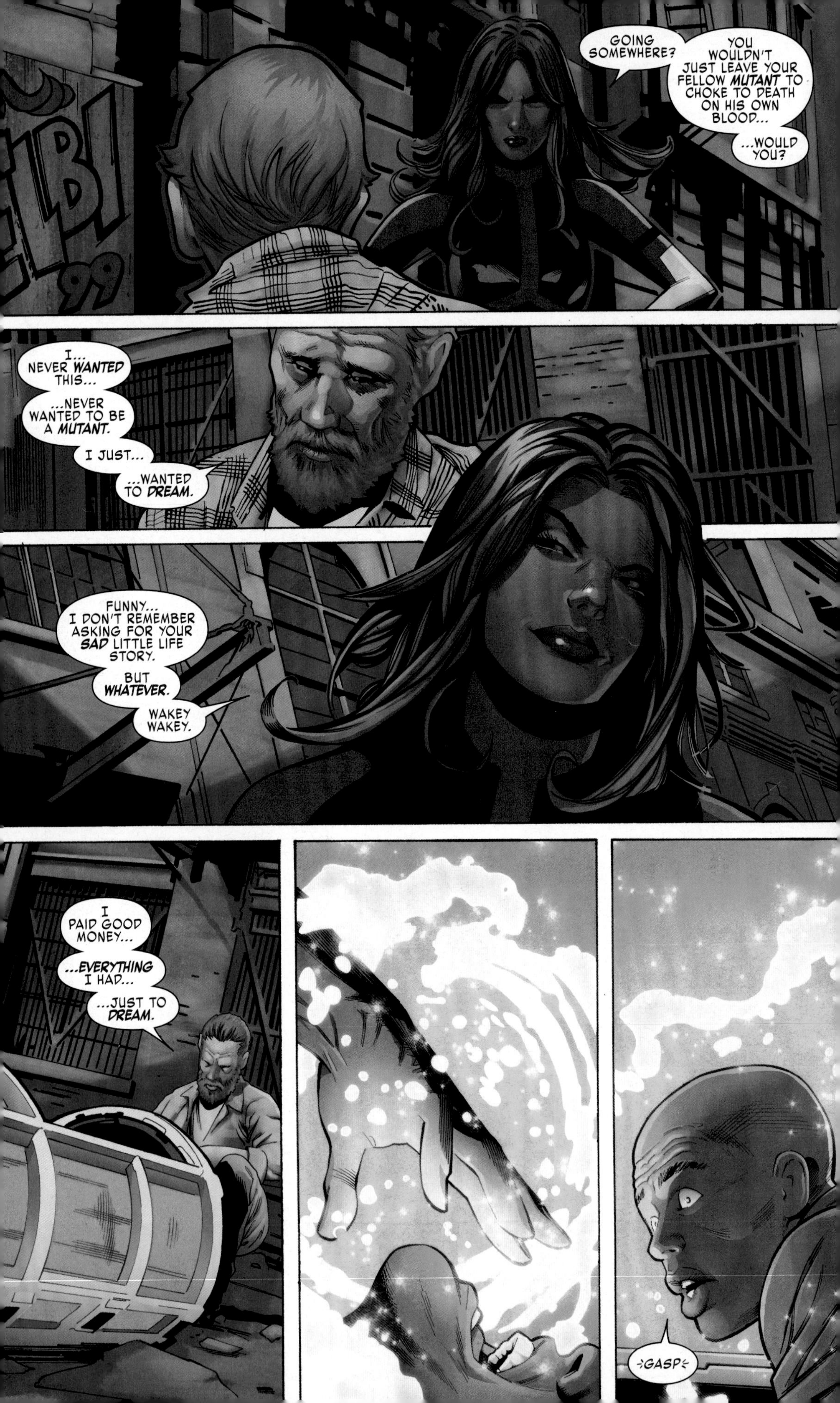
GOING SOMEWHERE?
YOU WOULDN'T JUST LEAVE YOUR FELLOW MUTANT TO CHOKE TO DEATH ON HIS OWN BLOOD...
...WOULD YOU?
I... NEVER WANTED THIS...
...NEVER WANTED TO BE A MUTANT.
I JUST...
...WANTED TO DREAM.
FUNNY... I DON'T REMEMBER ASKING FOR YOUR SAD LITTLE LIFE STORY.
BUT WHATEVER.
WAKEY WAKEY.
I PAID GOOD MONEY...
...EVERYTHING I HAD...
...JUST TO DREAM.
GASP

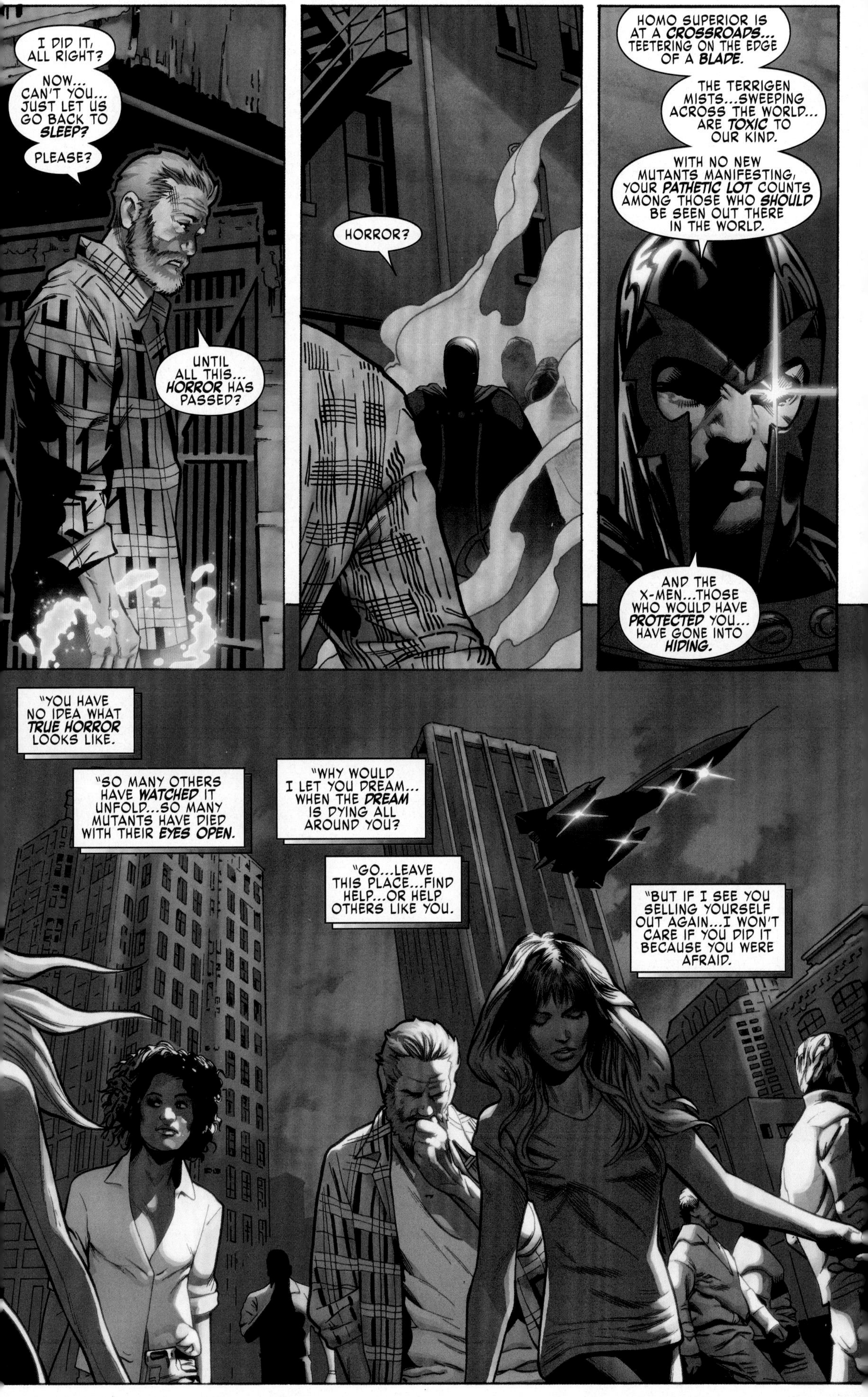
I DID IT, ALL RIGHT?
NOW... CAN'T YOU... JUST LET US GO BACK TO SLEEP?
PLEASE?
UNTIL ALL THIS... HORROR HAS PASSED?
HORROR?
HOMO SUPERIOR IS AT A CROSSROADS... TEETERING ON THE EDGE OF A BLADE.
THE TERRIGEN MISTS...SWEEPING ACROSS THE WORLD... ARE TOXIC TO OUR KIND.
WITH NO NEW MUTANTS MANIFESTING, YOUR PATHETIC LOT COUNTS AMONG THOSE WHO SHOULD BE SEEN OUT THERE IN THE WORLD.
AND THE X-MEN...THOSE WHO WOULD HAVE PROTECTED YOU... HAVE GONE INTO HIDING.
"YOU HAVE NO IDEA WHAT TRUE HORROR LOOKS LIKE.
"SO MANY OTHERS HAVE WATCHED IT UNFOLD...SO MANY MUTANTS HAVE DIED WITH THEIR EYES OPEN.
"WHY WOULD I LET YOU DREAM... WHEN THE DREAM IS DYING ALL AROUND YOU?
"GO...LEAVE THIS PLACE...FIND HELP...OR HELP OTHERS LIKE YOU.
"BUT IF I SEE YOU SELLING YOURSELF OUT AGAIN...I WON'T CARE IF YOU DID IT BECAUSE YOU WERE AFRAID.

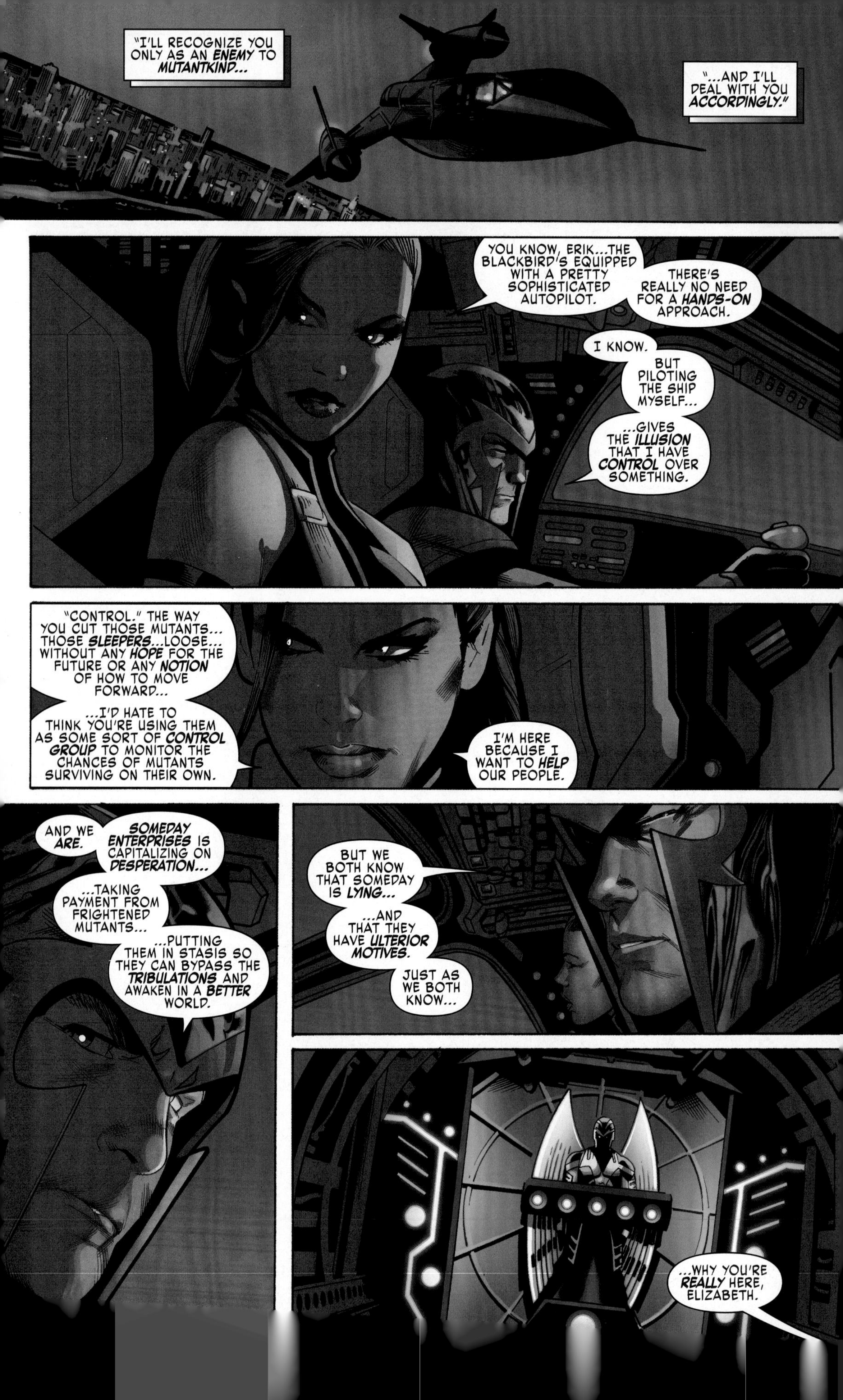
"I'LL RECOGNIZE YOU ONLY AS AN ENEMY TO MUTANTKIND...
"...AND I'LL DEAL WITH YOU ACCORDINGLY."
YOU KNOW, ERIK...THE BLACKBIRD'S EQUIPPED WITH A PRETTY SOPHISTICATED AUTOPILOT.
THERE'S REALLY NO NEED FOR A HANDS-ON APPROACH.
I KNOW.
BUT PILOTING THE SHIP MYSELF...
...GIVES THE ILLUSION THAT I HAVE CONTROL OVER SOMETHING.
"CONTROL." THE WAY YOU CUT THOSE MUTANTS... THOSE SLEEPERS...LOOSE... WITHOUT ANY HOPE FOR THE FUTURE OR ANY NOTION OF HOW TO MOVE FORWARD...
...I'D HATE TO THINK YOU'RE USING THEM AS SOME SORT OF CONTROL GROUP TO MONITOR THE CHANCES OF MUTANTS SURVIVING ON THEIR OWN.
I'M HERE BECAUSE I WANT TO HELP OUR PEOPLE.
AND WE ARE.
SOMEDAY ENTERPRISES IS CAPITALIZING ON DESPERATION...
...TAKING PAYMENT FROM FRIGHTENED MUTANTS...
...PUTTING THEM IN STASIS SO THEY CAN BYPASS THE TRIBULATIONS AND AWAKEN IN A BETTER WORLD.
BUT WE BOTH KNOW THAT SOMEDAY IS LYING...
...AND THAT THEY HAVE ULTERIOR MOTIVES.
JUST AS WE BOTH KNOW...
...WHY YOU'RE REALLY HERE, ELIZABETH.

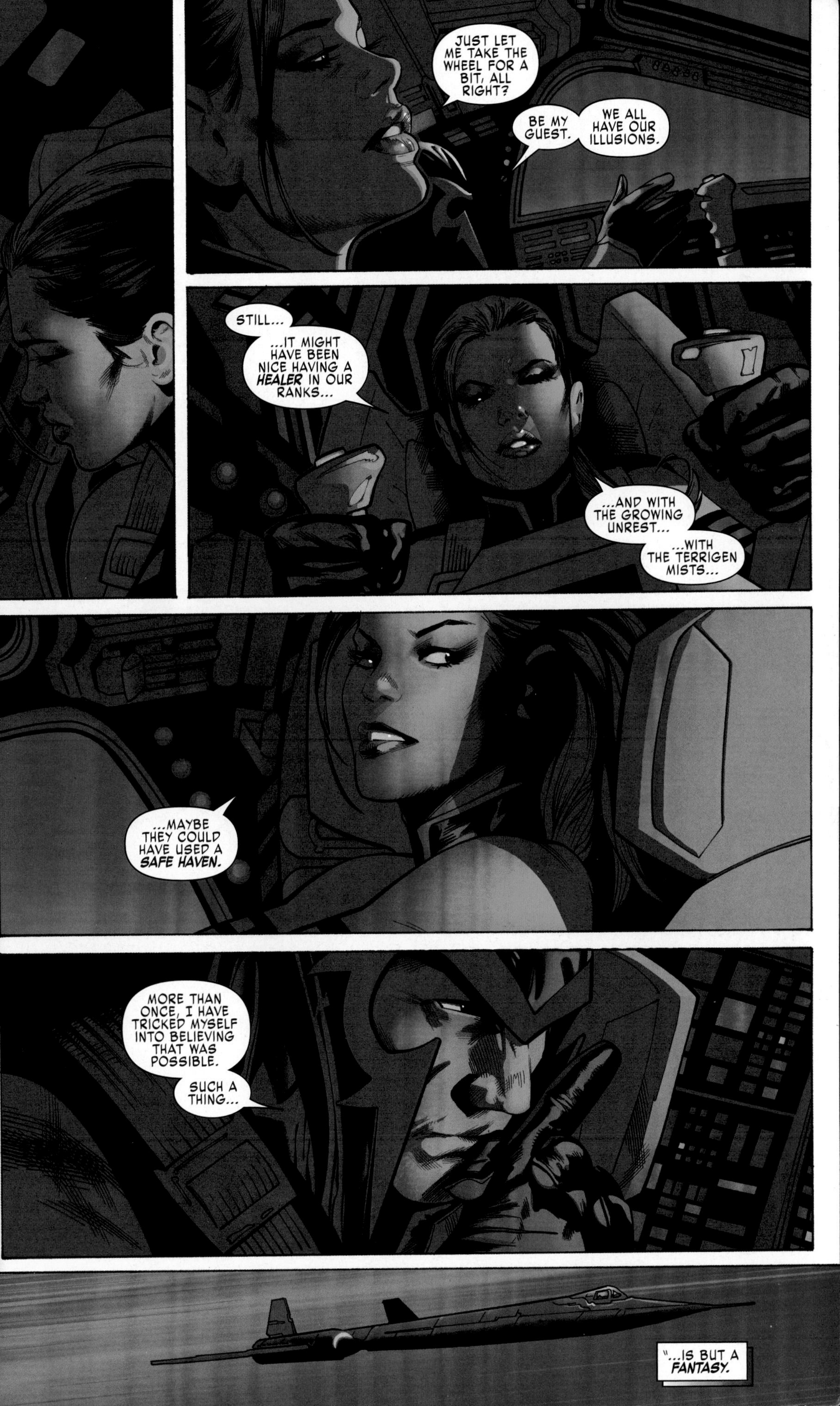

JUST LET ME TAKE THE WHEEL FOR A BIT, ALL RIGHT?
BE MY GUEST.
WE ALL HAVE OUR ILLUSIONS.
STILL...
...IT MIGHT HAVE BEEN NICE HAVING A *HEALER* IN OUR RANKS...
...AND WITH THE GROWING UNREST...
...WITH THE TERRIGEN MISTS...
...MAYBE THEY COULD HAVE USED A *SAFE HAVEN.*
MORE THAN ONCE, I HAVE TRICKED MYSELF INTO BELIEVING THAT WAS POSSIBLE.
SUCH A THING...
"...IS BUT A *FANTASY.*

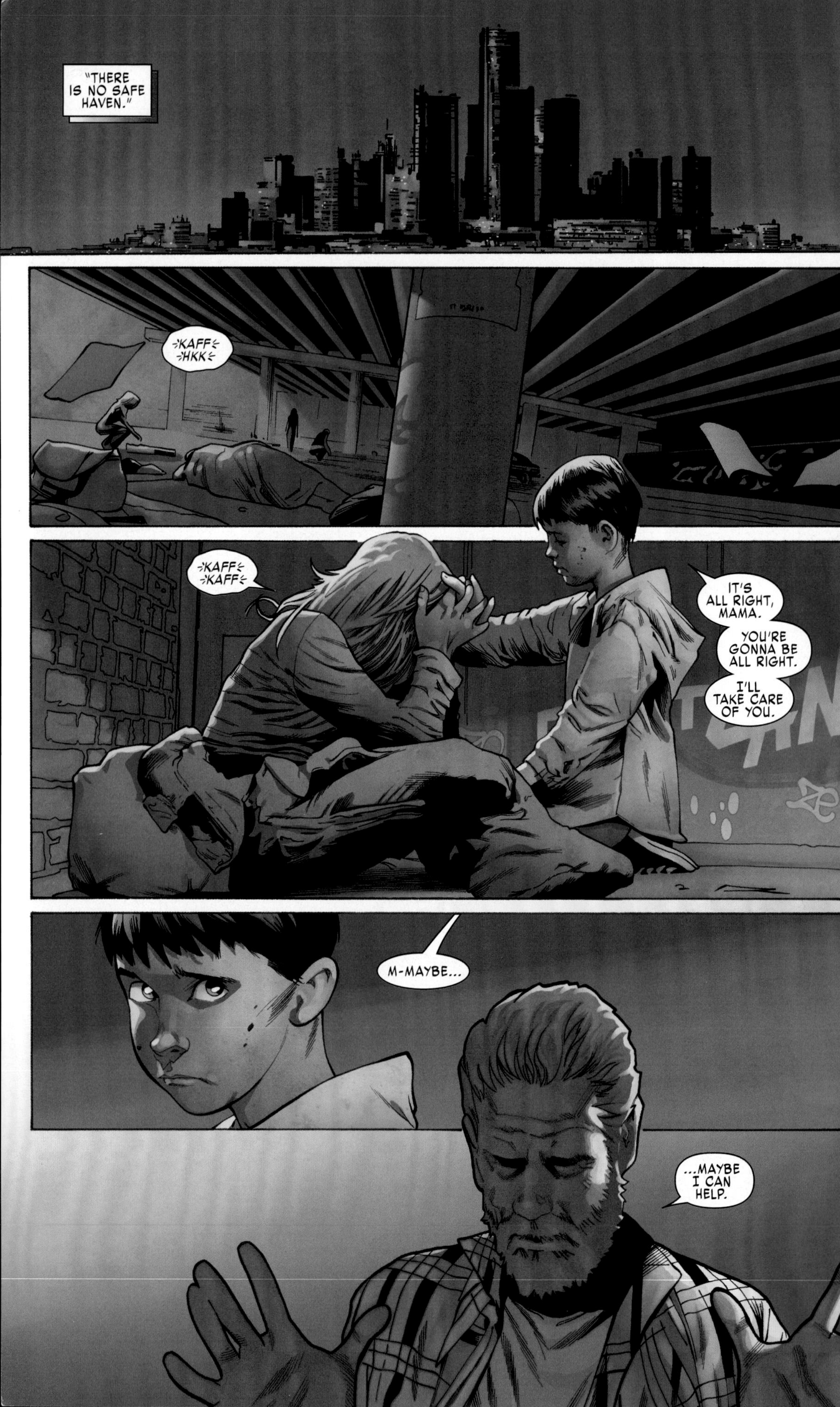
"THERE IS NO SAFE HAVEN."
KAFF HKK
KAFF KAFF
IT'S ALL RIGHT, MAMA.
YOU'RE GONNA BE ALL RIGHT.
I'LL TAKE CARE OF YOU.
M-MAYBE...
...MAYBE I CAN HELP.

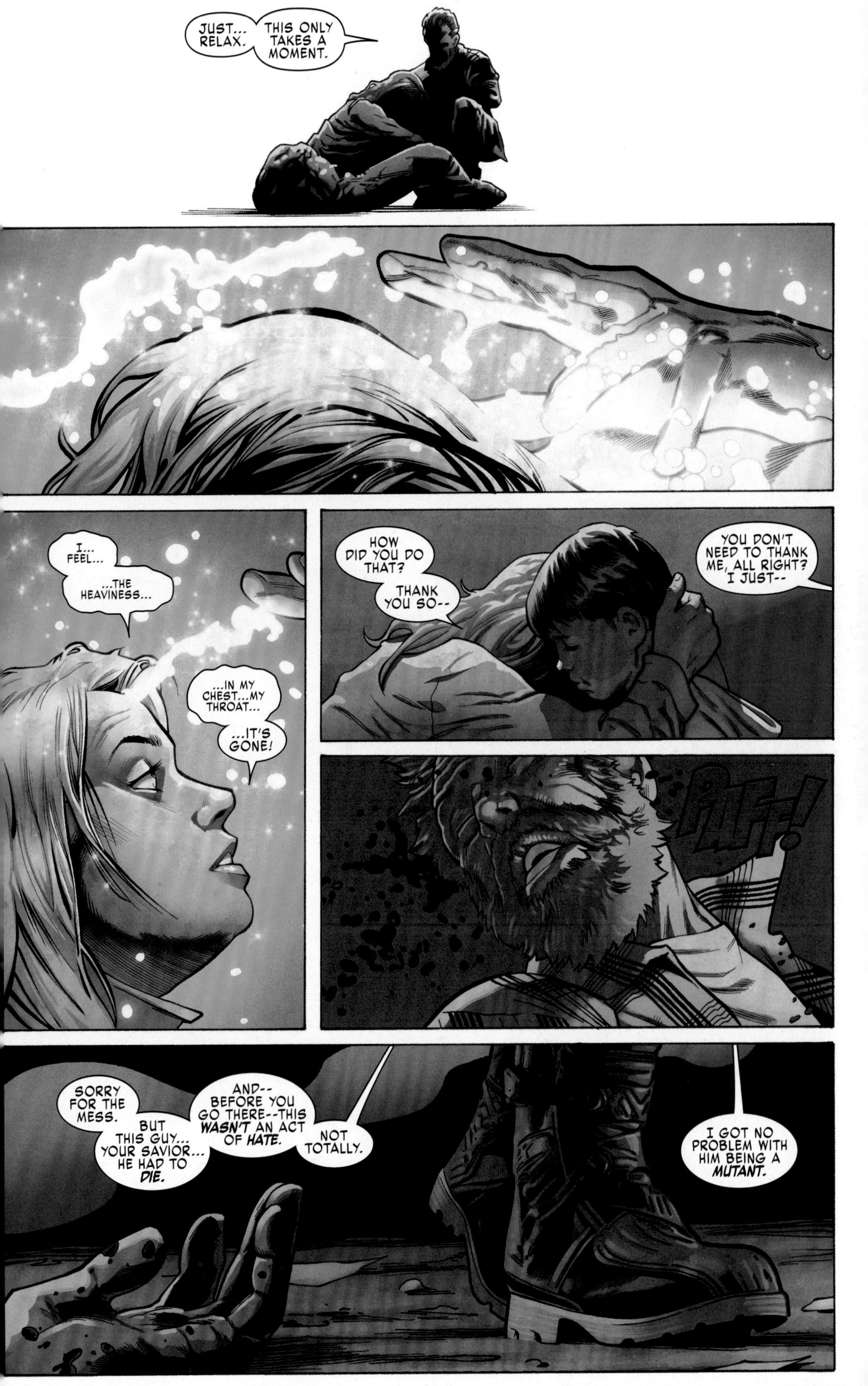
JUST... RELAX.
THIS ONLY TAKES A MOMENT.
I... FEEL...
...THE HEAVINESS...
...IN MY CHEST...MY THROAT...
...IT'S GONE!
HOW DID YOU DO THAT?
THANK YOU SO--
YOU DON'T NEED TO THANK ME, ALL RIGHT? I JUST--
PHFF!
SORRY FOR THE MESS.
BUT THIS GUY... YOUR SAVIOR... HE HAD TO DIE.
AND-- BEFORE YOU GO THERE--THIS WASN'T AN ACT OF HATE.
NOT TOTALLY.
I GOT NO PROBLEM WITH HIM BEING A MUTANT.

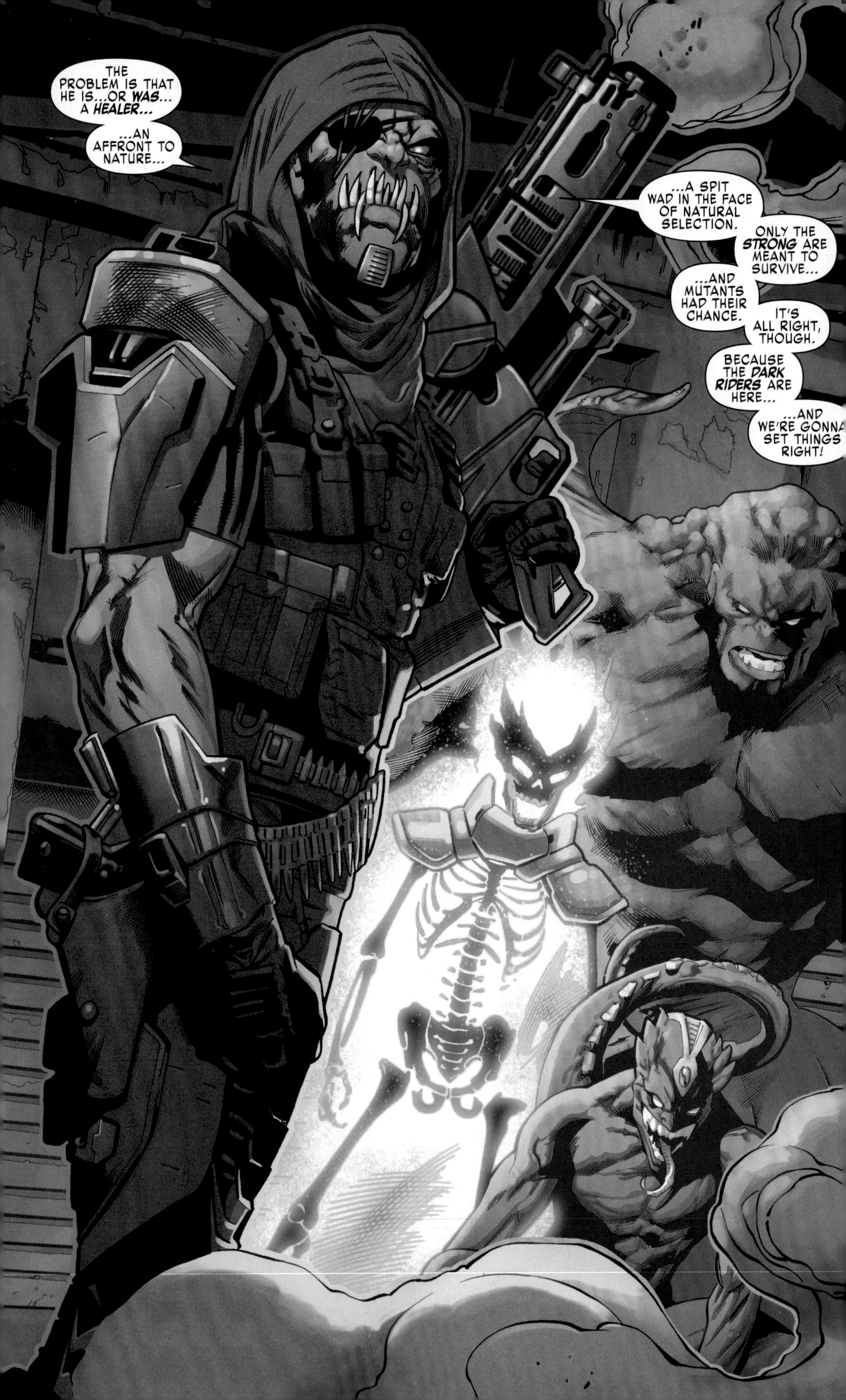
THE PROBLEM IS THAT HE IS...OR WAS... A HEALER...
...AN AFFRONT TO NATURE...
...A SPIT WAD IN THE FACE OF NATURAL SELECTION.
ONLY THE STRONG ARE MEANT TO SURVIVE...
...AND MUTANTS HAD THEIR CHANCE.
IT'S ALL RIGHT, THOUGH.
BECAUSE THE DARK RIDERS ARE HERE...
...AND WE'RE GONNA SET THINGS RIGHT!

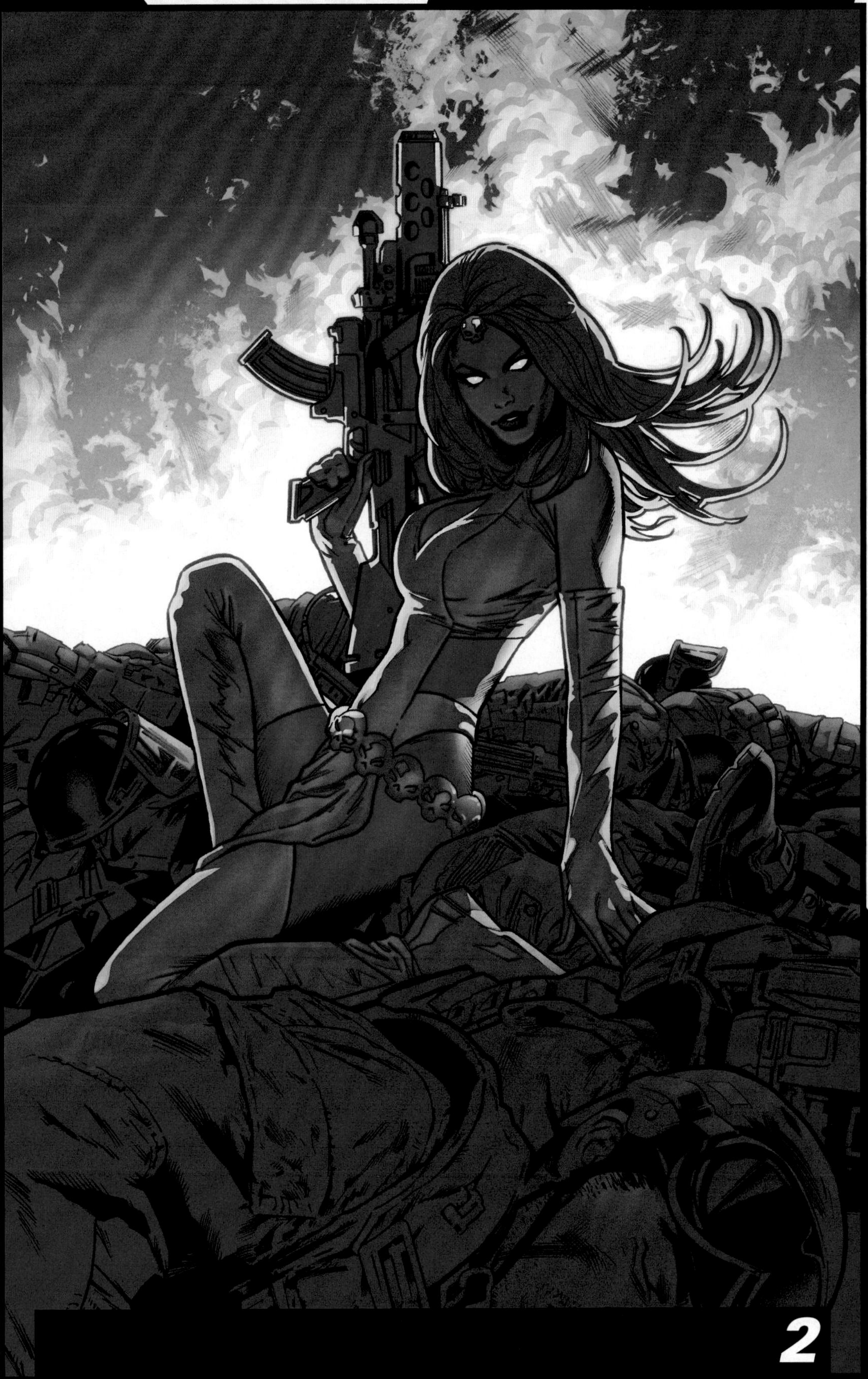
2

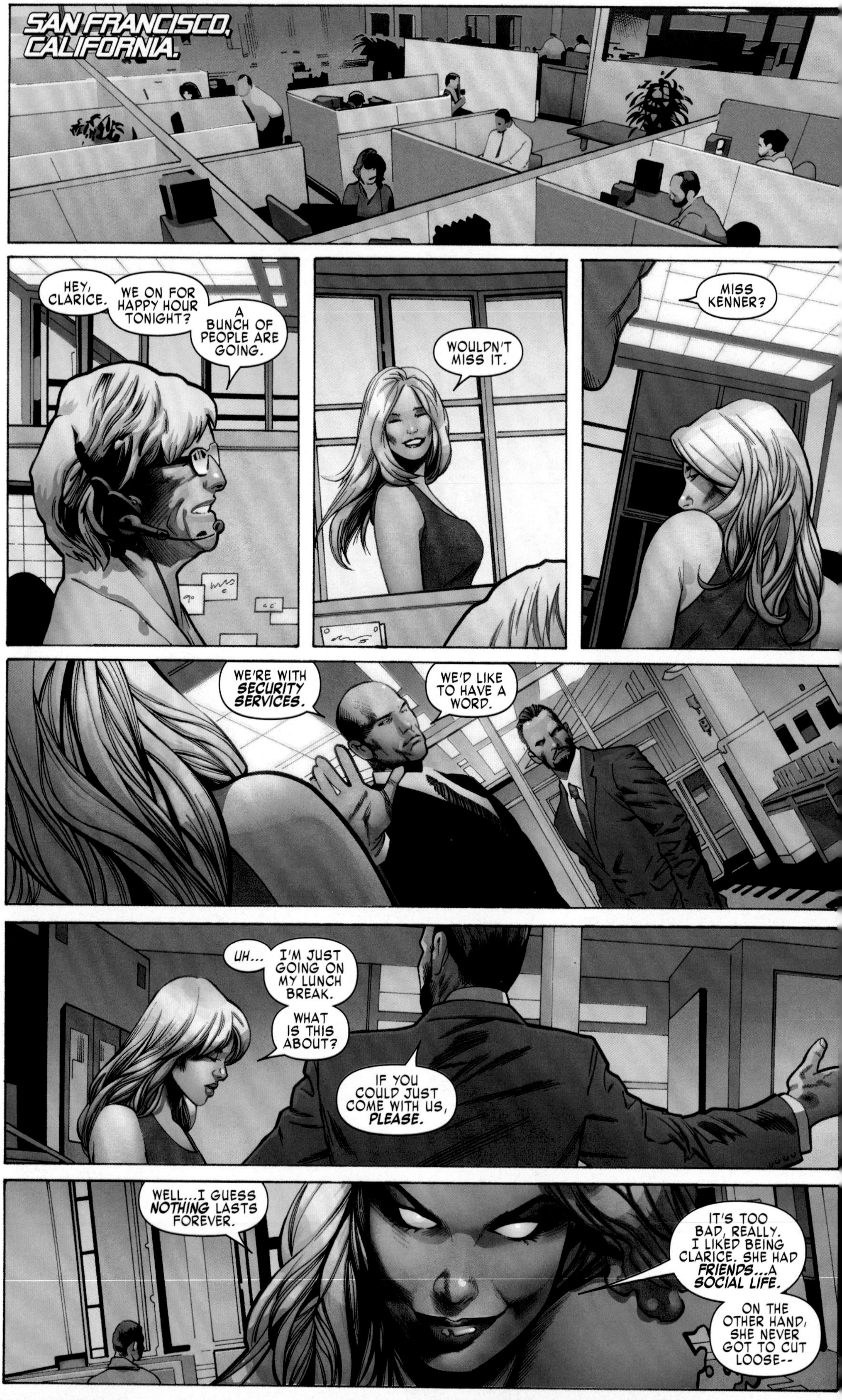
SAN FRANCISCO, CALIFORNIA.
HEY, CLARICE.
WE ON FOR HAPPY HOUR TONIGHT?
A BUNCH OF PEOPLE ARE GOING.
WOULDN'T MISS IT.
MISS KENNER?
WE'RE WITH SECURITY SERVICES.
WE'D LIKE TO HAVE A WORD.
UH...
I'M JUST GOING ON MY LUNCH BREAK.
WHAT IS THIS ABOUT?
IF YOU COULD JUST COME WITH US, PLEASE.
WELL...I GUESS NOTHING LASTS FOREVER.
IT'S TOO BAD, REALLY. I LIKED BEING CLARICE. SHE HAD FRIENDS...A SOCIAL LIFE.
ON THE OTHER HAND, SHE NEVER GOT TO CUT LOOSE--

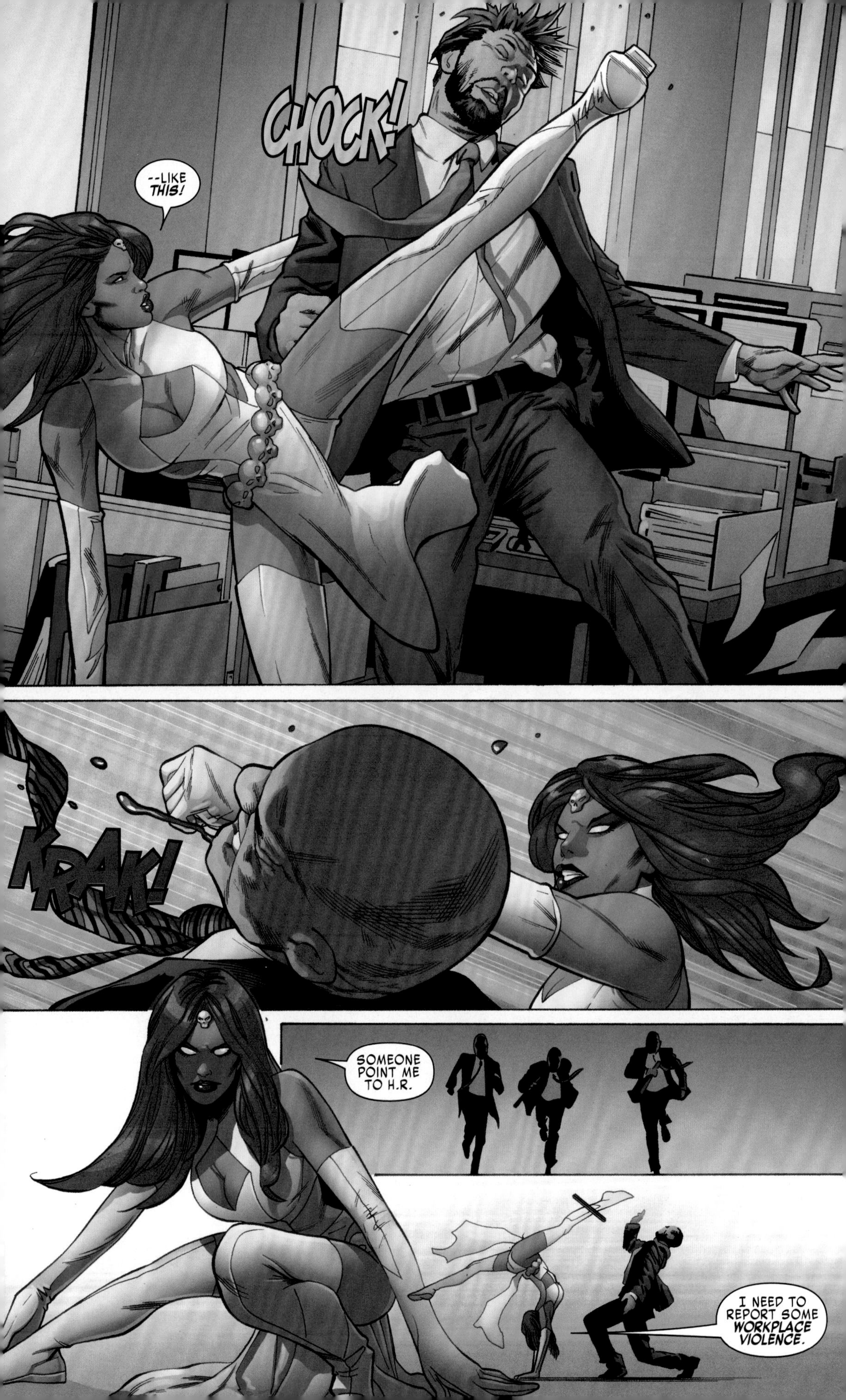
CHOCK!
--LIKE THIS!
KRAK!
SOMEONE POINT ME TO H.R.
I NEED TO REPORT SOME WORKPLACE VIOLENCE.

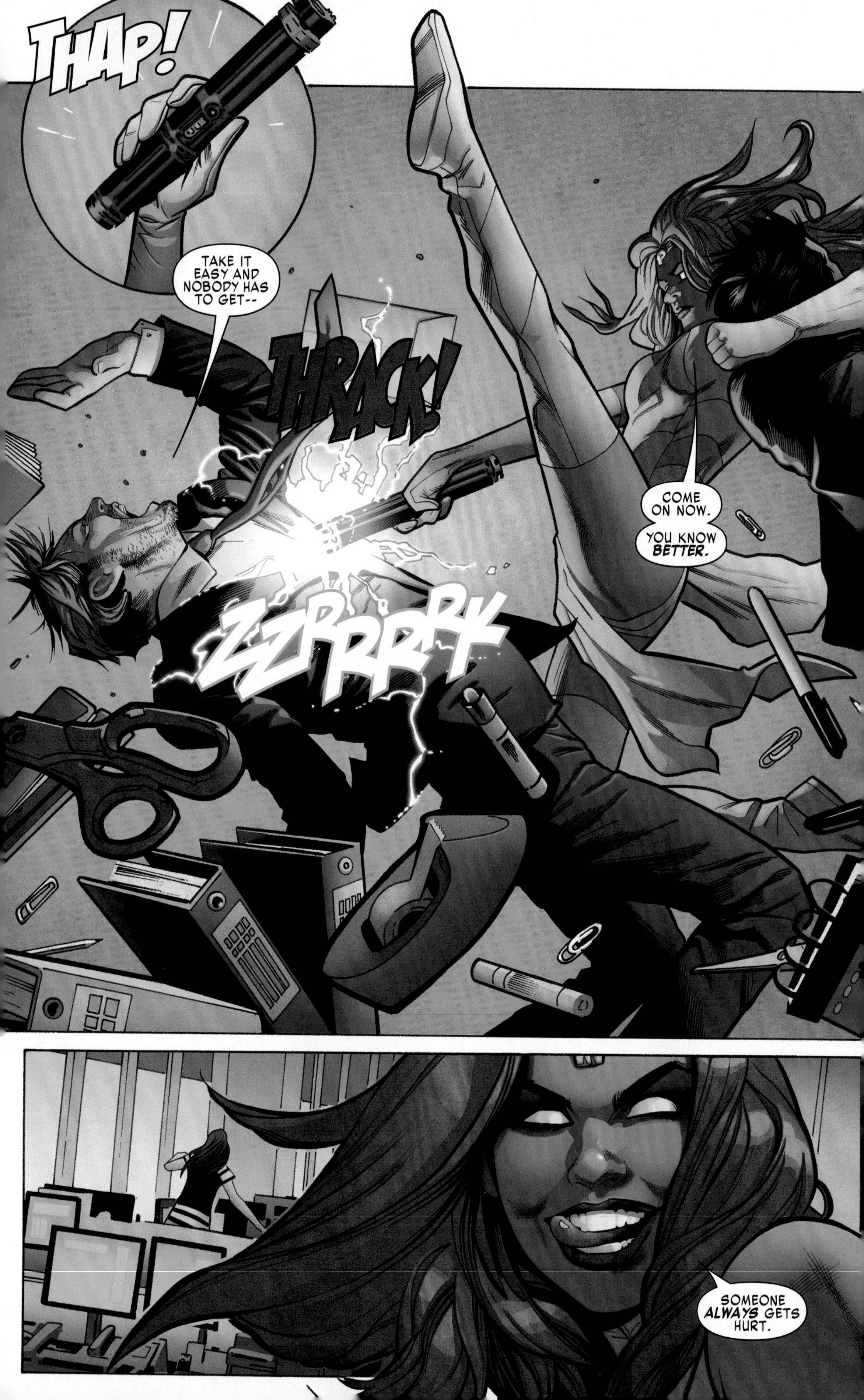
THAP!
TAKE IT EASY AND NOBODY HAS TO GET--
THRACK!
ZZRRRRK
COME ON NOW.
YOU KNOW BETTER.
SOMEONE ALWAYS GETS HURT.

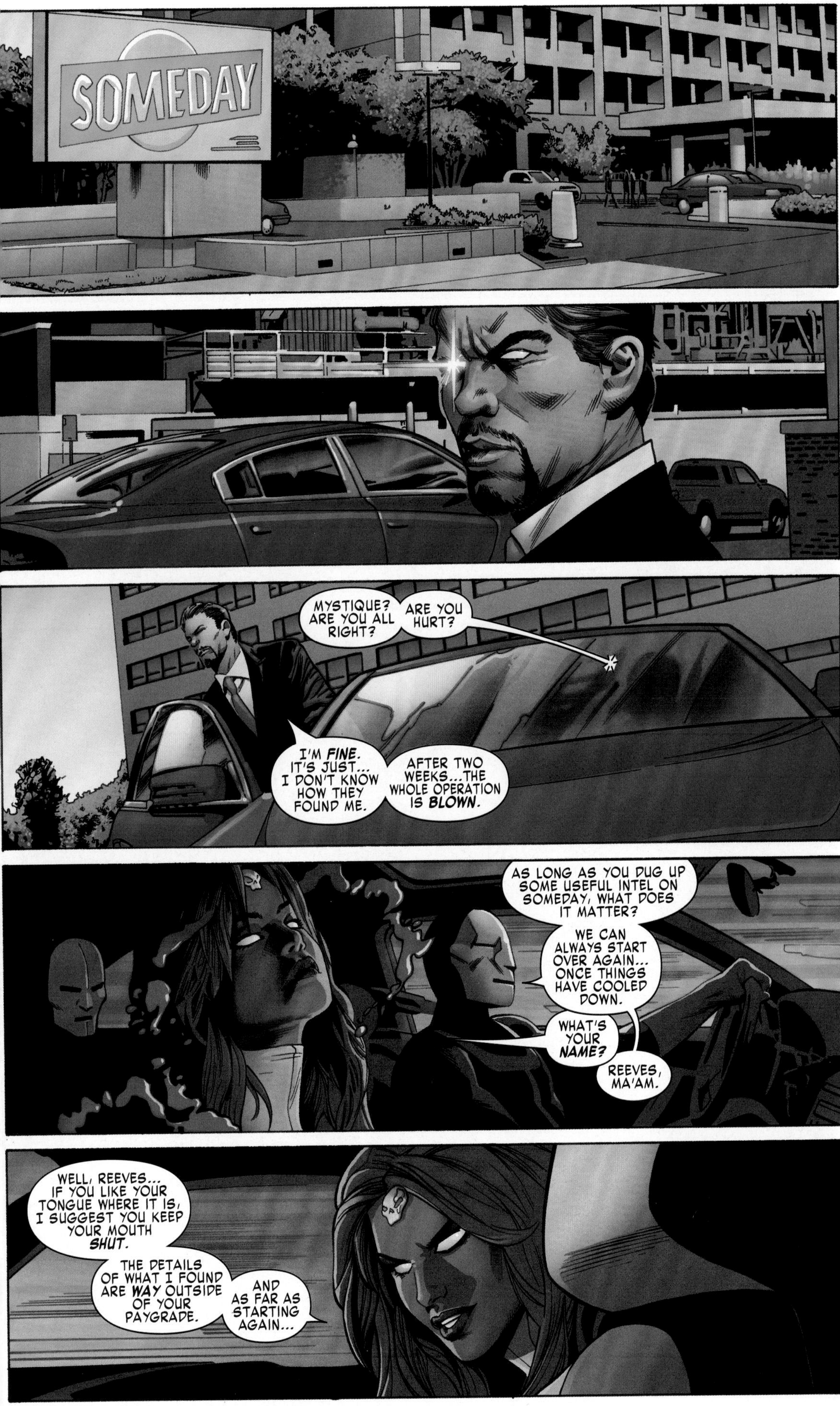
SOMEDAY
MYSTIQUE? ARE YOU ALL RIGHT?
ARE YOU HURT?
I'M FINE. IT'S JUST... I DON'T KNOW HOW THEY FOUND ME.
AFTER TWO WEEKS...THE WHOLE OPERATION IS BLOWN.
AS LONG AS YOU DUG UP SOME USEFUL INTEL ON SOMEDAY, WHAT DOES IT MATTER?
WE CAN ALWAYS START OVER AGAIN... ONCE THINGS HAVE COOLED DOWN.
WHAT'S YOUR NAME?
REEVES, MA'AM.
WELL, REEVES... IF YOU LIKE YOUR TONGUE WHERE IT IS, I SUGGEST YOU KEEP YOUR MOUTH SHUT.
THE DETAILS OF WHAT I FOUND ARE WAY OUTSIDE OF YOUR PAYGRADE.
AND AS FAR AS STARTING AGAIN...

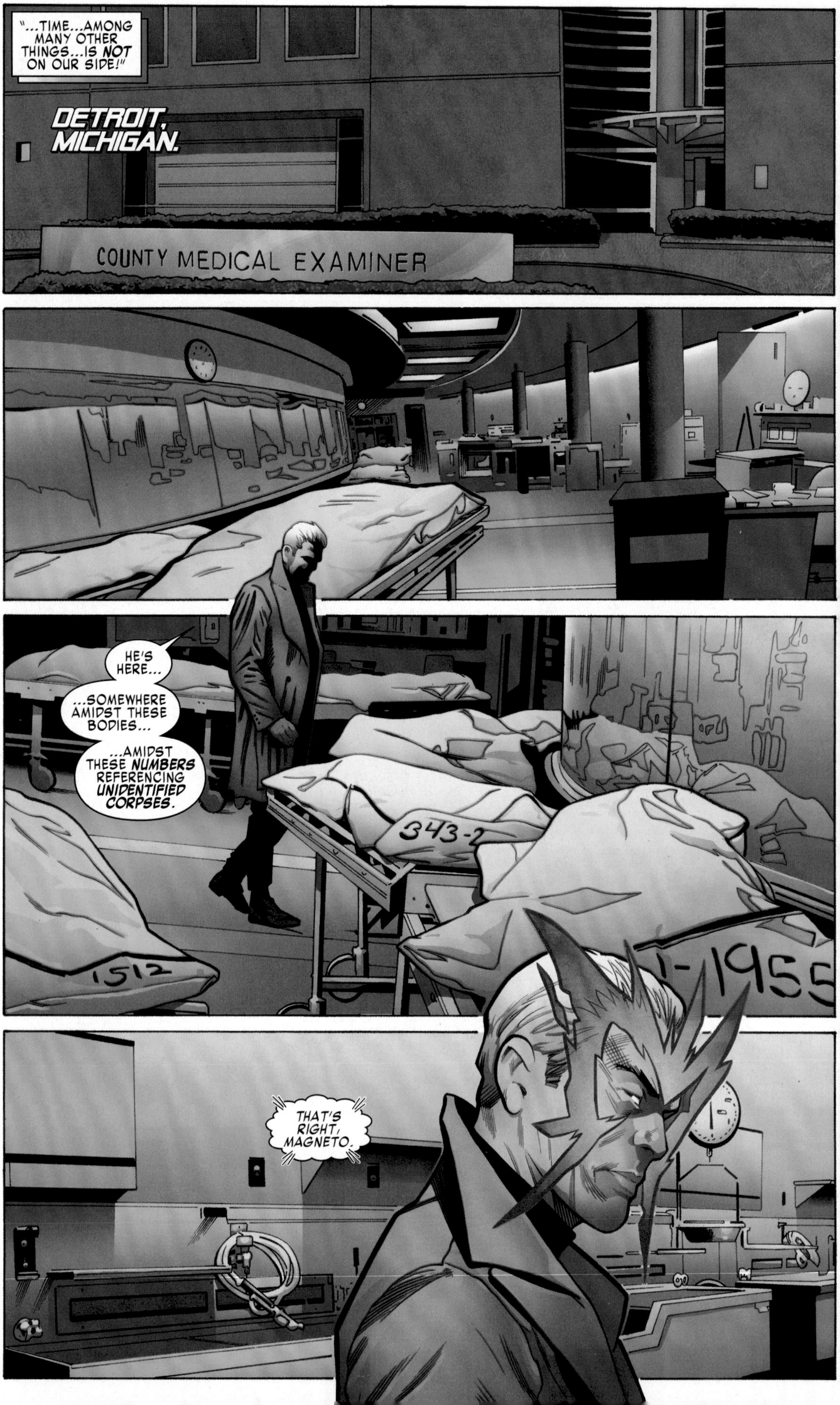
"...TIME...AMONG MANY OTHER THINGS...IS NOT ON OUR SIDE!"
DETROIT, MICHIGAN.
COUNTY MEDICAL EXAMINER
HE'S HERE...
...SOMEWHERE AMIDST THESE BODIES...
...AMIDST THESE NUMBERS REFERENCING UNIDENTIFIED CORPSES.
343-2
1512
1-1955
THAT'S RIGHT, MAGNETO.

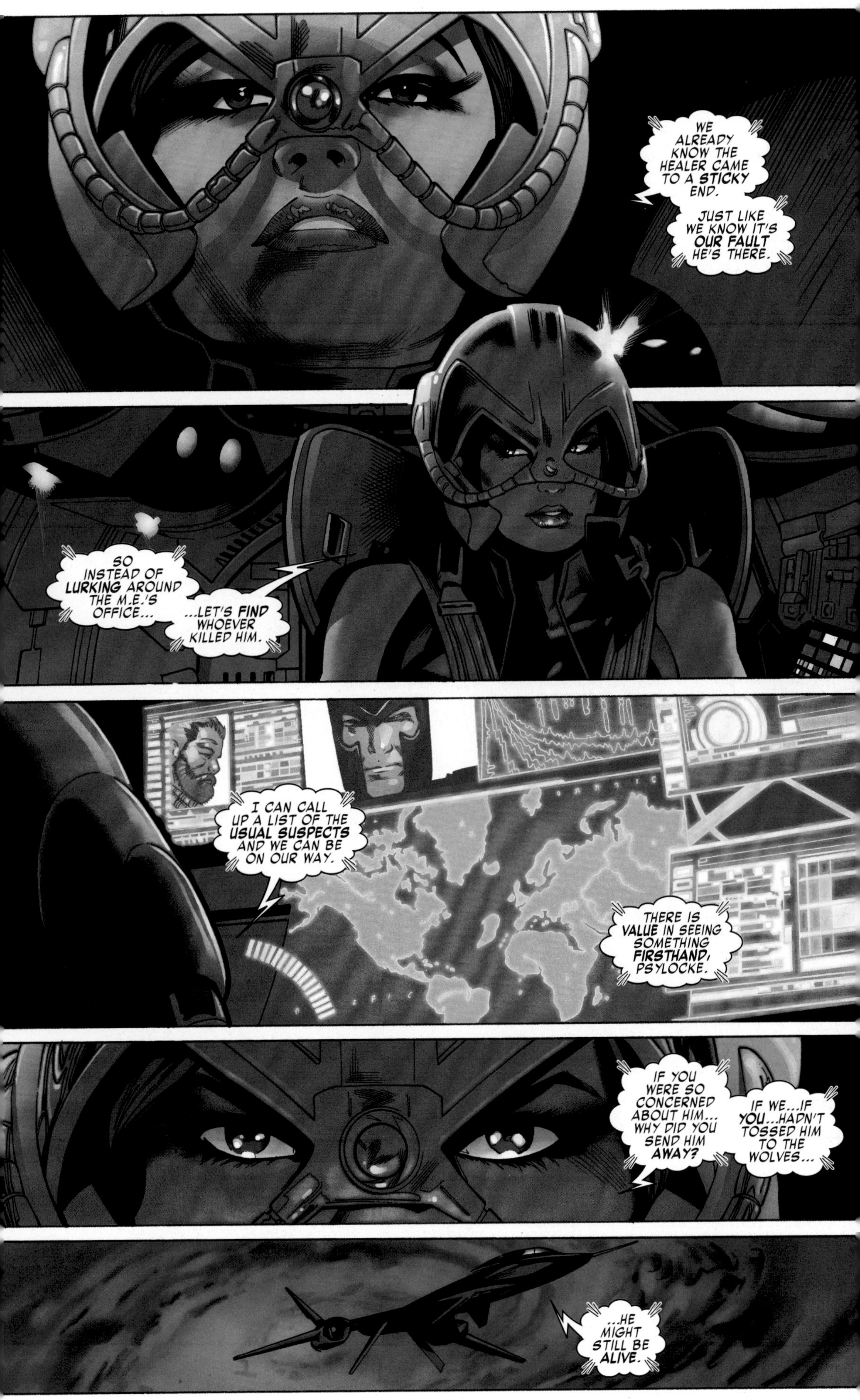

WE ALREADY KNOW THE HEALER CAME TO A STICKY END.
JUST LIKE WE KNOW IT'S OUR FAULT HE'S THERE.
SO INSTEAD OF LURKING AROUND THE M.E.'S OFFICE...
...LET'S FIND WHOEVER KILLED HIM.
I CAN CALL UP A LIST OF THE USUAL SUSPECTS AND WE CAN BE ON OUR WAY.
THERE IS VALUE IN SEEING SOMETHING FIRSTHAND, PSYLOCKE.
IF YOU WERE SO CONCERNED ABOUT HIM... WHY DID YOU SEND HIM AWAY?
IF WE...IF YOU...HADN'T TOSSED HIM TO THE WOLVES...
...HE MIGHT STILL BE ALIVE.

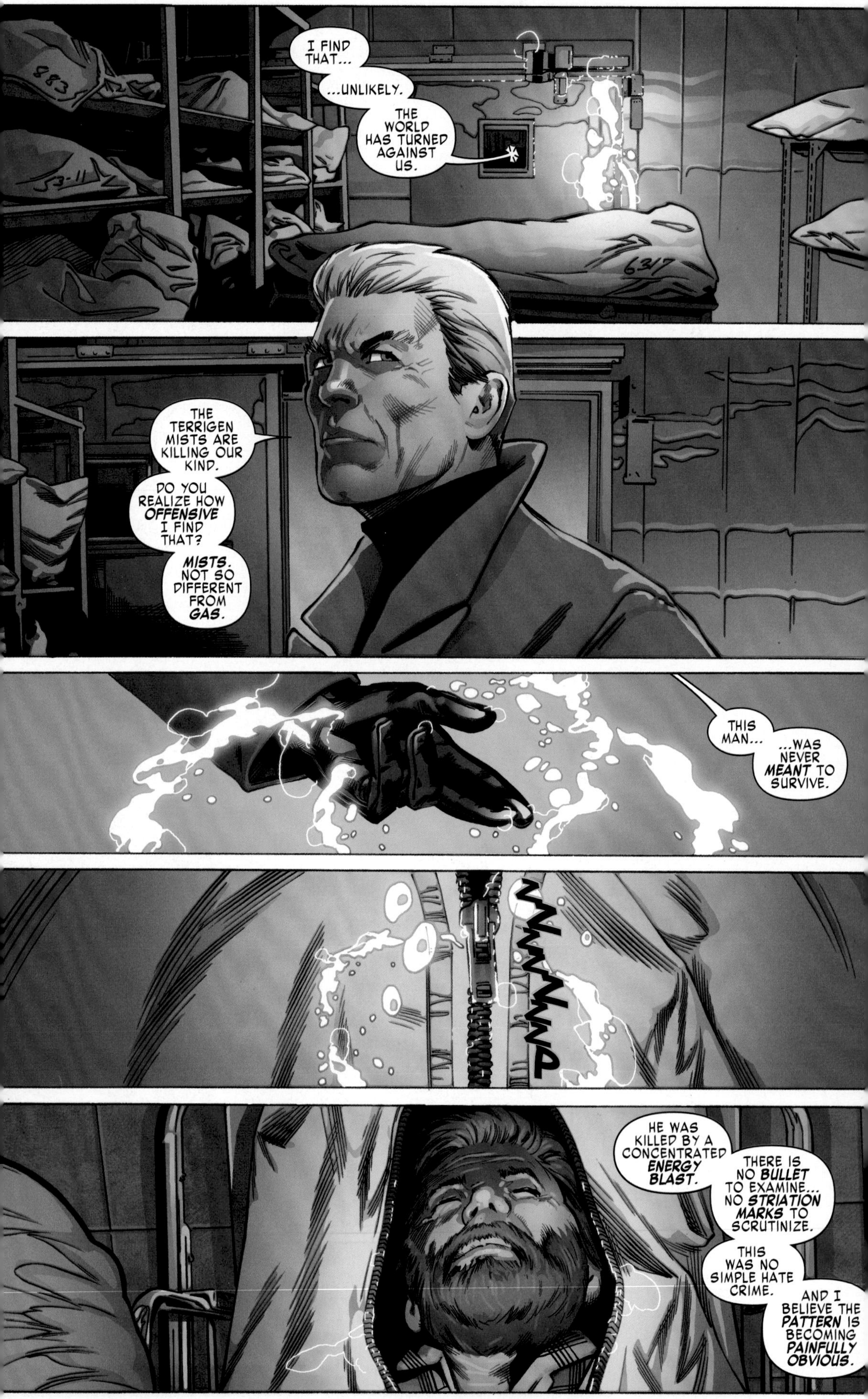

I FIND THAT...
...UNLIKELY.
THE WORLD HAS TURNED AGAINST US.
THE TERRIGEN MISTS ARE KILLING OUR KIND.
DO YOU REALIZE HOW OFFENSIVE I FIND THAT?
MISTS. NOT SO DIFFERENT FROM GAS.
THIS MAN...
...WAS NEVER MEANT TO SURVIVE.
VVVVVVVVP
HE WAS KILLED BY A CONCENTRATED ENERGY BLAST.
THERE IS NO BULLET TO EXAMINE... NO STRIATION MARKS TO SCRUTINIZE.
THIS WAS NO SIMPLE HATE CRIME.
AND I BELIEVE THE PATTERN IS BECOMING PAINFULLY OBVIOUS.

THREE OTHER DEATHS IN THE LAST COUPLE OF DAYS.

MARC DALE AND SISTER SALVATION... ALSO MUTANTS WITH THE POWER TO HEAL.

A THIRD PERSON...WE DON'T KNOW MUCH ABOUT HIM...BUT REPORTS INDICATE HE HAD A "HEALING VOICE."

ALL OF OUR OTHER ENDEAVORS WILL HAVE TO WAIT.

THIS TAKES PRECEDENCE.

WE NEED TO IDENTIFY AND LOCATE AS MANY OTHER POTENTIAL TARGETS AS POSSIBLE.

I'VE ALREADY PINPOINTED A COUPLE OF CANDIDATES WE MIGHT CONSIDER HIGH-RISK.

JOSHUA FOLEY. ELIXIR.

AND CHRISTOPHER MUSE. TRIAGE.

I CAN--

WARREN?

WHAT ARE YOU DOING HERE?

HOW DID YOU GET IN MY...

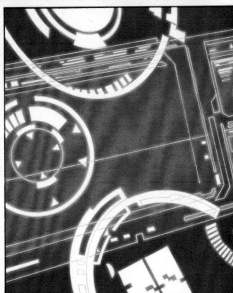

ELIZABETH? ARE YOU ALL RIGHT?

I'M FINE. JUST LOST FOCUS FOR A SECOND.

I'LL ALERT SABRETOOTH AND MONET.

WHILE WE TRACK DOWN TRIAGE...

"...WE'LL SEND *THEM* TO RETRIEVE ELIXIR."

COOPER'S MOUNTAIN, VERMONT.

SLOW DOWN, CREED.

YOU'RE AS *DANGEROUS* BEHIND THE WHEEL AS YOU ARE IN A FIGHT.

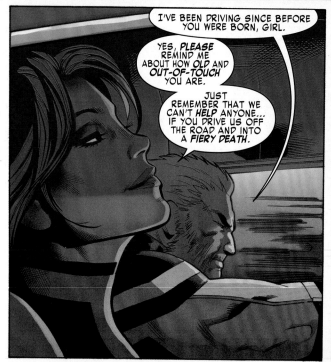

I'VE BEEN DRIVING SINCE BEFORE YOU WERE BORN, GIRL.

YES, *PLEASE* REMIND ME ABOUT HOW *OLD* AND *OUT-OF-TOUCH* YOU ARE.

JUST REMEMBER THAT WE CAN'T *HELP* ANYONE... IF YOU DRIVE US OFF THE ROAD AND INTO A *FIERY DEATH*.

HEALING FACTOR WOULD GET ME THROUGH A WRECK.

AND YOU'D BE ALL RIGHT, TOO.

YOU'RE *STURDY*.

SO ANNOYING.

I'M GUESSING, THOUGH, THAT THIS IS ALL A LITTLE *UNSETTLING* TO YOU...

...GOING ON A RESCUE OP...

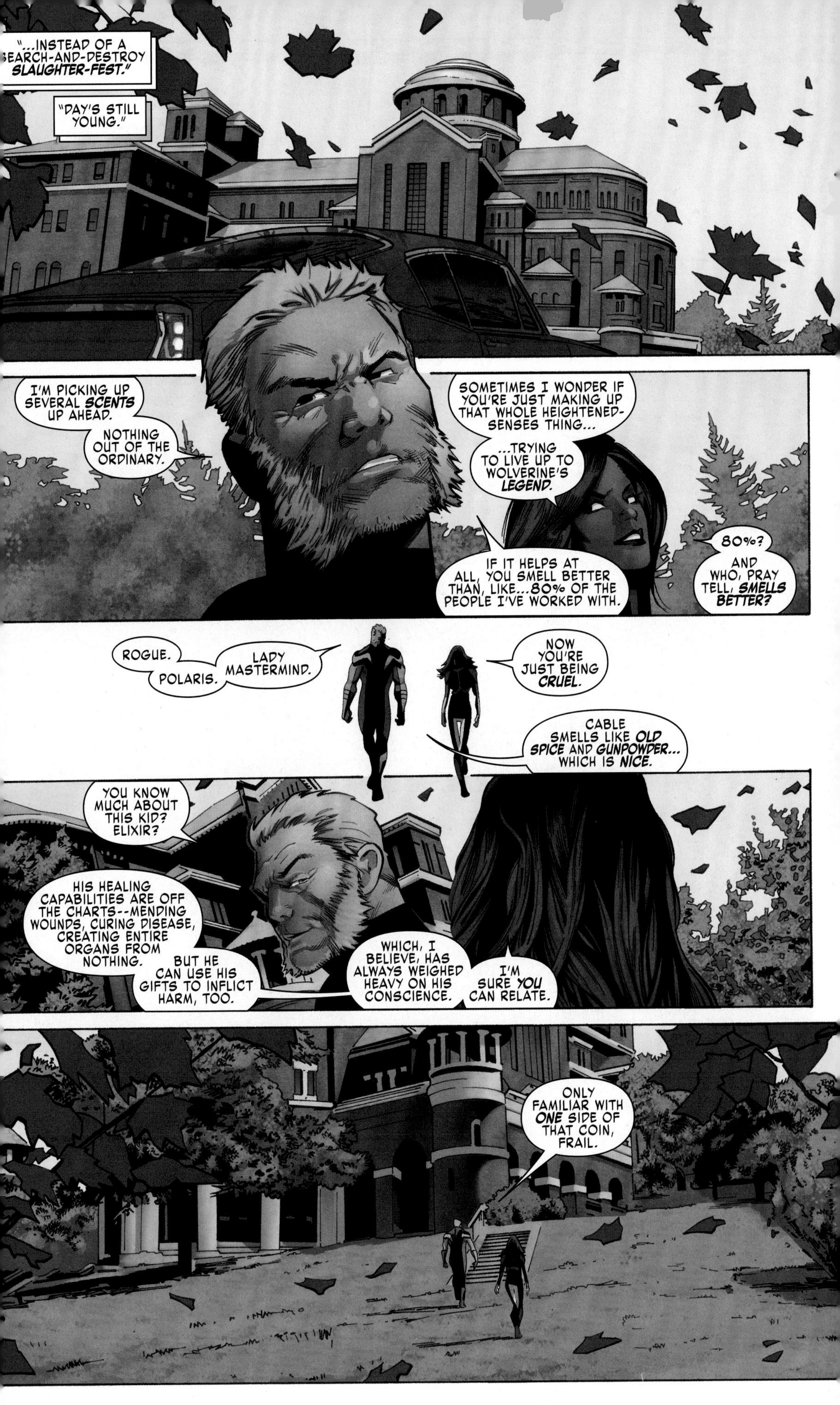
"...INSTEAD OF A SEARCH-AND-DESTROY SLAUGHTER-FEST."
"DAY'S STILL YOUNG."
I'M PICKING UP SEVERAL SCENTS UP AHEAD.
NOTHING OUT OF THE ORDINARY.
SOMETIMES I WONDER IF YOU'RE JUST MAKING UP THAT WHOLE HEIGHTENED-SENSES THING...
...TRYING TO LIVE UP TO WOLVERINE'S LEGEND.
IF IT HELPS AT ALL, YOU SMELL BETTER THAN, LIKE...80% OF THE PEOPLE I'VE WORKED WITH.
80%?
AND WHO, PRAY TELL, SMELLS BETTER?
ROGUE.
POLARIS.
LADY MASTERMIND.
NOW YOU'RE JUST BEING CRUEL.
CABLE SMELLS LIKE OLD SPICE AND GUNPOWDER... WHICH IS NICE.
YOU KNOW MUCH ABOUT THIS KID? ELIXIR?
HIS HEALING CAPABILITIES ARE OFF THE CHARTS--MENDING WOUNDS, CURING DISEASE, CREATING ENTIRE ORGANS FROM NOTHING.
BUT HE CAN USE HIS GIFTS TO INFLICT HARM, TOO.
WHICH, I BELIEVE, HAS ALWAYS WEIGHED HEAVY ON HIS CONSCIENCE.
I'M SURE YOU CAN RELATE.
ONLY FAMILIAR WITH ONE SIDE OF THAT COIN, FRAIL.

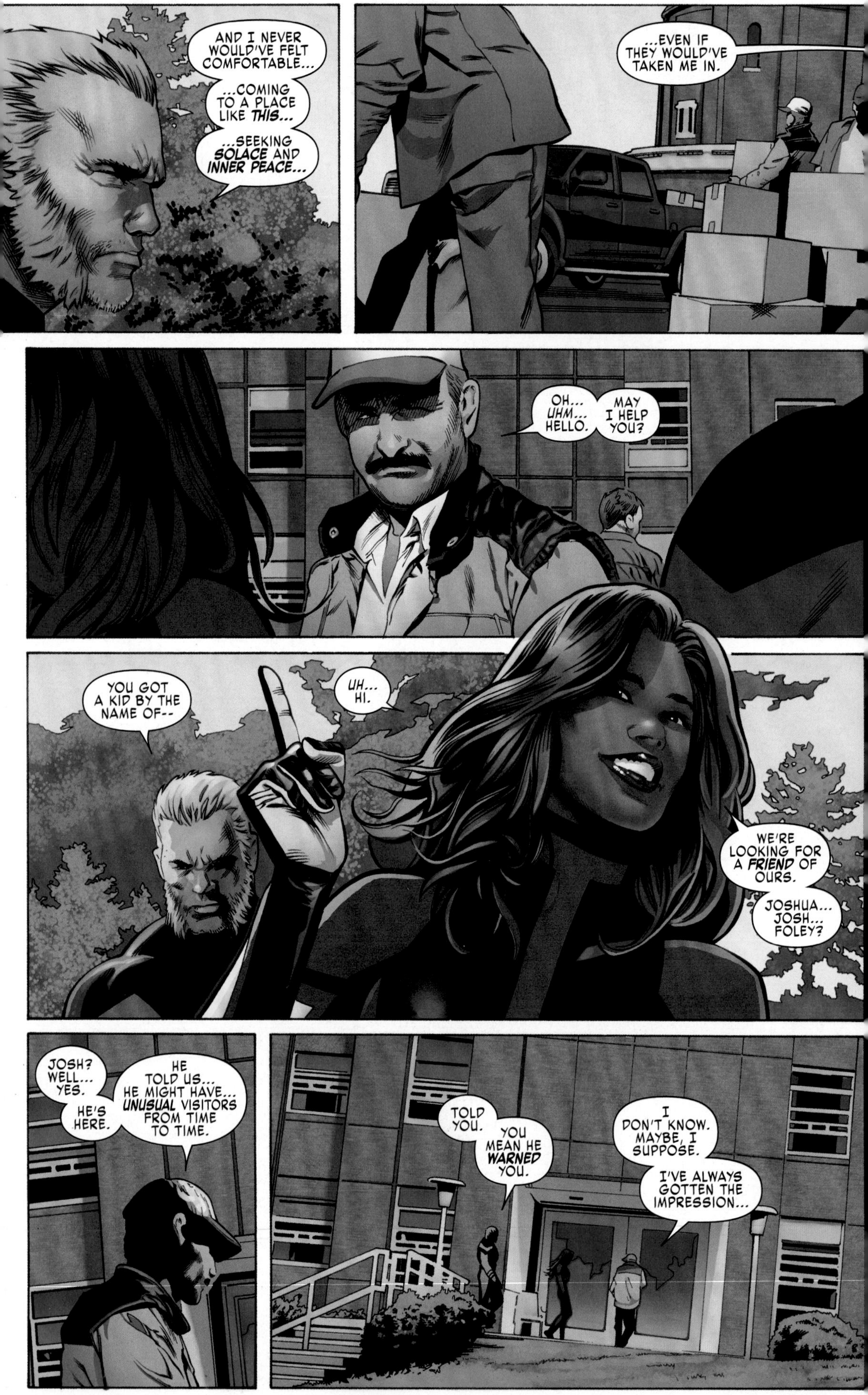
AND I NEVER WOULD'VE FELT COMFORTABLE...
...COMING TO A PLACE LIKE THIS...
...SEEKING SOLACE AND INNER PEACE...
...EVEN IF THEY WOULD'VE TAKEN ME IN.
OH... UHM... HELLO.
MAY I HELP YOU?
YOU GOT A KID BY THE NAME OF--
UH... HI.
WE'RE LOOKING FOR A FRIEND OF OURS.
JOSHUA... JOSH... FOLEY?
JOSH? WELL... YES.
HE'S HERE.
HE TOLD US... HE MIGHT HAVE... UNUSUAL VISITORS FROM TIME TO TIME.
TOLD YOU.
YOU MEAN HE WARNED YOU.
I DON'T KNOW. MAYBE, I SUPPOSE.
I'VE ALWAYS GOTTEN THE IMPRESSION...

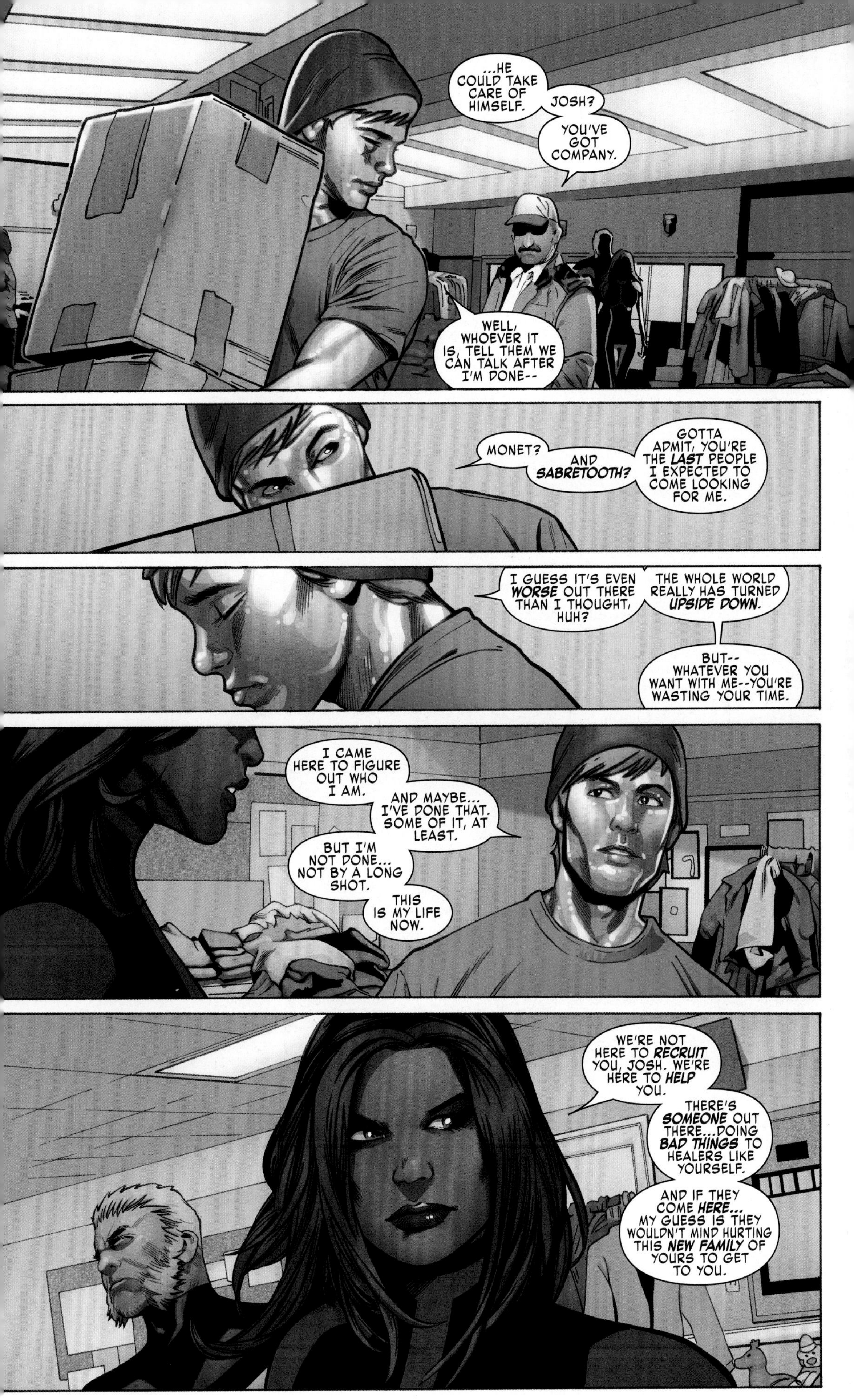
...HE COULD TAKE CARE OF HIMSELF.
JOSH?
YOU'VE GOT COMPANY.
WELL, WHOEVER IT IS, TELL THEM WE CAN TALK AFTER I'M DONE--
MONET?
AND SABRETOOTH?
GOTTA ADMIT, YOU'RE THE LAST PEOPLE I EXPECTED TO COME LOOKING FOR ME.
I GUESS IT'S EVEN WORSE OUT THERE THAN I THOUGHT, HUH?
THE WHOLE WORLD REALLY HAS TURNED UPSIDE DOWN.
BUT-- WHATEVER YOU WANT WITH ME--YOU'RE WASTING YOUR TIME.
I CAME HERE TO FIGURE OUT WHO I AM.
AND MAYBE... I'VE DONE THAT. SOME OF IT, AT LEAST.
BUT I'M NOT DONE... NOT BY A LONG SHOT.
THIS IS MY LIFE NOW.
WE'RE NOT HERE TO RECRUIT YOU, JOSH. WE'RE HERE TO HELP YOU.
THERE'S SOMEONE OUT THERE...DOING BAD THINGS TO HEALERS LIKE YOURSELF.
AND IF THEY COME HERE... MY GUESS IS THEY WOULDN'T MIND HURTING THIS NEW FAMILY OF YOURS TO GET TO YOU.

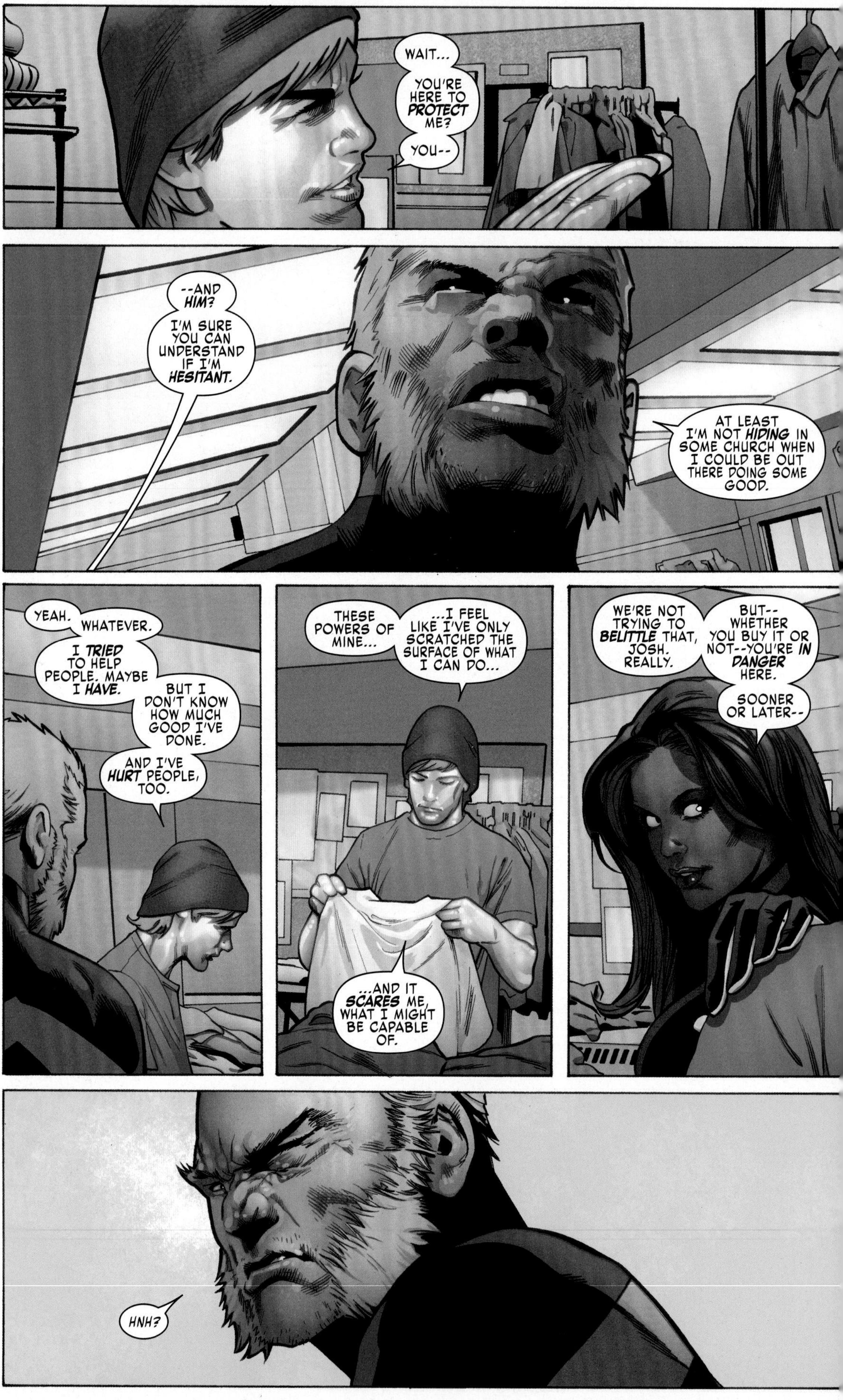
WAIT...
YOU'RE HERE TO PROTECT ME?
YOU--
--AND HIM?
I'M SURE YOU CAN UNDERSTAND IF I'M HESITANT.
AT LEAST I'M NOT HIDING IN SOME CHURCH WHEN I COULD BE OUT THERE DOING SOME GOOD.
YEAH.
WHATEVER.
I TRIED TO HELP PEOPLE. MAYBE I HAVE.
BUT I DON'T KNOW HOW MUCH GOOD I'VE DONE.
AND I'VE HURT PEOPLE, TOO.
THESE POWERS OF MINE...
...I FEEL LIKE I'VE ONLY SCRATCHED THE SURFACE OF WHAT I CAN DO...
...AND IT SCARES ME, WHAT I MIGHT BE CAPABLE OF.
WE'RE NOT TRYING TO BELITTLE THAT, JOSH. REALLY.
BUT-- WHETHER YOU BUY IT OR NOT--YOU'RE IN DANGER HERE.
SOONER OR LATER--
HNH?

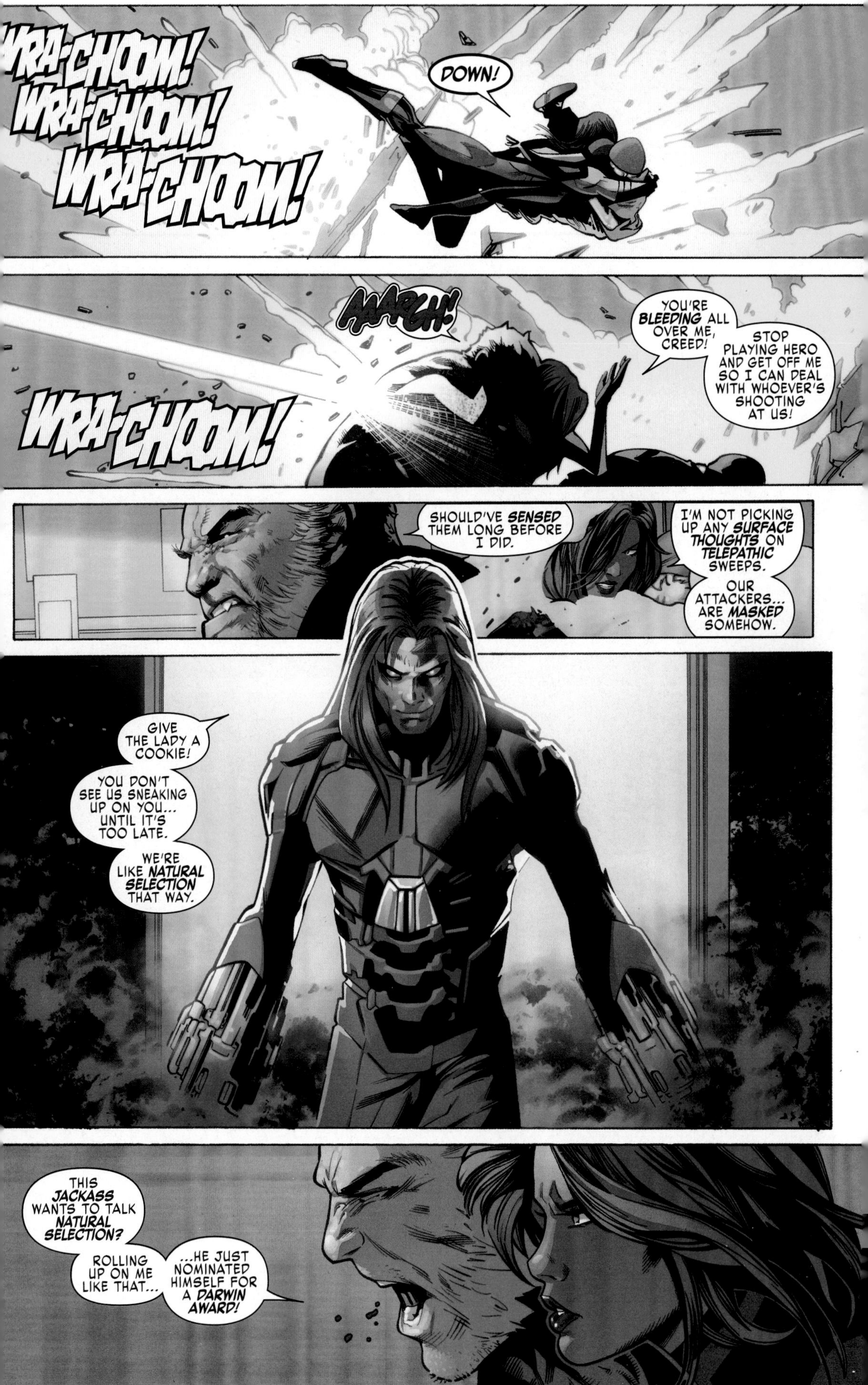

WRA-CHOOM! WRA-CHOOM! WRA-CHOOM!
DOWN!
AAARGH!
WRA-CHOOM!
YOU'RE BLEEDING ALL OVER ME, CREED!
STOP PLAYING HERO AND GET OFF ME SO I CAN DEAL WITH WHOEVER'S SHOOTING AT US!
SHOULD'VE SENSED THEM LONG BEFORE I DID.
I'M NOT PICKING UP ANY SURFACE THOUGHTS ON TELEPATHIC SWEEPS.
OUR ATTACKERS... ARE MASKED SOMEHOW.
GIVE THE LADY A COOKIE!
YOU DON'T SEE US SNEAKING UP ON YOU... UNTIL IT'S TOO LATE.
WE'RE LIKE NATURAL SELECTION THAT WAY.
THIS JACKASS WANTS TO TALK NATURAL SELECTION?
ROLLING UP ON ME LIKE THAT...
...HE JUST NOMINATED HIMSELF FOR A DARWIN AWARD!

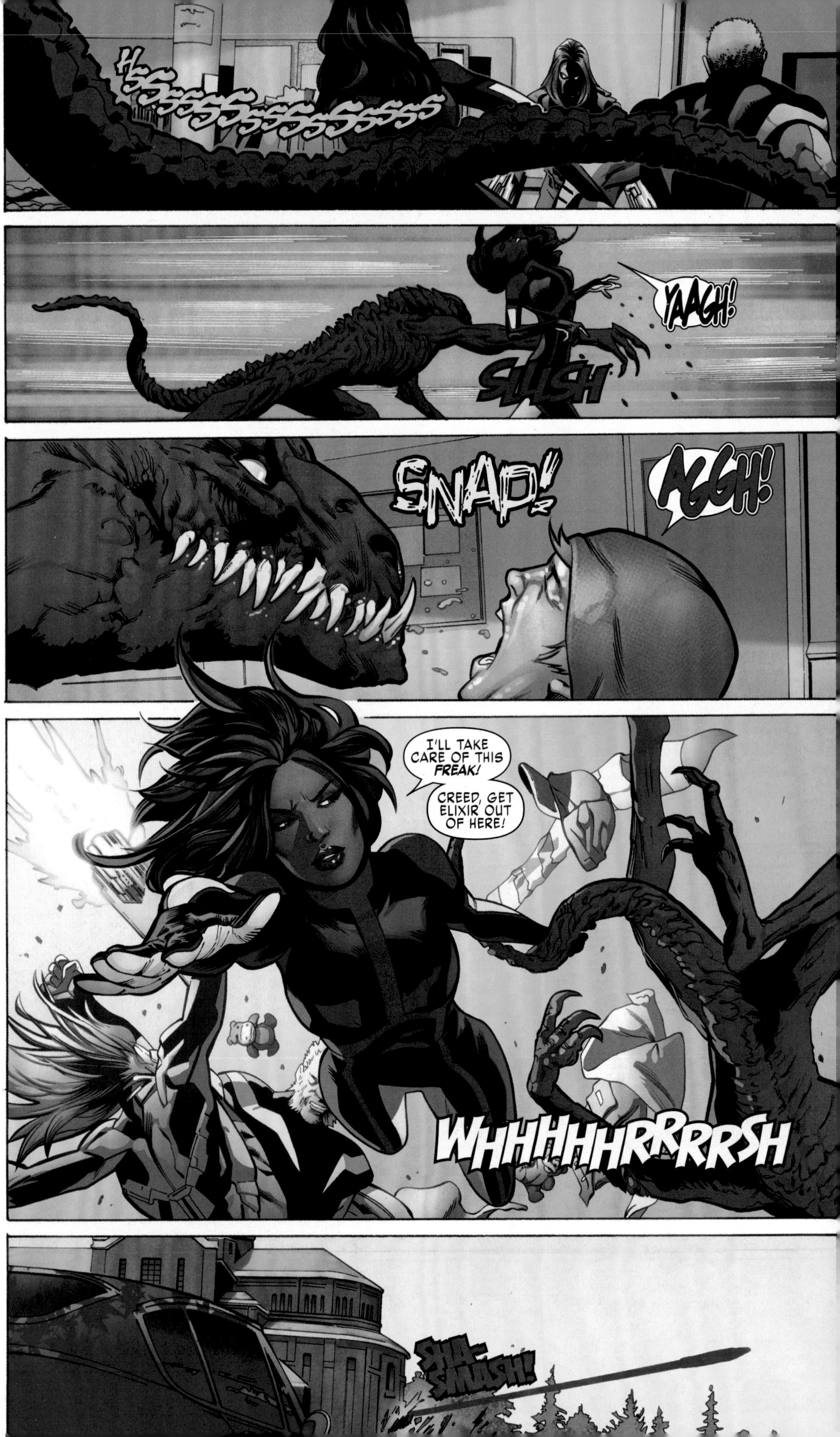
HSSSSSSSSSSSSSSSSS
YAAGH!
SHLISH
SNAP!
AGGH!
I'LL TAKE CARE OF THIS *FREAK!*
CREED, GET ELIXIR OUT OF HERE!
WHHHHHRRRRSH
SHA-SMASH!

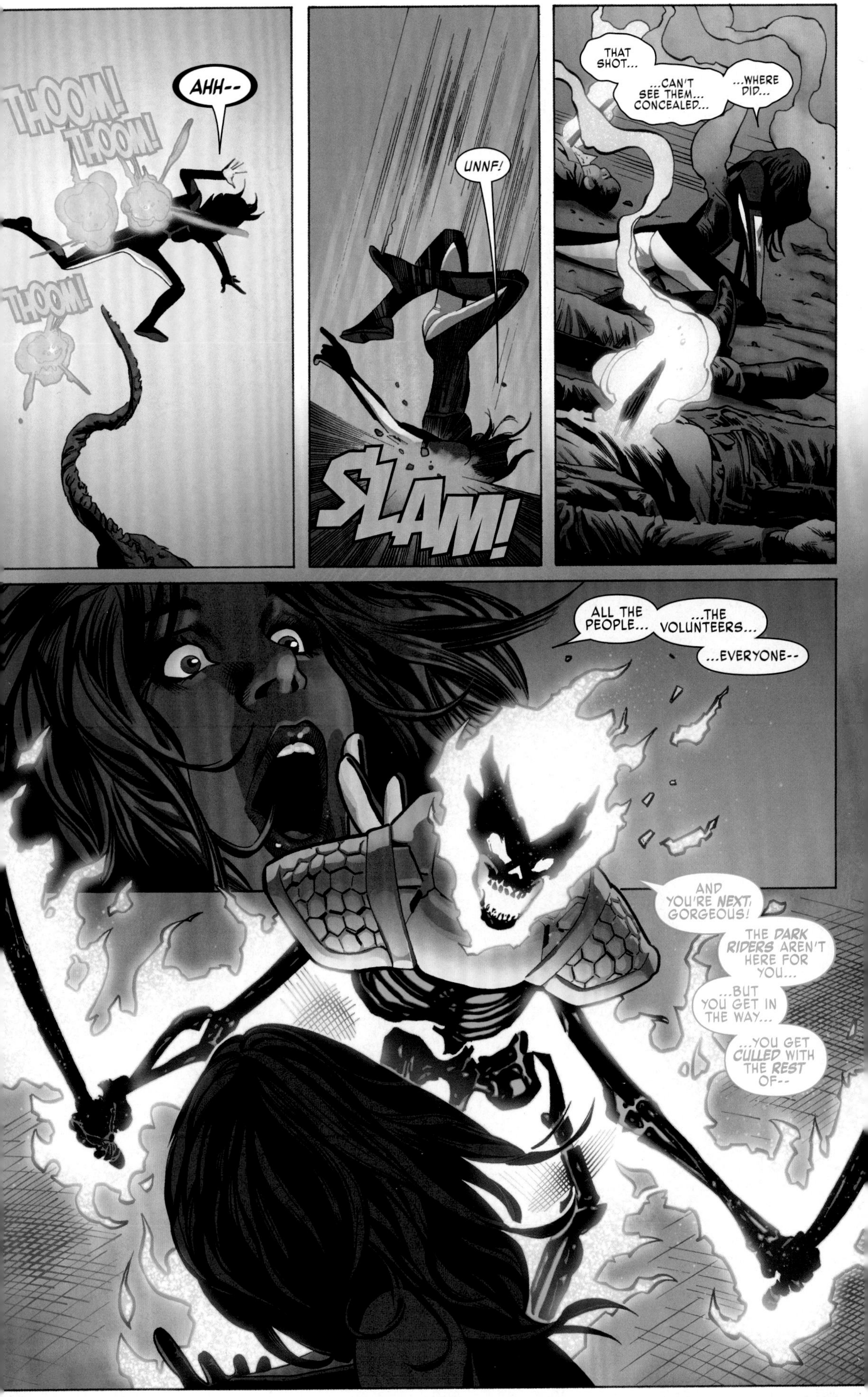

THOOM! THOOM!
AHH--
THOOM!
UNNF!
SLAM!
THAT SHOT...
...CAN'T SEE THEM... CONCEALED...
...WHERE DID...
ALL THE PEOPLE...
...THE VOLUNTEERS...
...EVERYONE--
AND YOU'RE NEXT, GORGEOUS!
THE DARK RIDERS AREN'T HERE FOR YOU...
...BUT YOU GET IN THE WAY...
...YOU GET CULLED WITH THE REST OF--

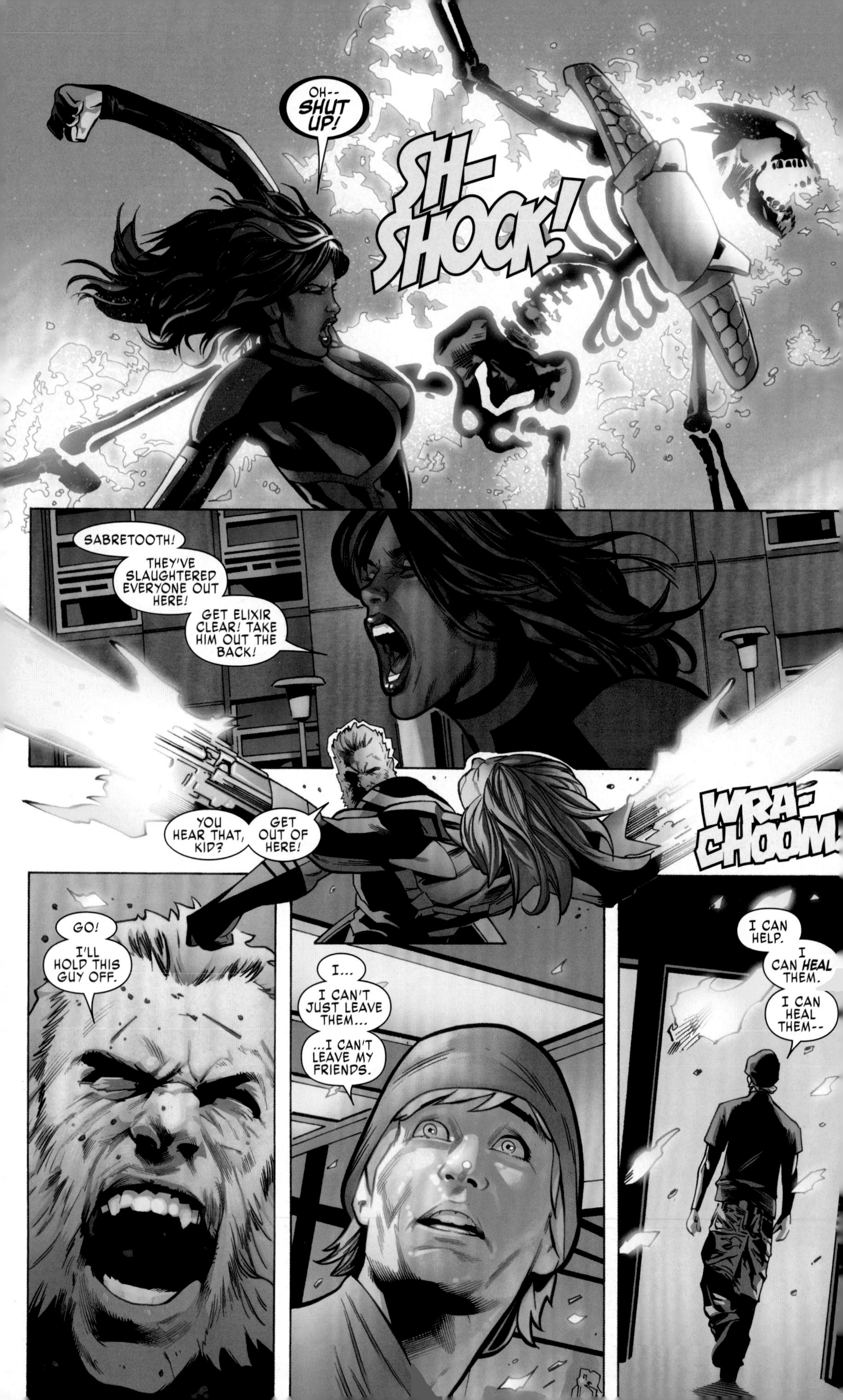
OH--
SHUT UP!
SH-SHOCK!
SABRETOOTH!
THEY'VE SLAUGHTERED EVERYONE OUT HERE!
GET ELIXIR CLEAR! TAKE HIM OUT THE BACK!
WRA-CHOOM
YOU HEAR THAT, KID?
GET OUT OF HERE!
GO!
I'LL HOLD THIS GUY OFF.
I...
I CAN'T JUST LEAVE THEM...
...I CAN'T LEAVE MY FRIENDS.
I CAN HELP.
I CAN HEAL THEM.
I CAN HEAL THEM--

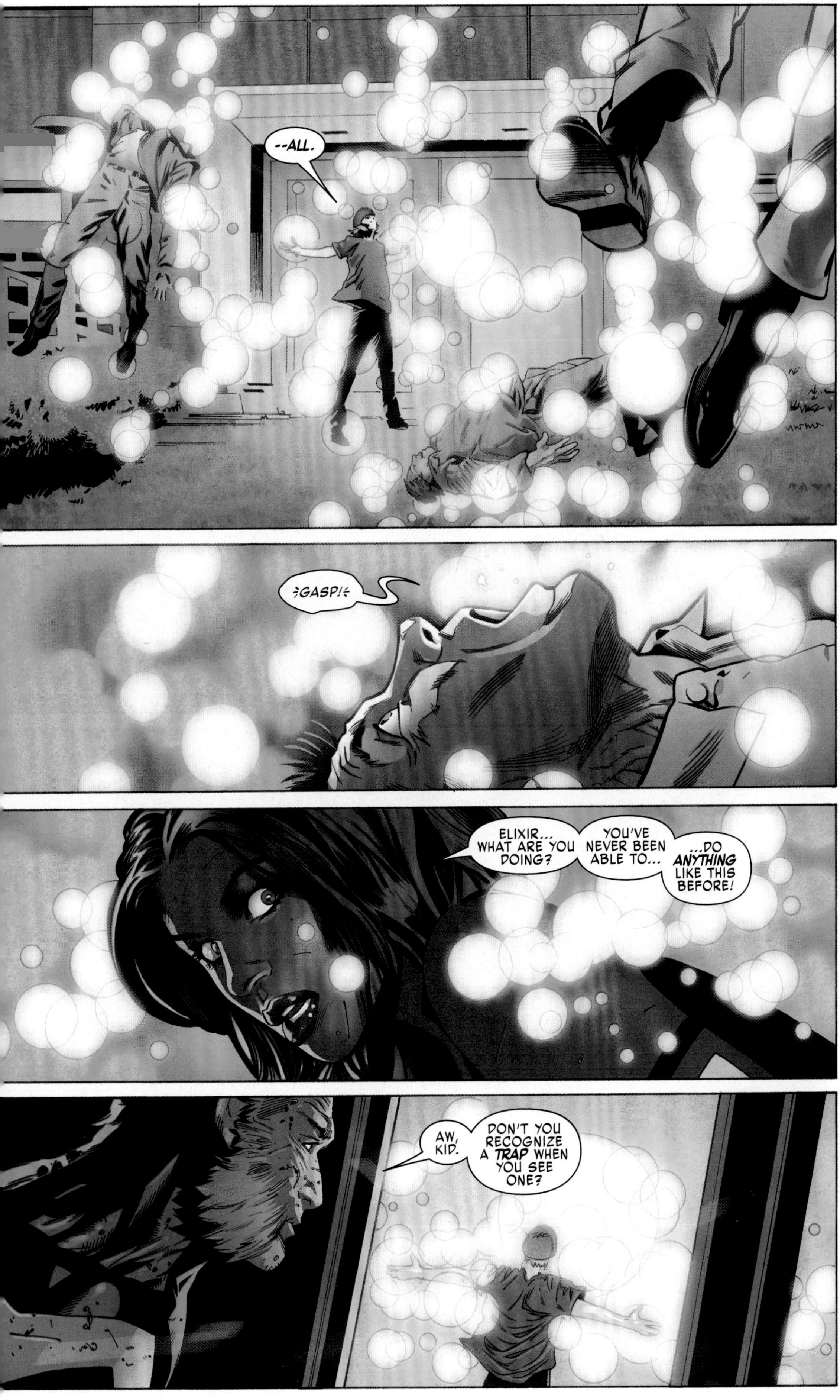
--ALL.
GASP!
ELIXIR... WHAT ARE YOU DOING?
YOU'VE NEVER BEEN ABLE TO...
...DO ANYTHING LIKE THIS BEFORE!
AW, KID.
DON'T YOU RECOGNIZE A TRAP WHEN YOU SEE ONE?

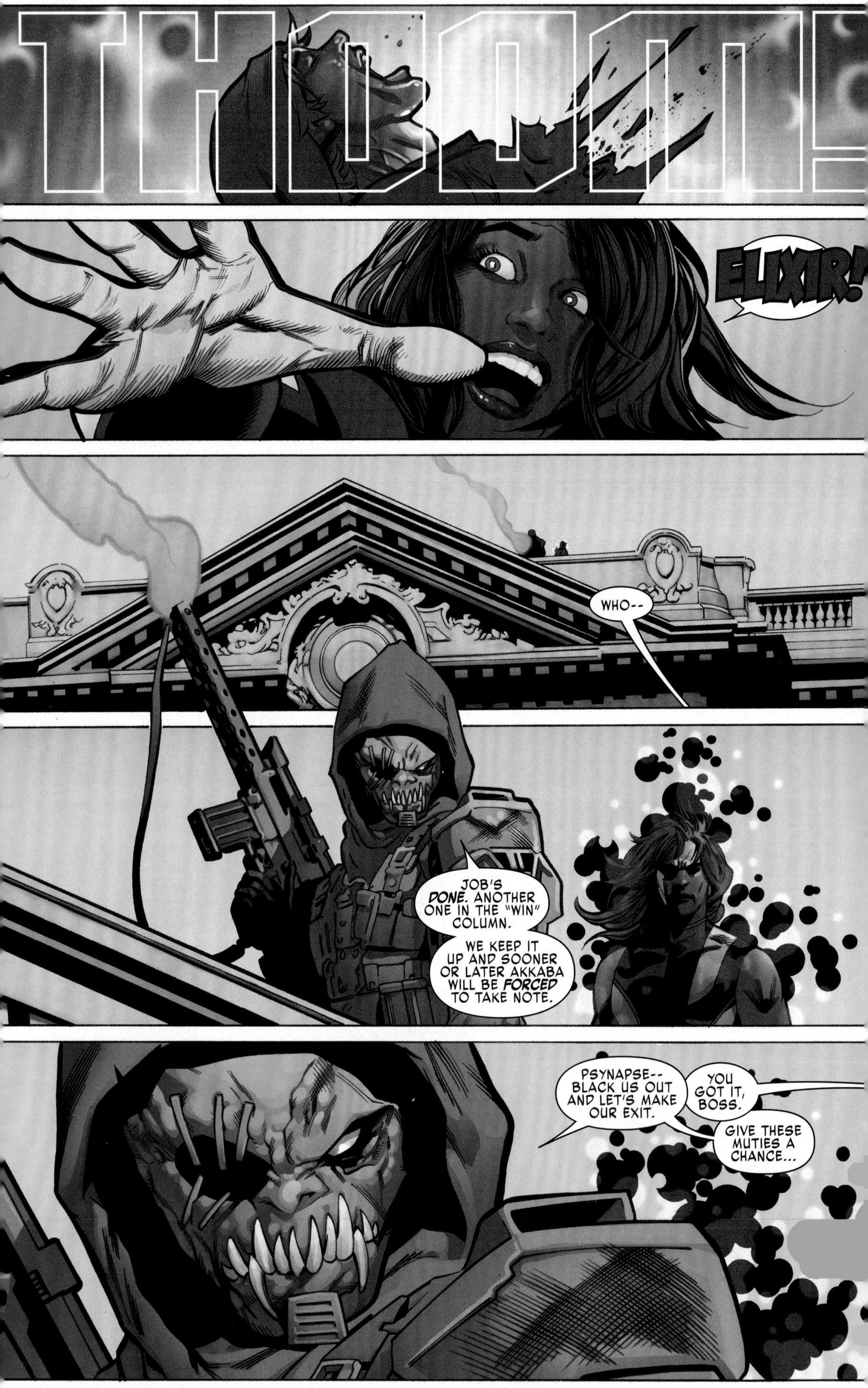
THOOM!
ELIXIR!
WHO--
JOB'S DONE. ANOTHER ONE IN THE "WIN" COLUMN.
WE KEEP IT UP AND SOONER OR LATER AKKABA WILL BE FORCED TO TAKE NOTE.
PSYNAPSE-- BLACK US OUT AND LET'S MAKE OUR EXIT.
YOU GOT IT, BOSS.
GIVE THESE MUTIES A CHANCE...

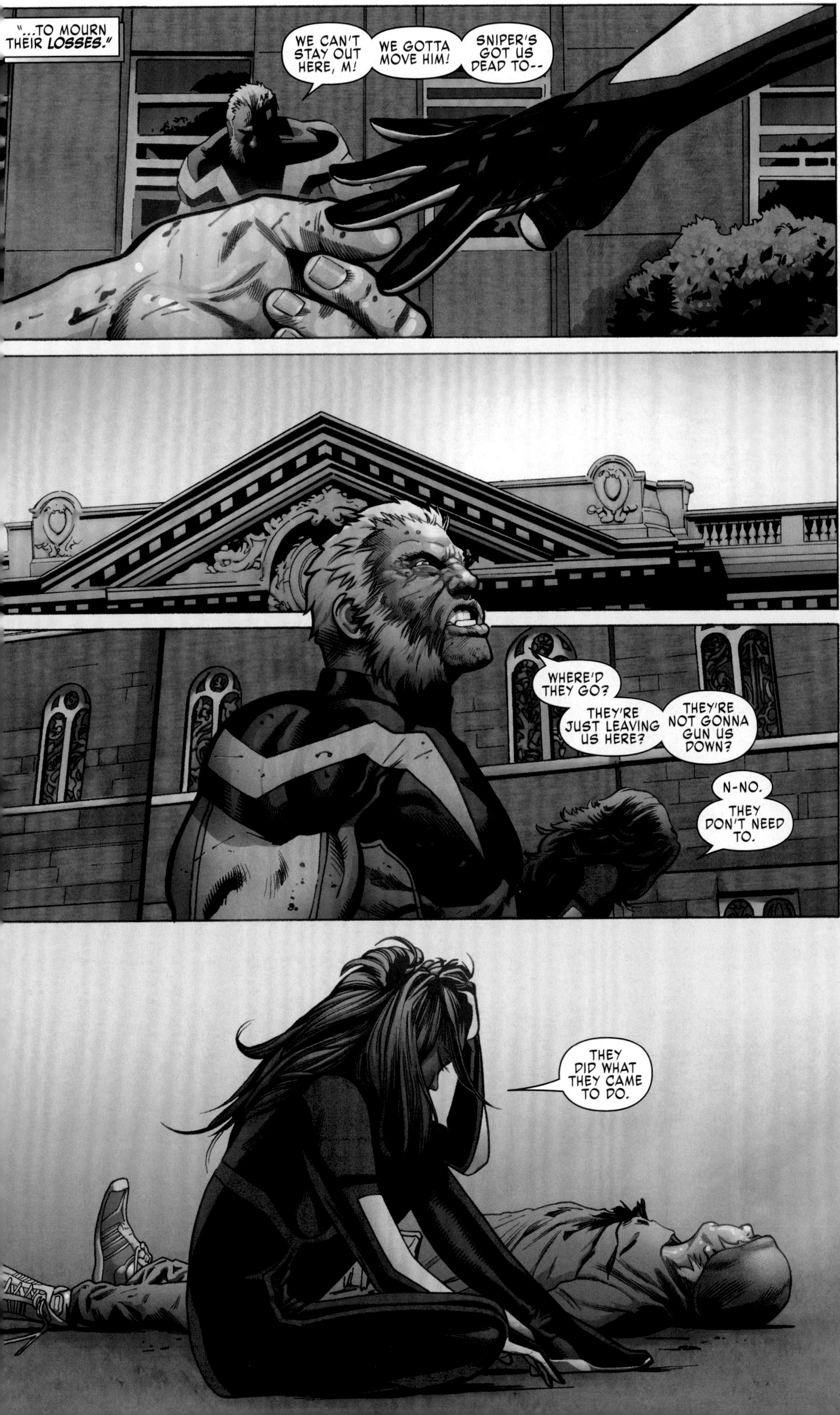
"...TO MOURN THEIR LOSSES."
WE CAN'T STAY OUT HERE, M!
WE GOTTA MOVE HIM!
SNIPER'S GOT US DEAD TO--
WHERE'D THEY GO?
THEY'RE JUST LEAVING US HERE?
THEY'RE NOT GONNA GUN US DOWN?
N-NO.
THEY DON'T NEED TO.
THEY DID WHAT THEY CAME TO DO.

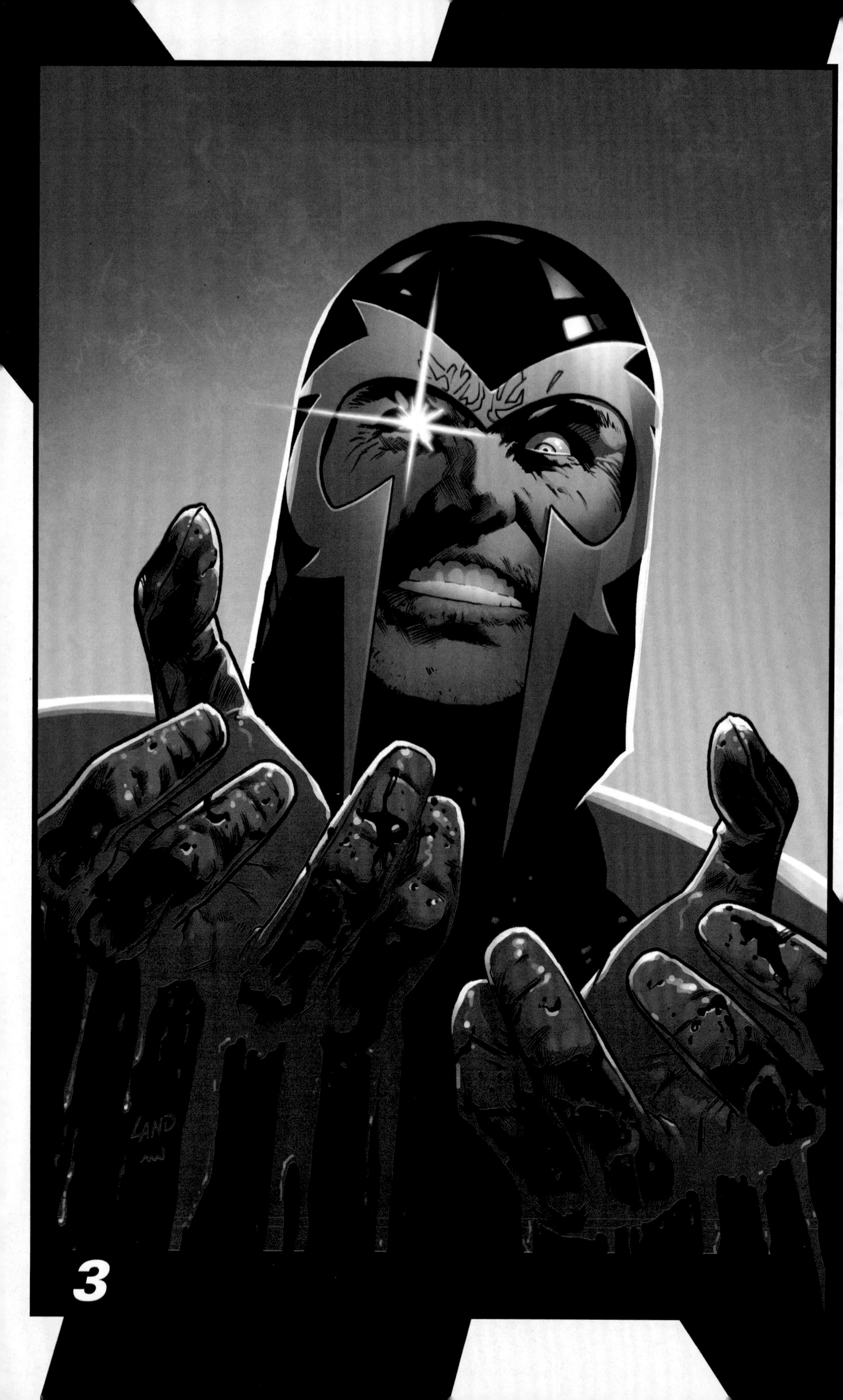
3

I KNOW WHAT YOU'RE THINKING, MAGNETO, BUT TRY TO KEEP YOURSELF IN CHECK.

MUTANTS= DISEASE

NO MUTANTS, NO M-POX

DON'T B SICKN

WE DON'T NEED THE ATTENTION RIGHT NOW.

I CAN TWEAK THE SURFACE THOUGHTS OF EVERYONE IN THE CROWD AS LONG AS THEY'RE DISTRACTED.

THEY CAN'T SEE US.

TINES LIVES!

HI THE AW

DON'T BRING SICKNESS

MAYBE THEY SHOULD, ELIZABETH.

MAYBE. BUT WE'RE NOT HERE TO TERRORIZE THESE PEOPLE.

I HAVEN'T ABANDONED THOSE IDEALS.

IT'S MORE LIKE I'VE PUT THEM ON HOLD.

PLEASE, DON'T TRY TO JOKE.

IT ONLY MAKES YOU SOUND EVEN BARMIER THAN USUAL.

WHO'S JOKING?

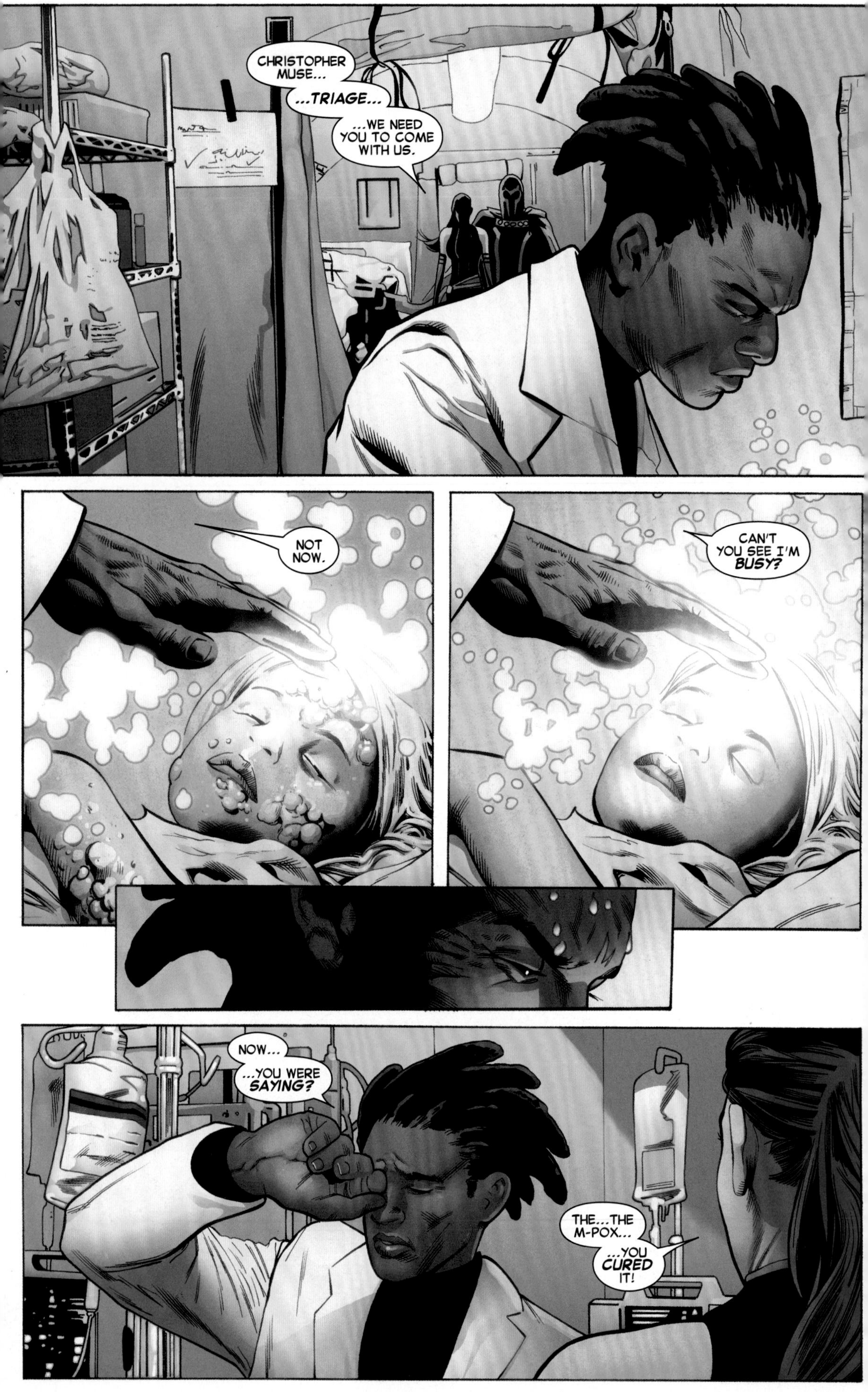
CHRISTOPHER MUSE...
...TRIAGE...
...WE NEED YOU TO COME WITH US.
NOT NOW.
CAN'T YOU SEE I'M BUSY?
NOW...
...YOU WERE SAYING?
THE...THE M-POX...
...YOU CURED IT!

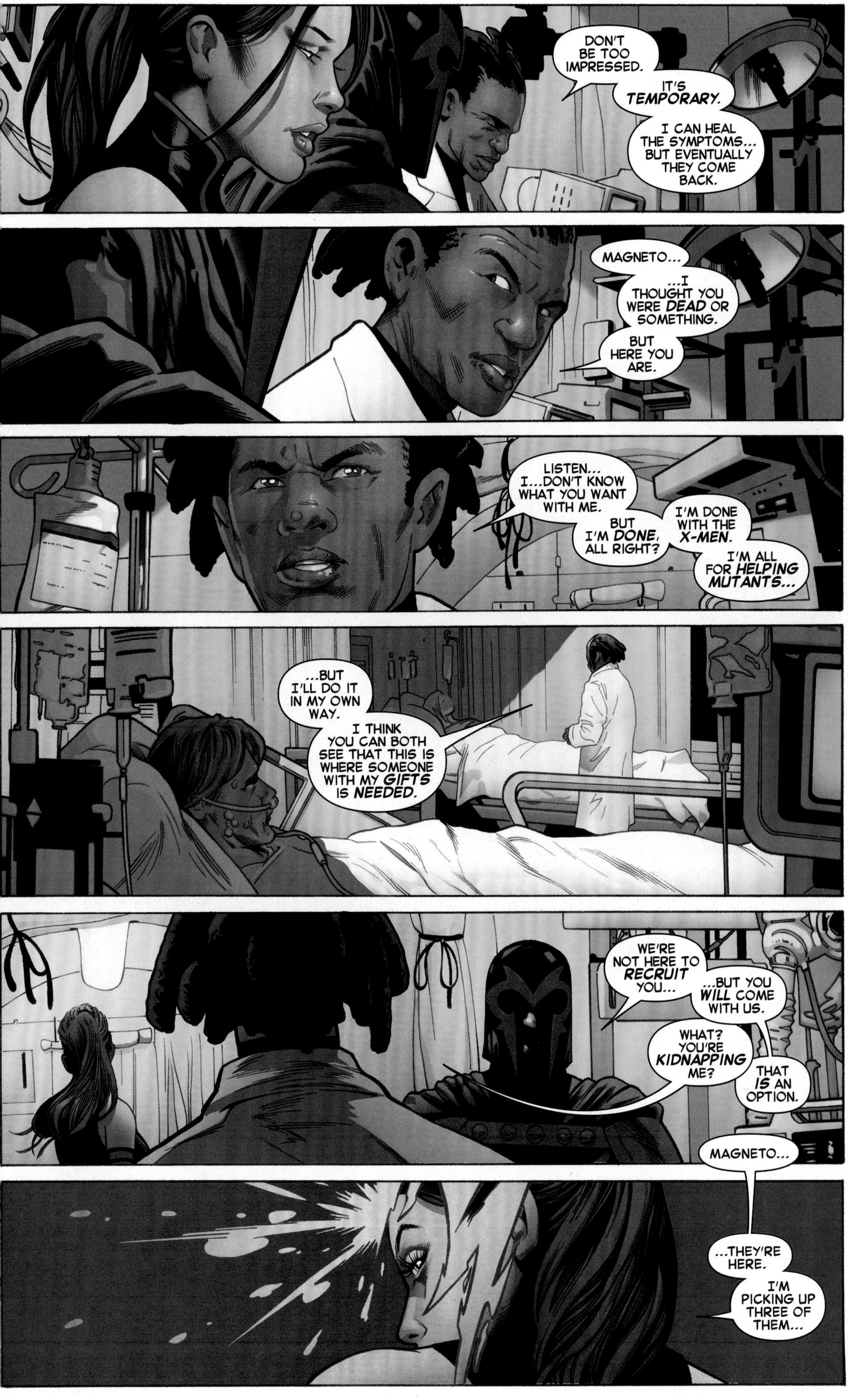
DON'T BE TOO IMPRESSED.
IT'S TEMPORARY.
I CAN HEAL THE SYMPTOMS... BUT EVENTUALLY THEY COME BACK.
MAGNETO...
...I THOUGHT YOU WERE DEAD OR SOMETHING.
BUT HERE YOU ARE.
LISTEN... I...DON'T KNOW WHAT YOU WANT WITH ME.
BUT I'M DONE, ALL RIGHT?
I'M DONE WITH THE X-MEN.
I'M ALL FOR HELPING MUTANTS...
...BUT I'LL DO IT IN MY OWN WAY.
I THINK YOU CAN BOTH SEE THAT THIS IS WHERE SOMEONE WITH MY GIFTS IS NEEDED.
WE'RE NOT HERE TO RECRUIT YOU...
...BUT YOU WILL COME WITH US.
WHAT? YOU'RE KIDNAPPING ME?
THAT IS AN OPTION.
MAGNETO...
...THEY'RE HERE.
I'M PICKING UP THREE OF THEM...

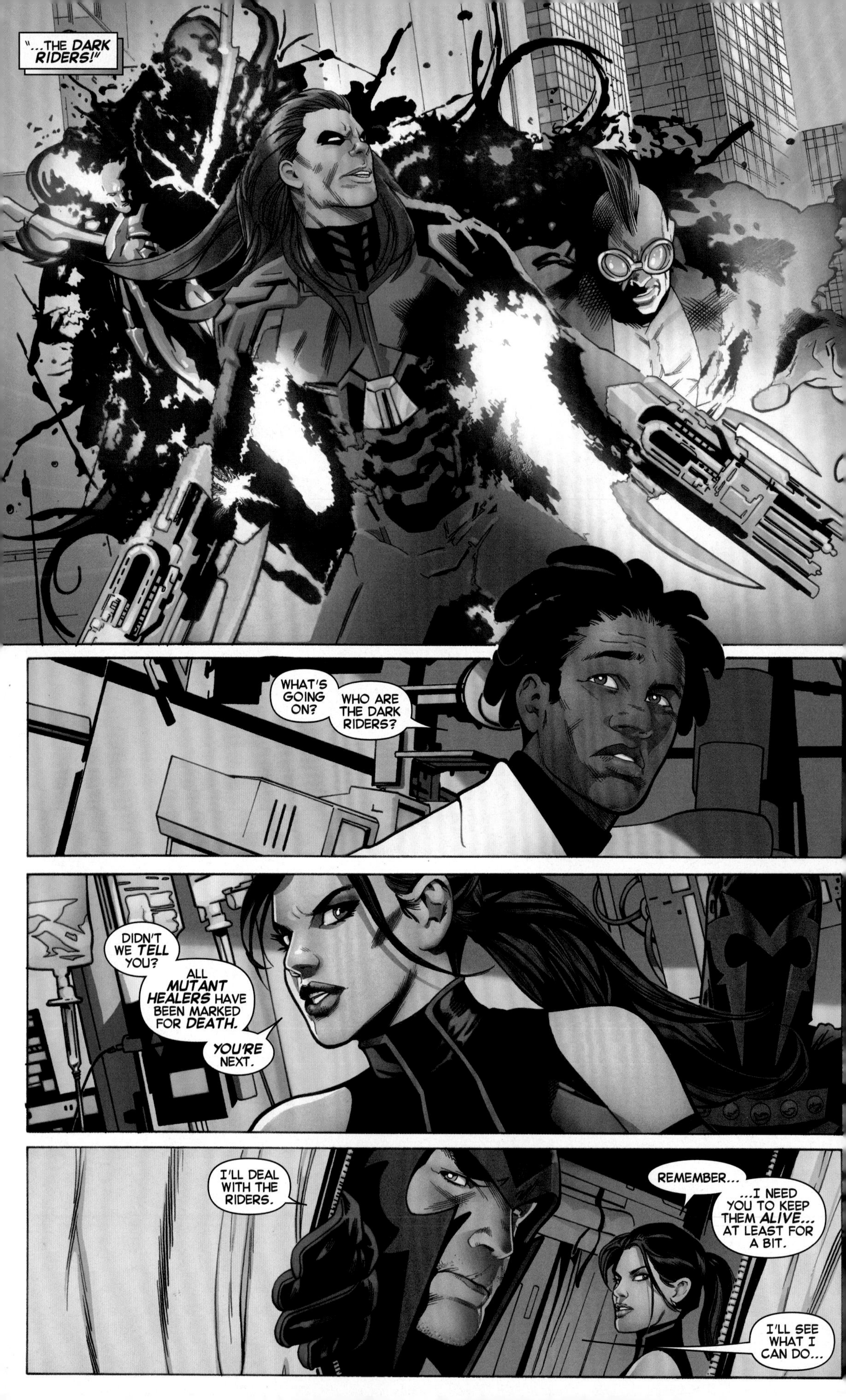
"...THE DARK RIDERS!"
WHAT'S GOING ON?
WHO ARE THE DARK RIDERS?
DIDN'T WE TELL YOU?
ALL MUTANT HEALERS HAVE BEEN MARKED FOR DEATH.
YOU'RE NEXT.
I'LL DEAL WITH THE RIDERS.
REMEMBER...
...I NEED YOU TO KEEP THEM ALIVE... AT LEAST FOR A BIT.
I'LL SEE WHAT I CAN DO...

"...BUT I MAKE NO PROMISES."

OUR QUARRY'S NEARBY.

FLUSH HIM OUT, HURRICANE!

WRRRRSSSSHHHH

WHAT IS THIS?

--THE MUTANTS?

AAAAH!

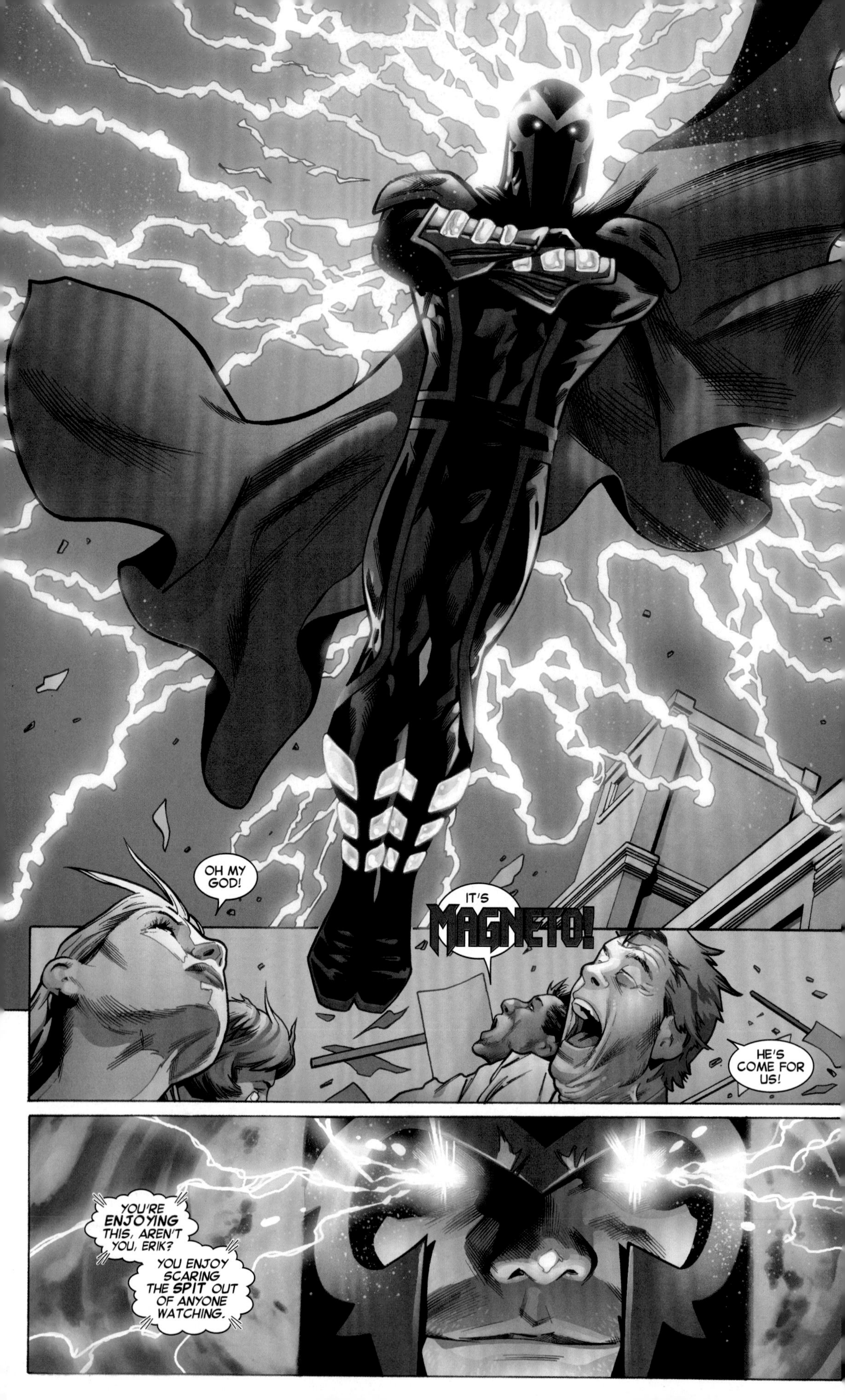
OH MY GOD!
IT'S MAGNETO!
HE'S COME FOR US!
YOU'RE ENJOYING THIS, AREN'T YOU, ERIK?
YOU ENJOY SCARING THE SPIT OUT OF ANYONE WATCHING.

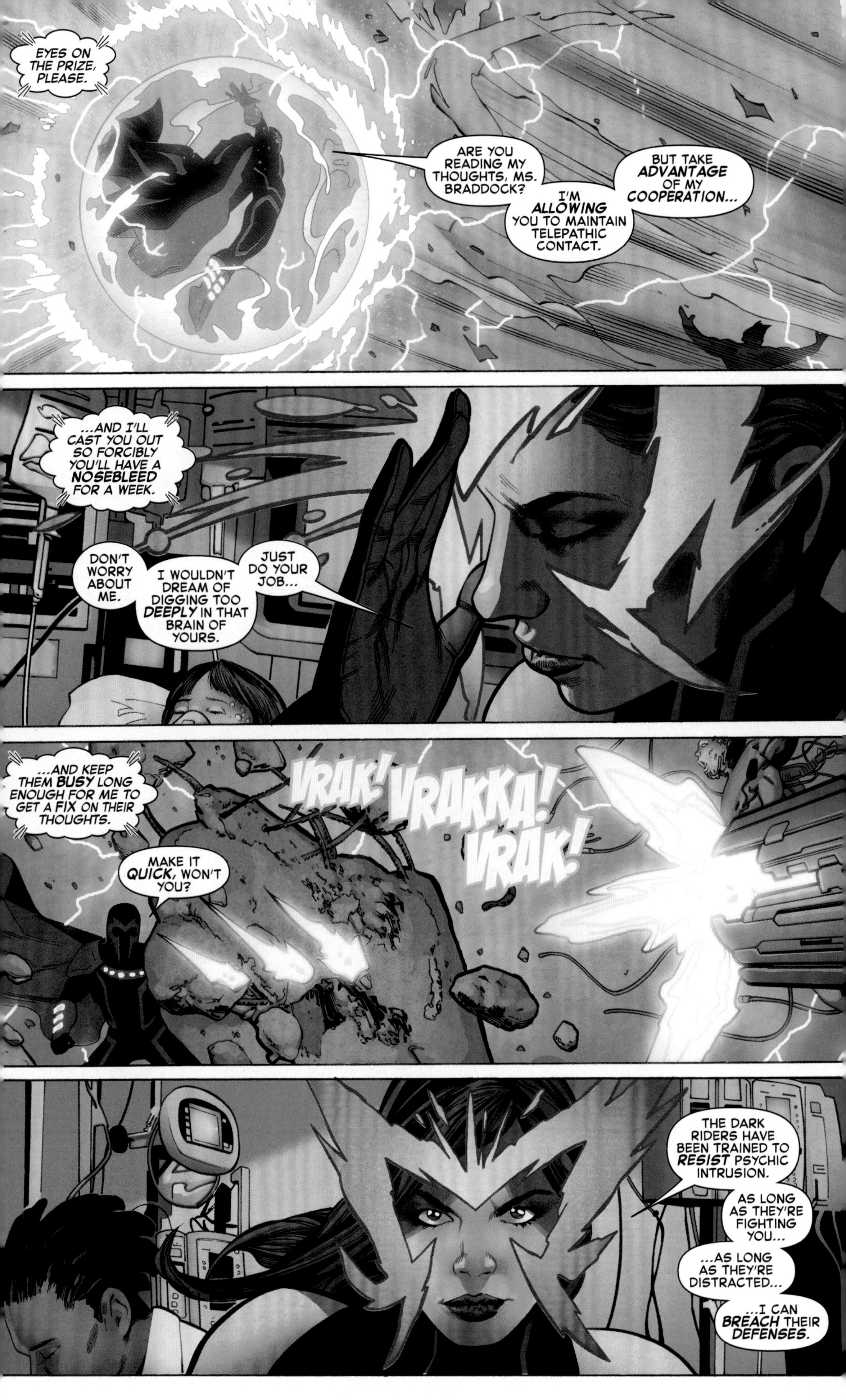

EYES ON THE PRIZE, PLEASE.
ARE YOU READING MY THOUGHTS, MS. BRADDOCK?
I'M ALLOWING YOU TO MAINTAIN TELEPATHIC CONTACT.
BUT TAKE ADVANTAGE OF MY COOPERATION...
...AND I'LL CAST YOU OUT SO FORCIBLY YOU'LL HAVE A NOSEBLEED FOR A WEEK.
DON'T WORRY ABOUT ME.
I WOULDN'T DREAM OF DIGGING TOO DEEPLY IN THAT BRAIN OF YOURS.
JUST DO YOUR JOB...
...AND KEEP THEM BUSY LONG ENOUGH FOR ME TO GET A FIX ON THEIR THOUGHTS.
VRAK! VRAKKA! VRAK!
MAKE IT QUICK, WON'T YOU?
THE DARK RIDERS HAVE BEEN TRAINED TO RESIST PSYCHIC INTRUSION.
AS LONG AS THEY'RE FIGHTING YOU...
...AS LONG AS THEY'RE DISTRACTED...
...I CAN BREACH THEIR DEFENSES.

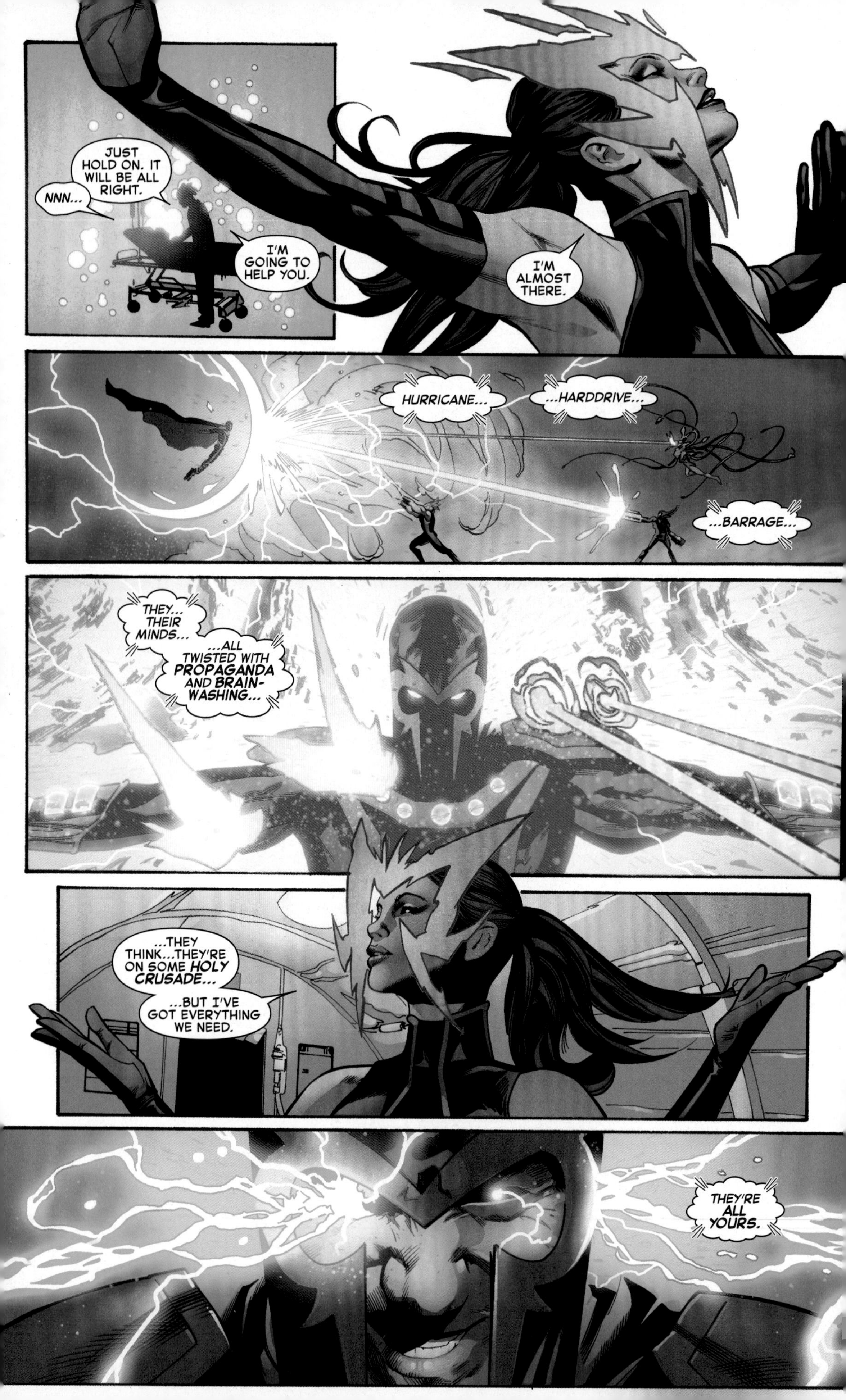

JUST HOLD ON. IT WILL BE ALL RIGHT.
NNN...
I'M GOING TO HELP YOU.
I'M ALMOST THERE.
HURRICANE...
...HARDDRIVE...
...BARRAGE...
THEY... THEIR MINDS...
...ALL TWISTED WITH PROPAGANDA AND BRAIN-WASHING...
...THEY THINK...THEY'RE ON SOME HOLY CRUSADE...
...BUT I'VE GOT EVERYTHING WE NEED.
THEY'RE ALL YOURS.

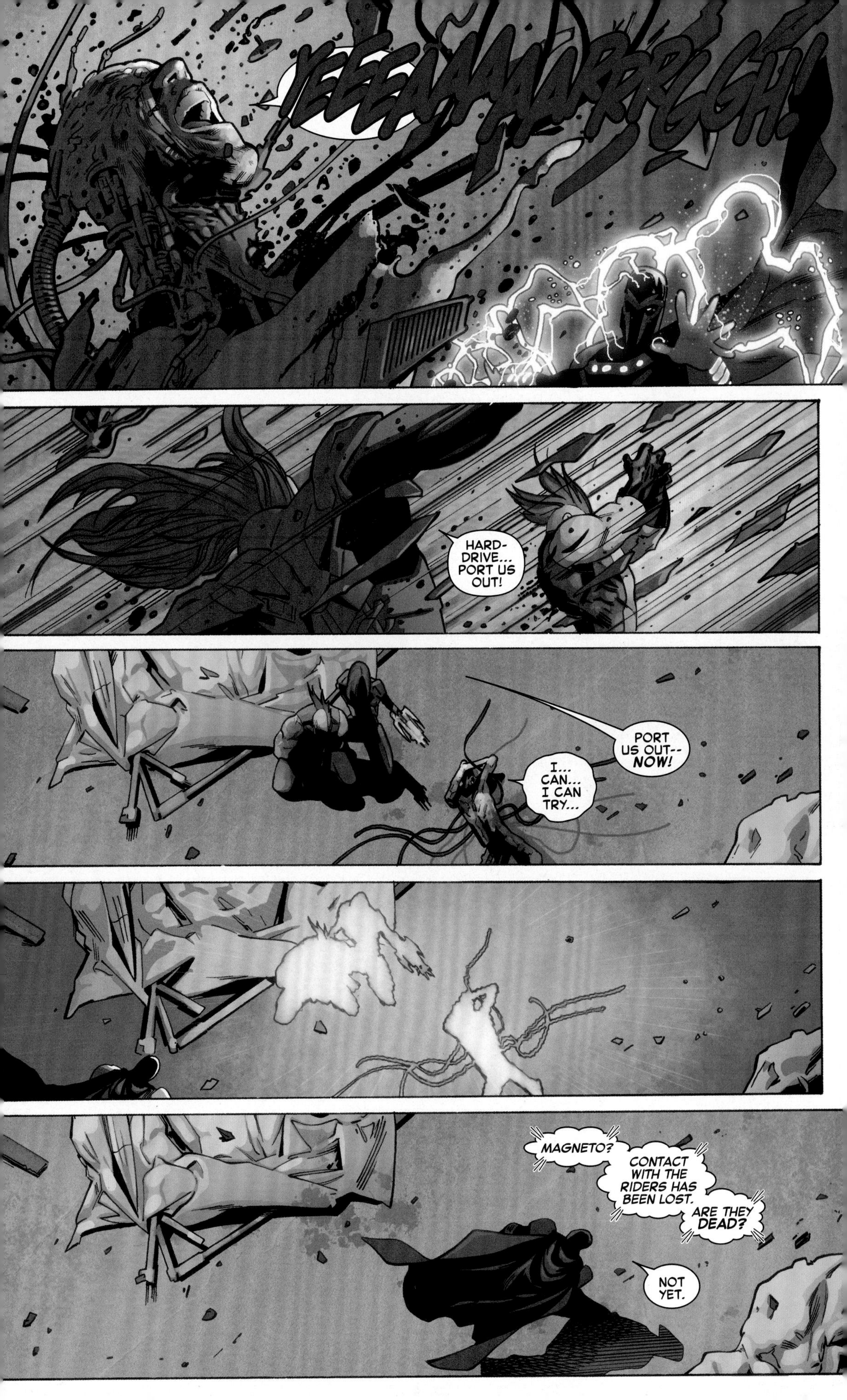
YEEEAAAAARRRGGH!
HARD-DRIVE... PORT US OUT!
PORT US OUT--NOW!
I... CAN... I CAN TRY...
MAGNETO?
CONTACT WITH THE RIDERS HAS BEEN LOST.
ARE THEY DEAD?
NOT YET.

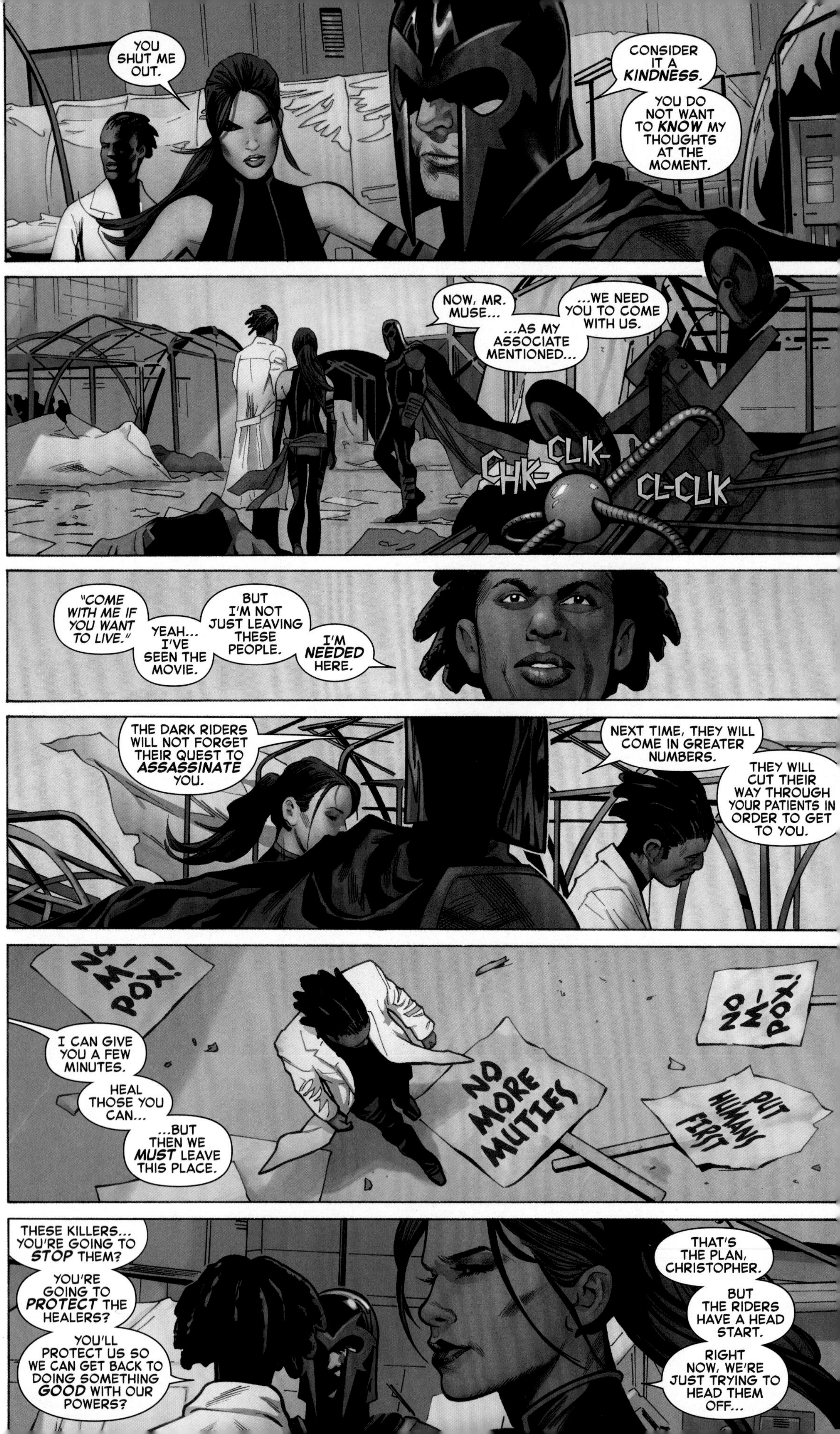

YOU SHUT ME OUT.
CONSIDER IT A KINDNESS.
YOU DO NOT WANT TO KNOW MY THOUGHTS AT THE MOMENT.
NOW, MR. MUSE...
...AS MY ASSOCIATE MENTIONED...
...WE NEED YOU TO COME WITH US.
CHK-
CLIK-
CL-CLIK
"COME WITH ME IF YOU WANT TO LIVE."
YEAH... I'VE SEEN THE MOVIE.
BUT I'M NOT JUST LEAVING THESE PEOPLE.
I'M NEEDED HERE.
THE DARK RIDERS WILL NOT FORGET THEIR QUEST TO ASSASSINATE YOU.
NEXT TIME, THEY WILL COME IN GREATER NUMBERS.
THEY WILL CUT THEIR WAY THROUGH YOUR PATIENTS IN ORDER TO GET TO YOU.
NO M-POX!
NO M-POX!
I CAN GIVE YOU A FEW MINUTES.
HEAL THOSE YOU CAN...
...BUT THEN WE MUST LEAVE THIS PLACE.
NO MORE MUTIES
PUT HUMANS FIRST
THESE KILLERS... YOU'RE GOING TO STOP THEM?
YOU'RE GOING TO PROTECT THE HEALERS?
YOU'LL PROTECT US SO WE CAN GET BACK TO DOING SOMETHING GOOD WITH OUR POWERS?
THAT'S THE PLAN, CHRISTOPHER.
BUT THE RIDERS HAVE A HEAD START.
RIGHT NOW, WE'RE JUST TRYING TO HEAD THEM OFF...

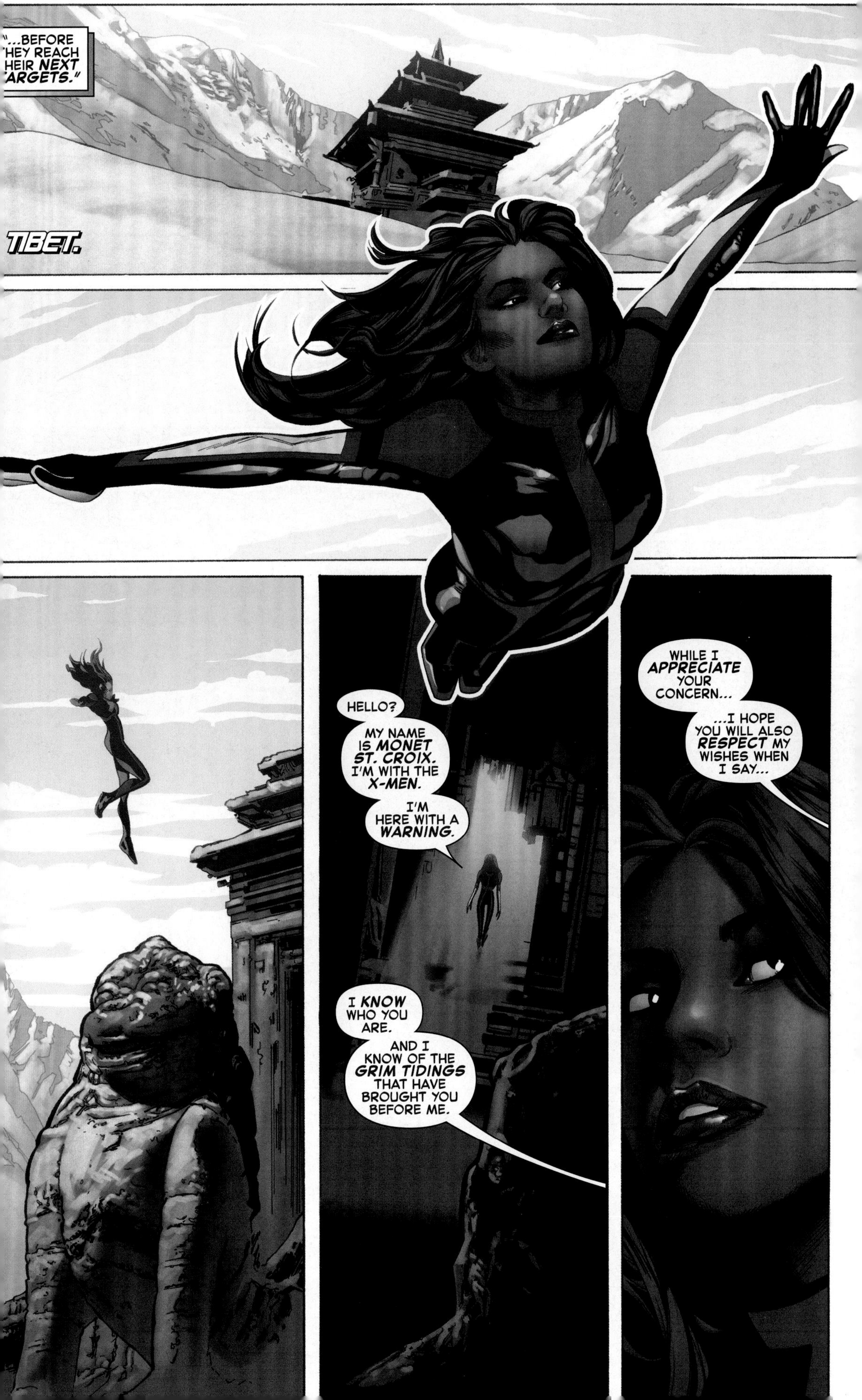
"...BEFORE
THEY REACH
THEIR NEXT
TARGETS."
TIBET.
HELLO?
MY NAME IS MONET ST. CROIX. I'M WITH THE X-MEN.
I'M HERE WITH A WARNING.
I KNOW WHO YOU ARE.
AND I KNOW OF THE GRIM TIDINGS THAT HAVE BROUGHT YOU BEFORE ME.
WHILE I APPRECIATE YOUR CONCERN...
...I HOPE YOU WILL ALSO RESPECT MY WISHES WHEN I SAY...

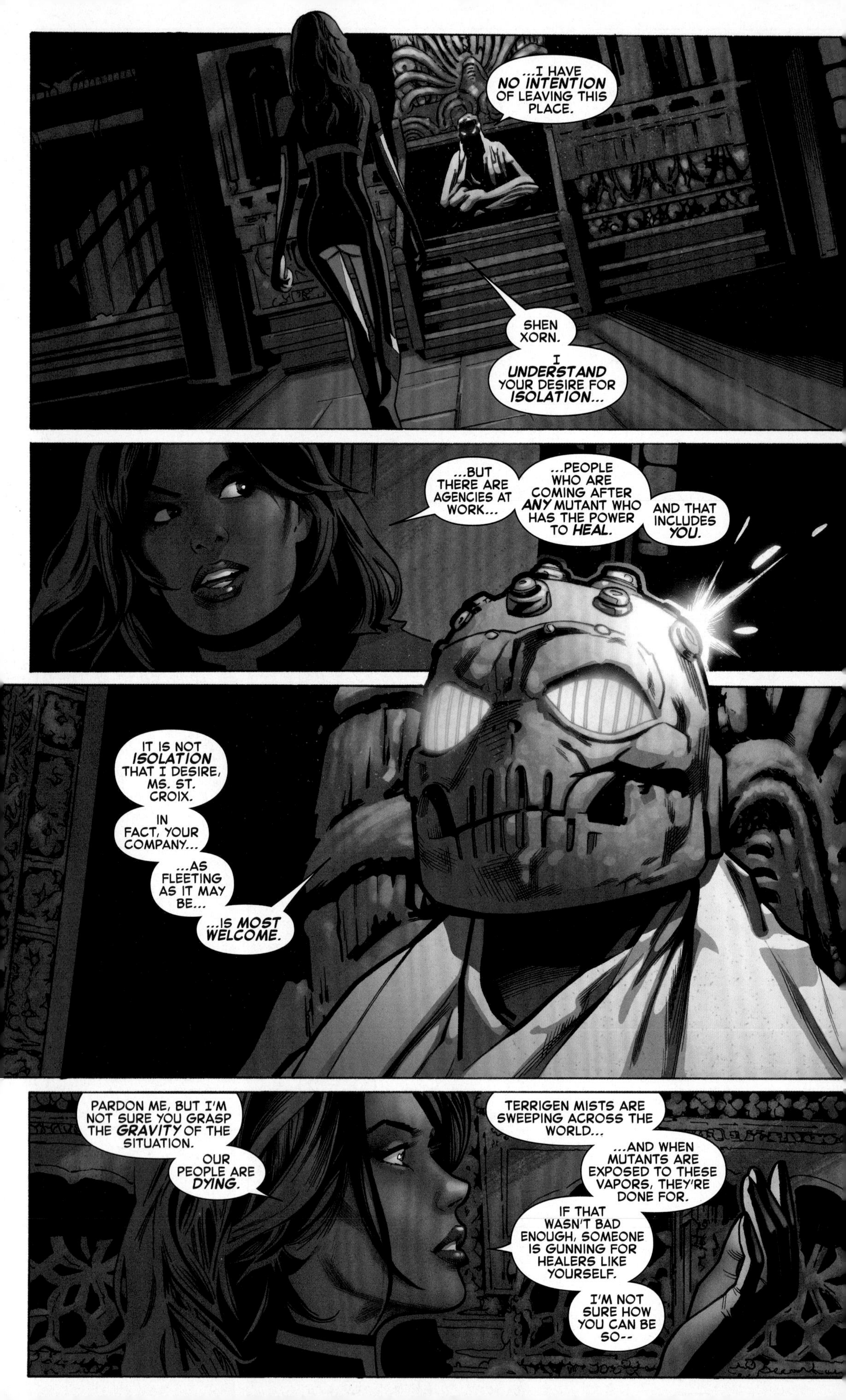

...I HAVE NO INTENTION OF LEAVING THIS PLACE.
SHEN XORN.
I UNDERSTAND YOUR DESIRE FOR ISOLATION...
...BUT THERE ARE AGENCIES AT WORK...
...PEOPLE WHO ARE COMING AFTER ANY MUTANT WHO HAS THE POWER TO HEAL.
AND THAT INCLUDES YOU.
IT IS NOT ISOLATION THAT I DESIRE, MS. ST. CROIX.
IN FACT, YOUR COMPANY...
...AS FLEETING AS IT MAY BE...
...IS MOST WELCOME.
PARDON ME, BUT I'M NOT SURE YOU GRASP THE GRAVITY OF THE SITUATION.
OUR PEOPLE ARE DYING.
TERRIGEN MISTS ARE SWEEPING ACROSS THE WORLD...
...AND WHEN MUTANTS ARE EXPOSED TO THESE VAPORS, THEY'RE DONE FOR.
IF THAT WASN'T BAD ENOUGH, SOMEONE IS GUNNING FOR HEALERS LIKE YOURSELF.
I'M NOT SURE HOW YOU CAN BE SO--

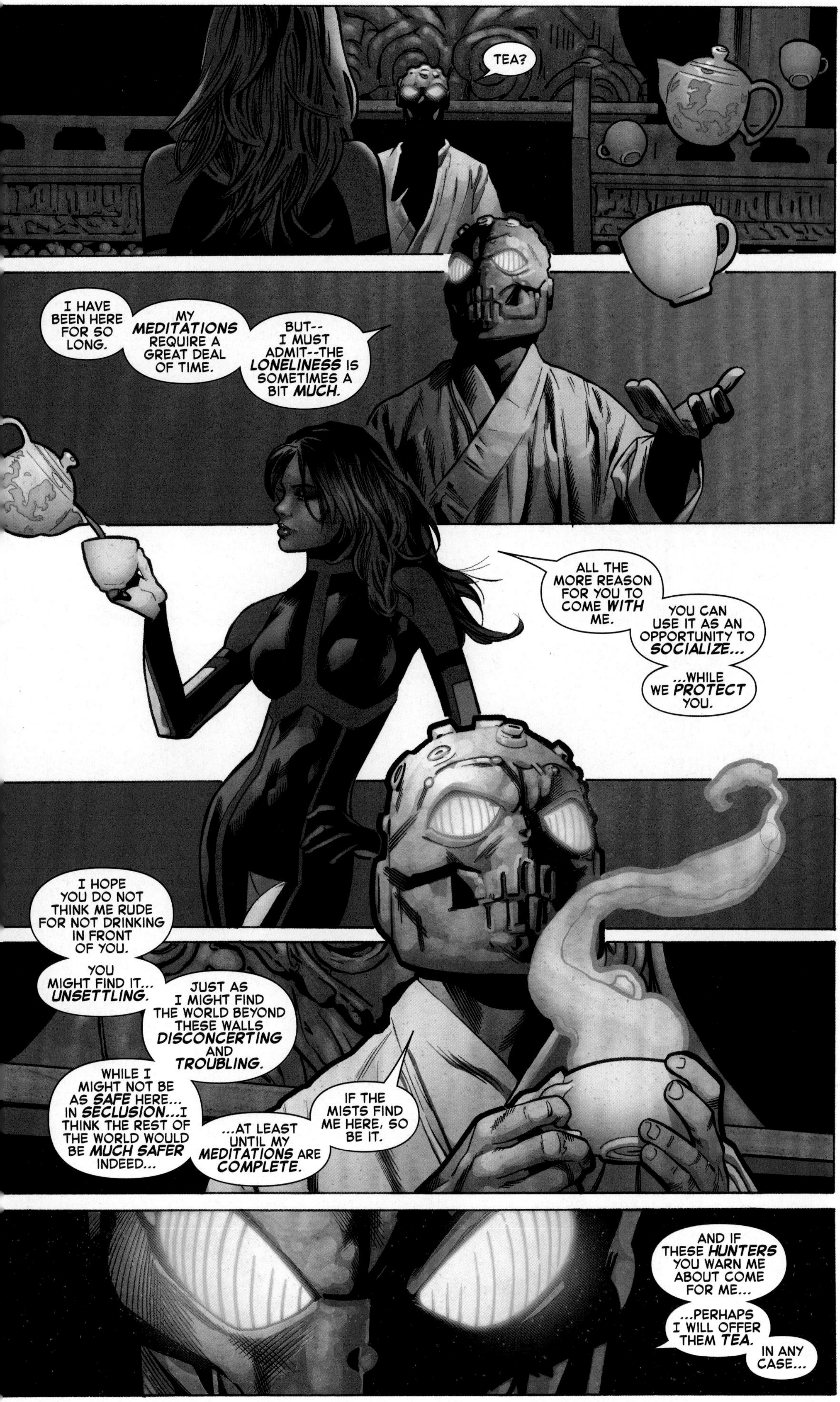
TEA?
I HAVE BEEN HERE FOR SO LONG.
MY MEDITATIONS REQUIRE A GREAT DEAL OF TIME.
BUT-- I MUST ADMIT--THE LONELINESS IS SOMETIMES A BIT MUCH.
ALL THE MORE REASON FOR YOU TO COME WITH ME.
YOU CAN USE IT AS AN OPPORTUNITY TO SOCIALIZE...
...WHILE WE PROTECT YOU.
I HOPE YOU DO NOT THINK ME RUDE FOR NOT DRINKING IN FRONT OF YOU.
YOU MIGHT FIND IT... UNSETTLING.
JUST AS I MIGHT FIND THE WORLD BEYOND THESE WALLS DISCONCERTING AND TROUBLING.
WHILE I MIGHT NOT BE AS SAFE HERE... IN SECLUSION...I THINK THE REST OF THE WORLD WOULD BE MUCH SAFER INDEED...
...AT LEAST UNTIL MY MEDITATIONS ARE COMPLETE.
IF THE MISTS FIND ME HERE, SO BE IT.
AND IF THESE HUNTERS YOU WARN ME ABOUT COME FOR ME...
...PERHAPS I WILL OFFER THEM TEA.
IN ANY CASE...

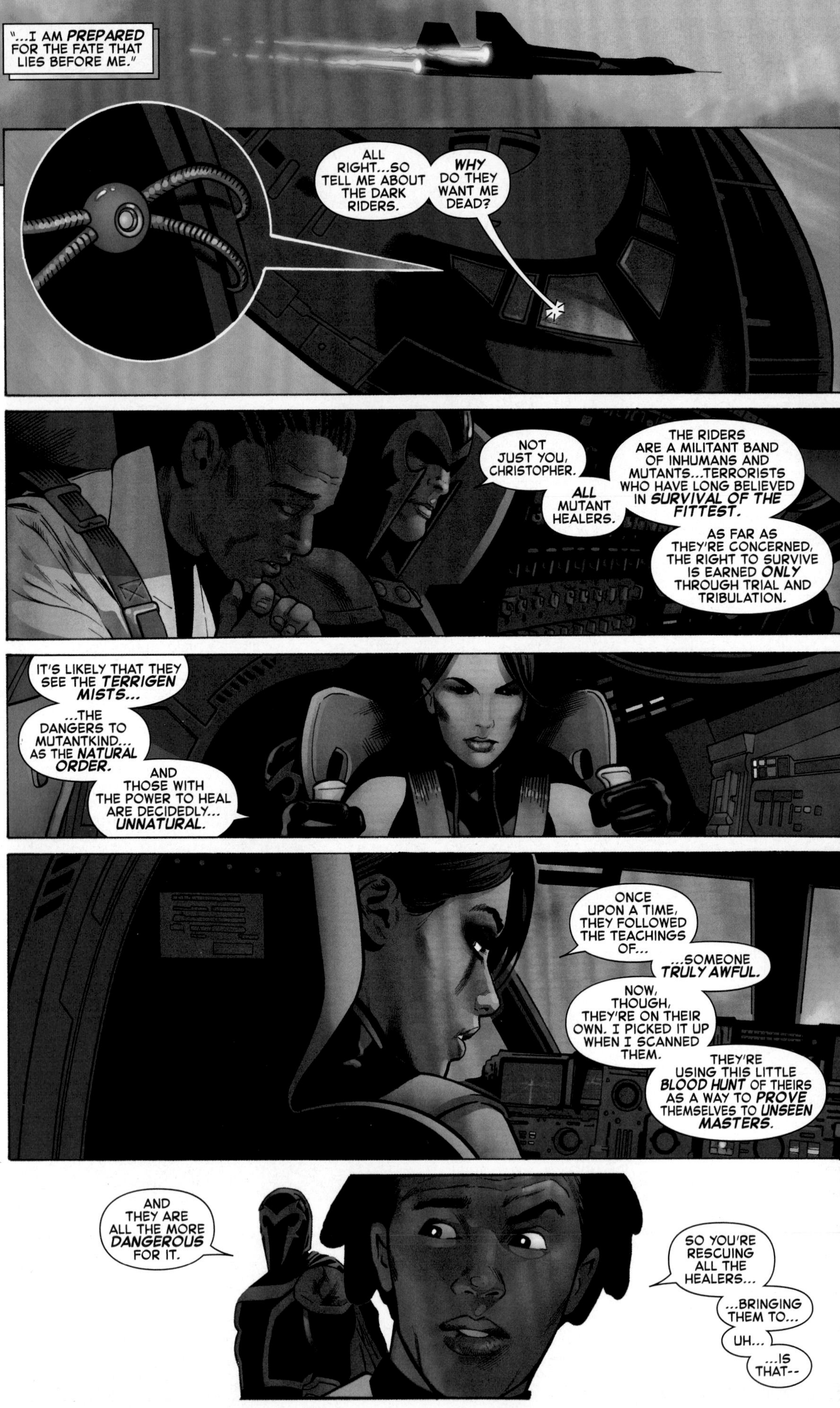
"...I AM PREPARED FOR THE FATE THAT LIES BEFORE ME."
ALL RIGHT...SO TELL ME ABOUT THE DARK RIDERS.
WHY DO THEY WANT ME DEAD?
NOT JUST YOU, CHRISTOPHER.
ALL MUTANT HEALERS.
THE RIDERS ARE A MILITANT BAND OF INHUMANS AND MUTANTS...TERRORISTS WHO HAVE LONG BELIEVED IN SURVIVAL OF THE FITTEST.
AS FAR AS THEY'RE CONCERNED, THE RIGHT TO SURVIVE IS EARNED ONLY THROUGH TRIAL AND TRIBULATION.
IT'S LIKELY THAT THEY SEE THE TERRIGEN MISTS...
...THE DANGERS TO MUTANTKIND... AS THE NATURAL ORDER.
AND THOSE WITH THE POWER TO HEAL ARE DECIDEDLY... UNNATURAL.
ONCE UPON A TIME, THEY FOLLOWED THE TEACHINGS OF...
...SOMEONE TRULY AWFUL.
NOW, THOUGH, THEY'RE ON THEIR OWN. I PICKED IT UP WHEN I SCANNED THEM.
THEY'RE USING THIS LITTLE BLOOD HUNT OF THEIRS AS A WAY TO PROVE THEMSELVES TO UNSEEN MASTERS.
AND THEY ARE ALL THE MORE DANGEROUS FOR IT.
SO YOU'RE RESCUING ALL THE HEALERS...
...BRINGING THEM TO...
UH...
...IS THAT--

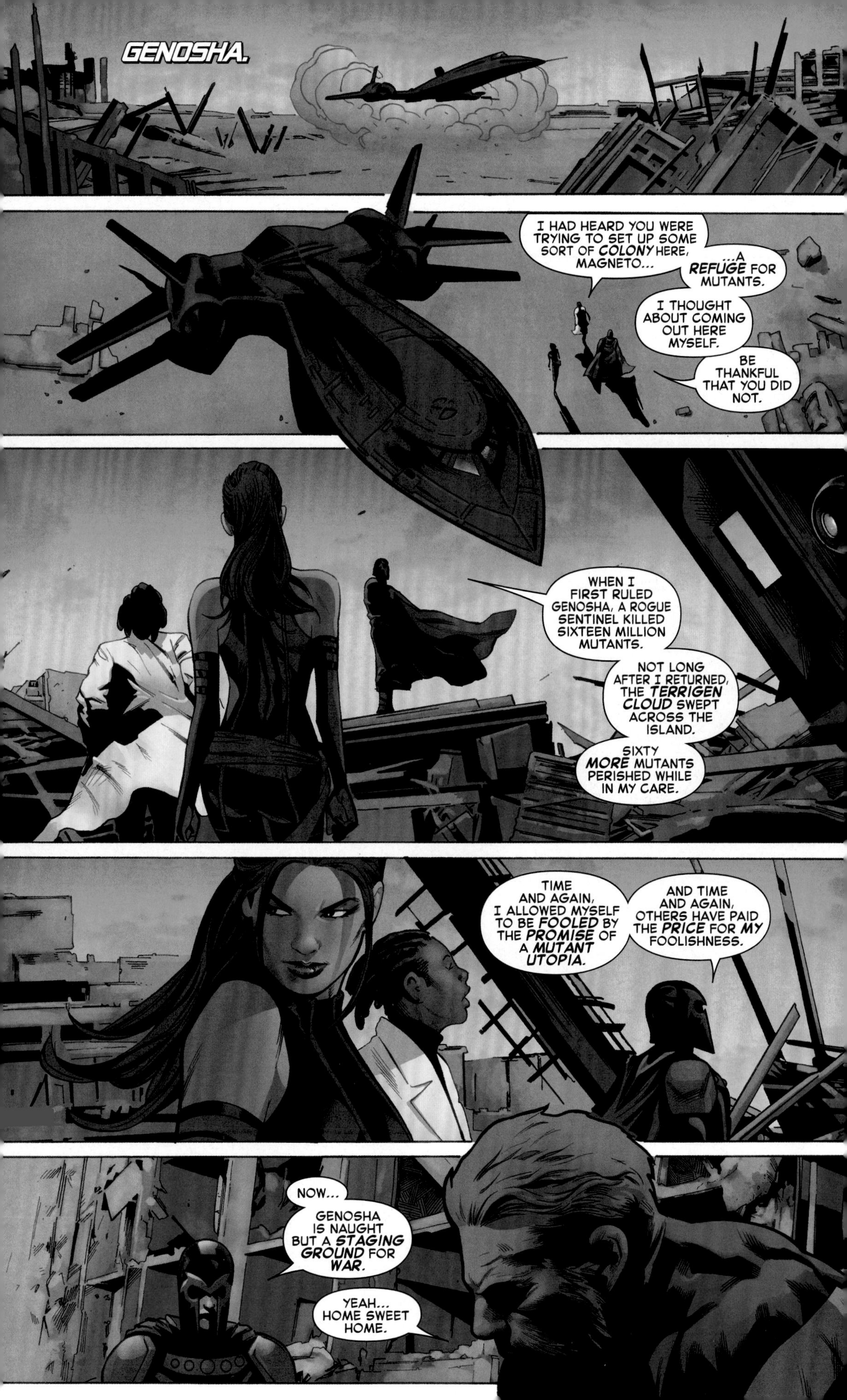
GENOSHA.
I HAD HEARD YOU WERE TRYING TO SET UP SOME SORT OF COLONY HERE, MAGNETO...
...A REFUGE FOR MUTANTS.
I THOUGHT ABOUT COMING OUT HERE MYSELF.
BE THANKFUL THAT YOU DID NOT.
WHEN I FIRST RULED GENOSHA, A ROGUE SENTINEL KILLED SIXTEEN MILLION MUTANTS.
NOT LONG AFTER I RETURNED, THE TERRIGEN CLOUD SWEPT ACROSS THE ISLAND.
SIXTY MORE MUTANTS PERISHED WHILE IN MY CARE.
TIME AND AGAIN, I ALLOWED MYSELF TO BE FOOLED BY THE PROMISE OF A MUTANT UTOPIA.
AND TIME AND AGAIN, OTHERS HAVE PAID THE PRICE FOR MY FOOLISHNESS.
NOW...
GENOSHA IS NAUGHT BUT A STAGING GROUND FOR WAR.
YEAH... HOME SWEET HOME.

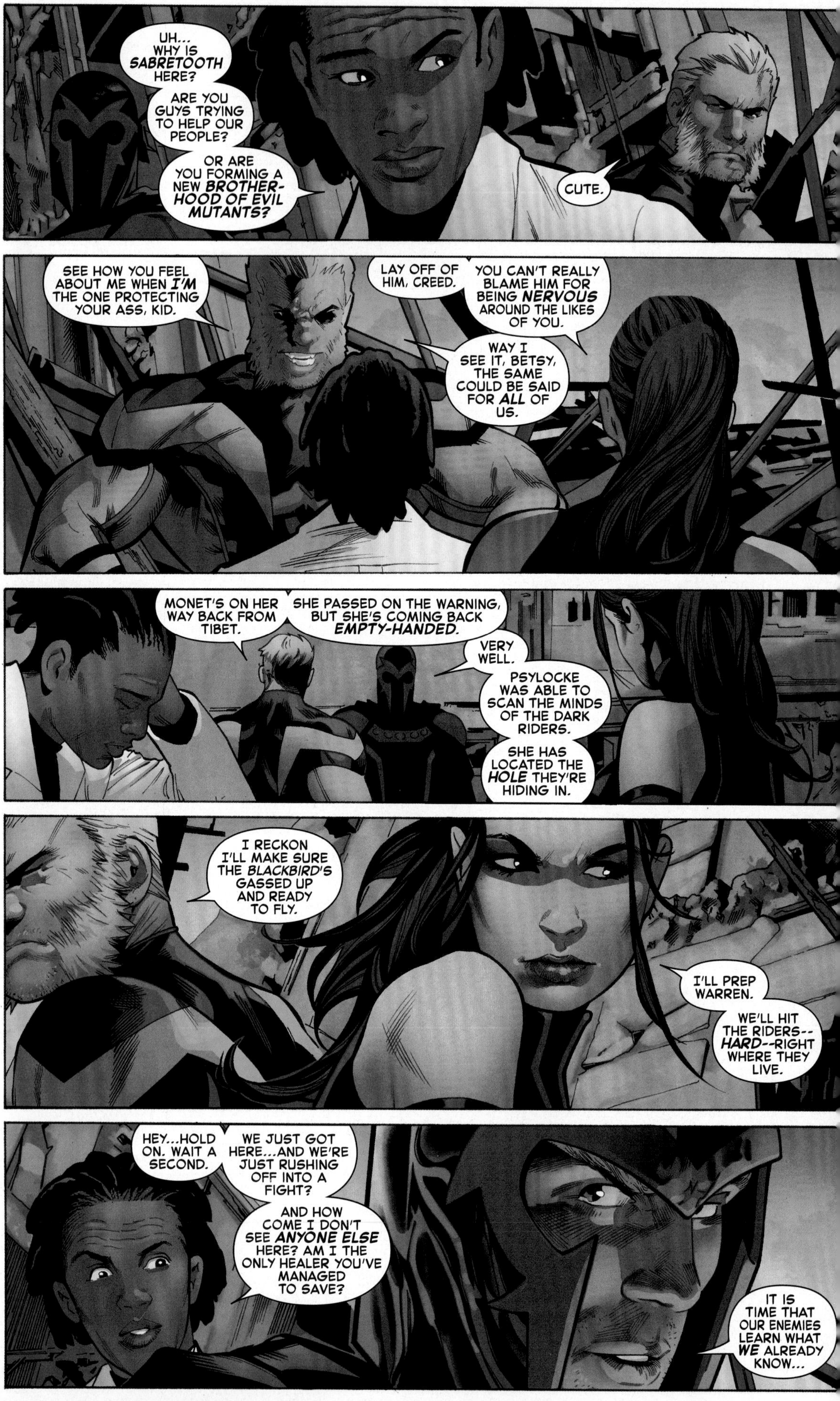
UH... WHY IS SABRETOOTH HERE?
ARE YOU GUYS TRYING TO HELP OUR PEOPLE?
OR ARE YOU FORMING A NEW BROTHERHOOD OF EVIL MUTANTS?
CUTE.
SEE HOW YOU FEEL ABOUT ME WHEN I'M THE ONE PROTECTING YOUR ASS, KID.
LAY OFF OF HIM, CREED.
YOU CAN'T REALLY BLAME HIM FOR BEING NERVOUS AROUND THE LIKES OF YOU.
WAY I SEE IT, BETSY, THE SAME COULD BE SAID FOR ALL OF US.
MONET'S ON HER WAY BACK FROM TIBET.
SHE PASSED ON THE WARNING, BUT SHE'S COMING BACK EMPTY-HANDED.
VERY WELL.
PSYLOCKE WAS ABLE TO SCAN THE MINDS OF THE DARK RIDERS.
SHE HAS LOCATED THE HOLE THEY'RE HIDING IN.
I RECKON I'LL MAKE SURE THE BLACKBIRD'S GASSED UP AND READY TO FLY.
I'LL PREP WARREN.
WE'LL HIT THE RIDERS--HARD--RIGHT WHERE THEY LIVE.
HEY...HOLD ON. WAIT A SECOND.
WE JUST GOT HERE...AND WE'RE JUST RUSHING OFF INTO A FIGHT?
AND HOW COME I DON'T SEE ANYONE ELSE HERE? AM I THE ONLY HEALER YOU'VE MANAGED TO SAVE?
IT IS TIME THAT OUR ENEMIES LEARN WHAT WE ALREADY KNOW...

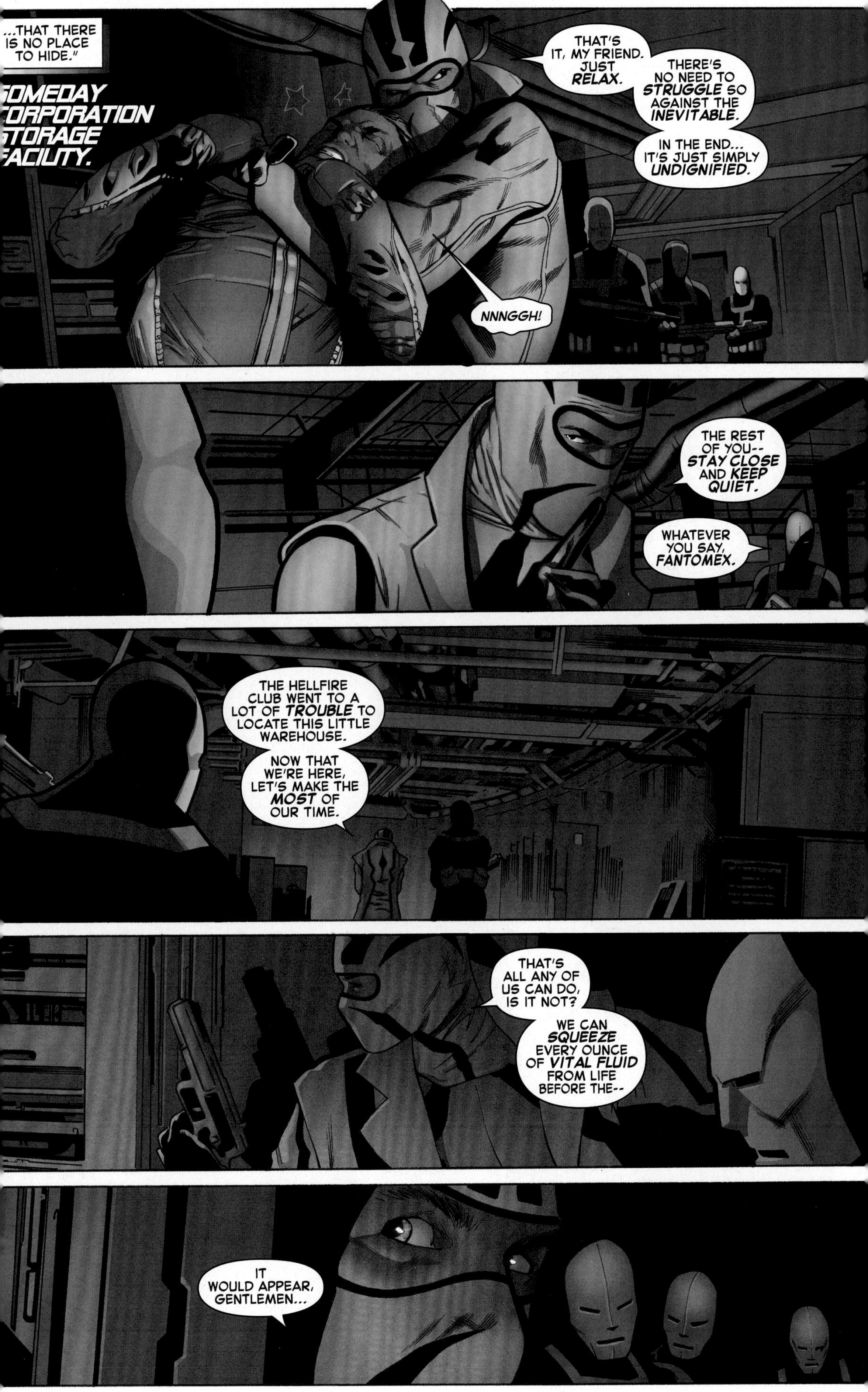

...THAT THERE IS NO PLACE TO HIDE."
SOMEDAY CORPORATION STORAGE FACILITY.
THAT'S IT, MY FRIEND. JUST RELAX.
THERE'S NO NEED TO STRUGGLE SO AGAINST THE INEVITABLE.
IN THE END... IT'S JUST SIMPLY UNDIGNIFIED.
NNNGGH!
THE REST OF YOU-- STAY CLOSE AND KEEP QUIET.
WHATEVER YOU SAY, FANTOMEX.
THE HELLFIRE CLUB WENT TO A LOT OF TROUBLE TO LOCATE THIS LITTLE WAREHOUSE.
NOW THAT WE'RE HERE, LET'S MAKE THE MOST OF OUR TIME.
THAT'S ALL ANY OF US CAN DO, IS IT NOT?
WE CAN SQUEEZE EVERY OUNCE OF VITAL FLUID FROM LIFE BEFORE THE--
IT WOULD APPEAR, GENTLEMEN...

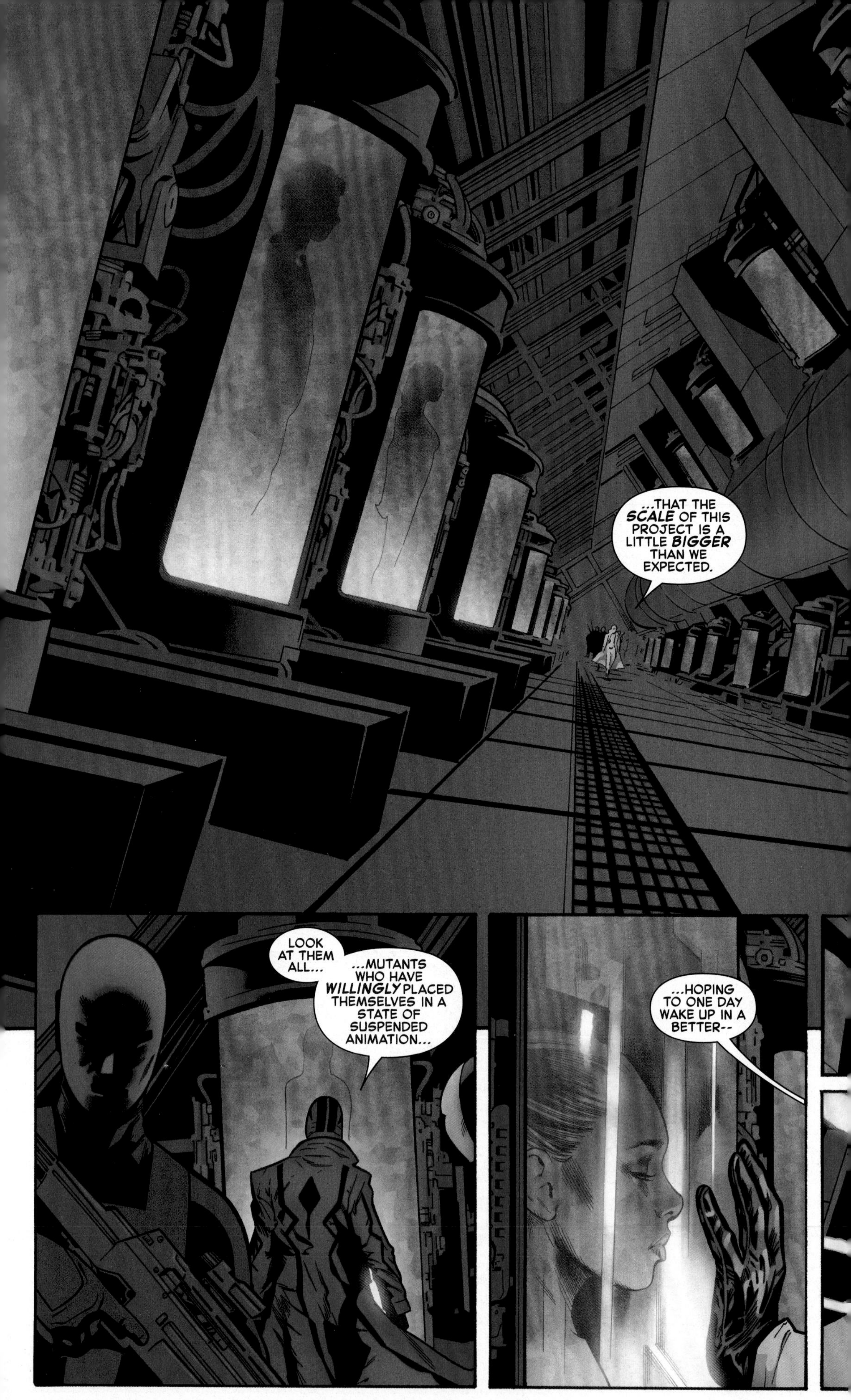
...THAT THE SCALE OF THIS PROJECT IS A LITTLE BIGGER THAN WE EXPECTED.
LOOK AT THEM ALL...
...MUTANTS WHO HAVE WILLINGLY PLACED THEMSELVES IN A STATE OF SUSPENDED ANIMATION...
...HOPING TO ONE DAY WAKE UP IN A BETTER--

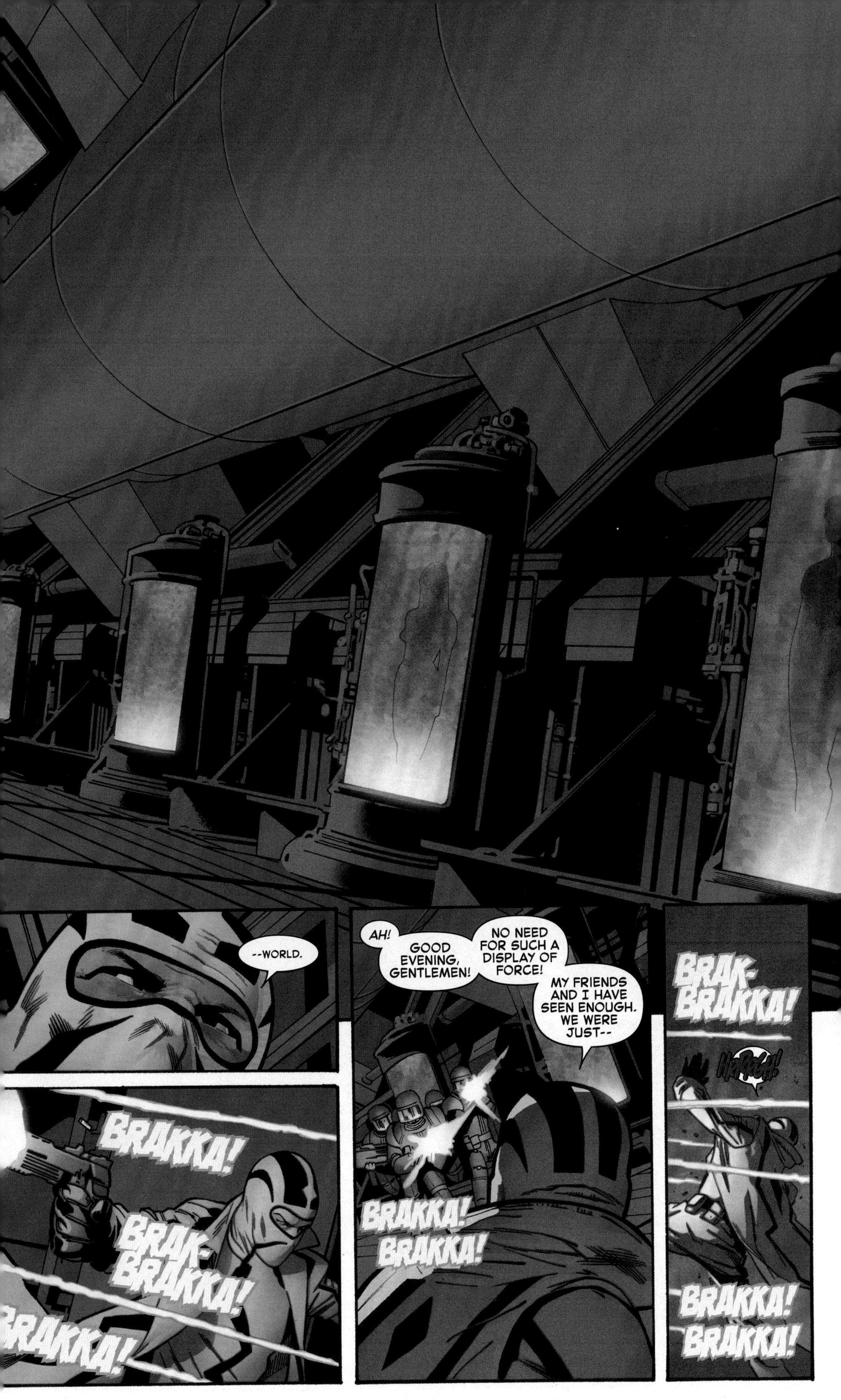
--WORLD.
AH!
GOOD EVENING, GENTLEMEN!
NO NEED FOR SUCH A DISPLAY OF FORCE!
MY FRIENDS AND I HAVE SEEN ENOUGH. WE WERE JUST--
BRAK-BRAKKA!
HRAAGH!
BRAKKA!
BRAKKA!
BRAKKA!
BRAKKA!
BRAK-BRAKKA!
BRAKKA!
BRAKKA! BRAKKA!

BRAKKA!

BRAK-BRAKKA!

SQUAD LEADER IS DOWN!

NO WAY OUT-- THEY'VE GOT US SURROUNDED!

BRAKKA!

BRAKKA! BRAKKA!

BRAKKA!

IT'S...NOT HIM... ...HE...

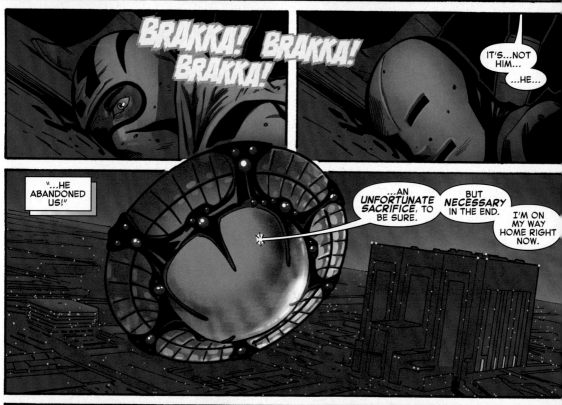

"...HE ABANDONED US!"

...AN UNFORTUNATE SACRIFICE, TO BE SURE.

BUT NECESSARY IN THE END.

I'M ON MY WAY HOME RIGHT NOW.

MYSTIQUE-- TELL OUR "MASTERS" THAT I'D LIKE AN AUDIENCE.

ANYTHING ELSE I CAN DO FOR YOU WHILE YOU'VE FORGOTTEN I'M NOT A MESSENGER SERVICE?

DON'T BE LIKE THAT, MY DEAR. MAYBE THEY'LL GIVE YOU SOME SCRAPS FOR BEING A GOOD LITTLE MINION.

AFTER ALL, I BELIEVE THEY WILL BE QUITE INTERESTED IN WHAT I HAVE TO SAY.

#1 VARIANT BY
KEN LASHLEY & NOLAN WOODARD

UNCANNY X-MEN

MAGNETO:
TXM11963

MYSTIQUE:
MM161978

SABRETOOTH:
IF141977

FANTOMEX:
NXM1282002

#1 HIP-HOP VARIANT BY
GREG LAND, JAY LEISTEN & GURU-eFX

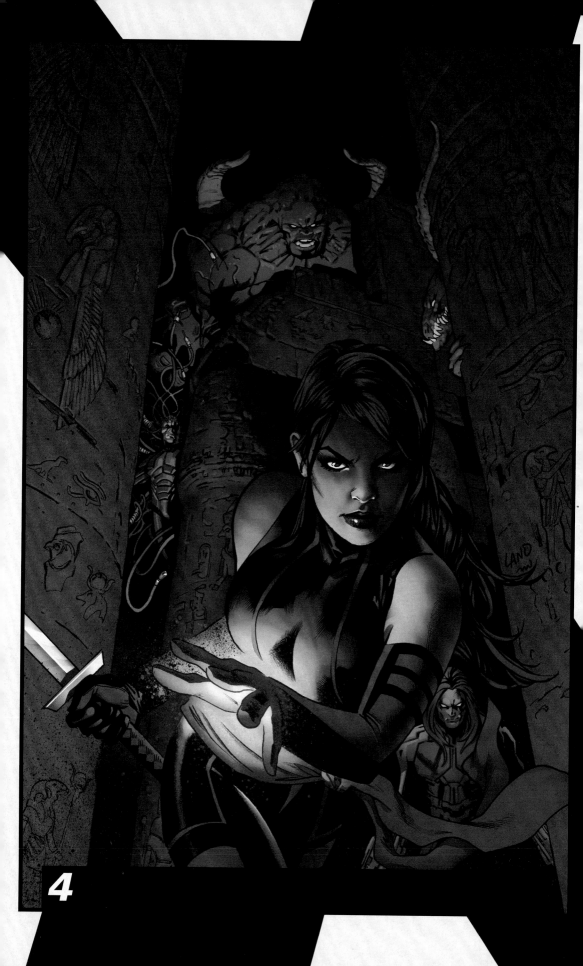

4

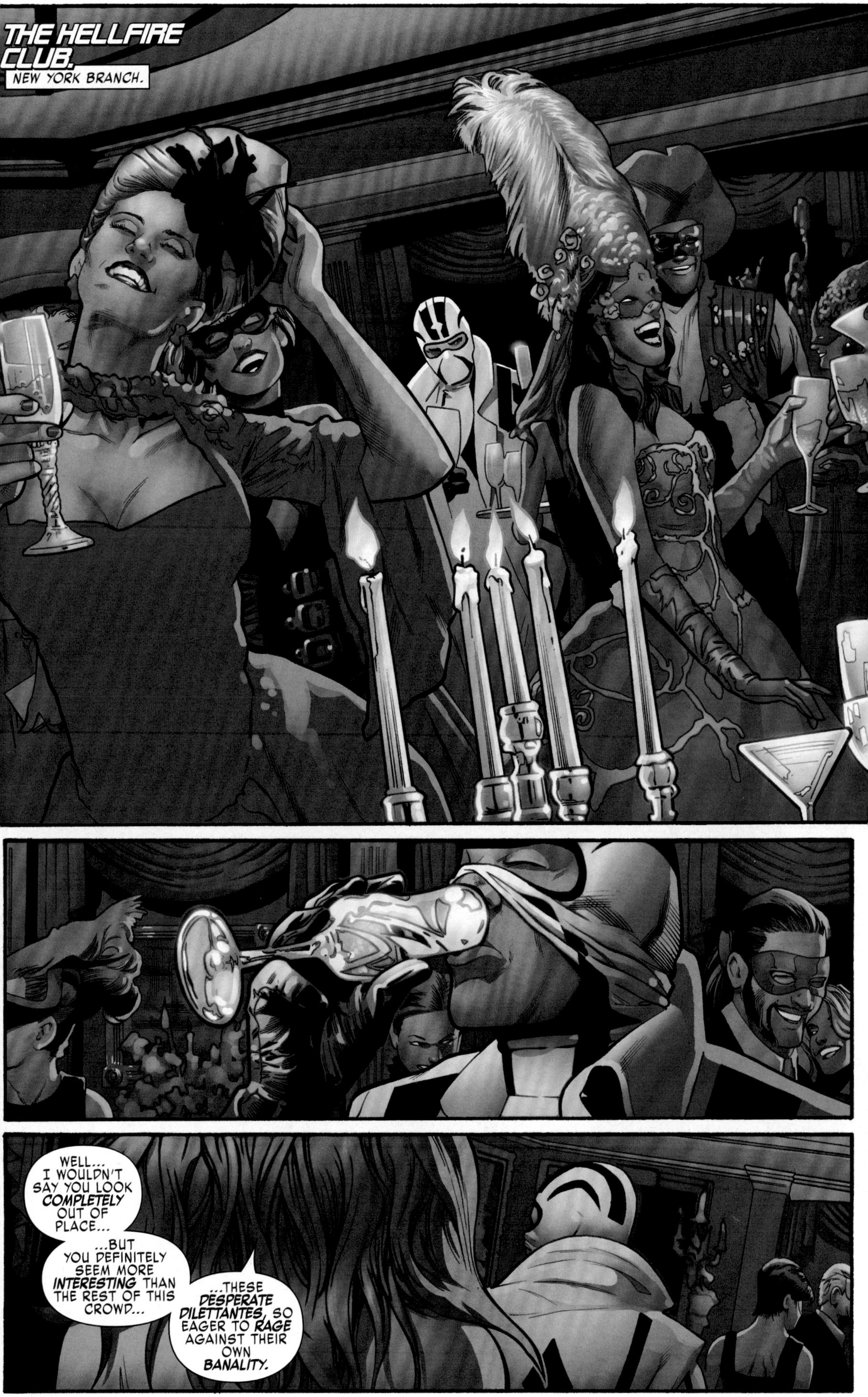
THE HELLFIRE CLUB.
NEW YORK BRANCH.
WELL... I WOULDN'T SAY YOU LOOK COMPLETELY OUT OF PLACE...
...BUT YOU DEFINITELY SEEM MORE INTERESTING THAN THE REST OF THIS CROWD...
...THESE DESPERATE DILETTANTES, SO EAGER TO RAGE AGAINST THEIR OWN BANALITY.

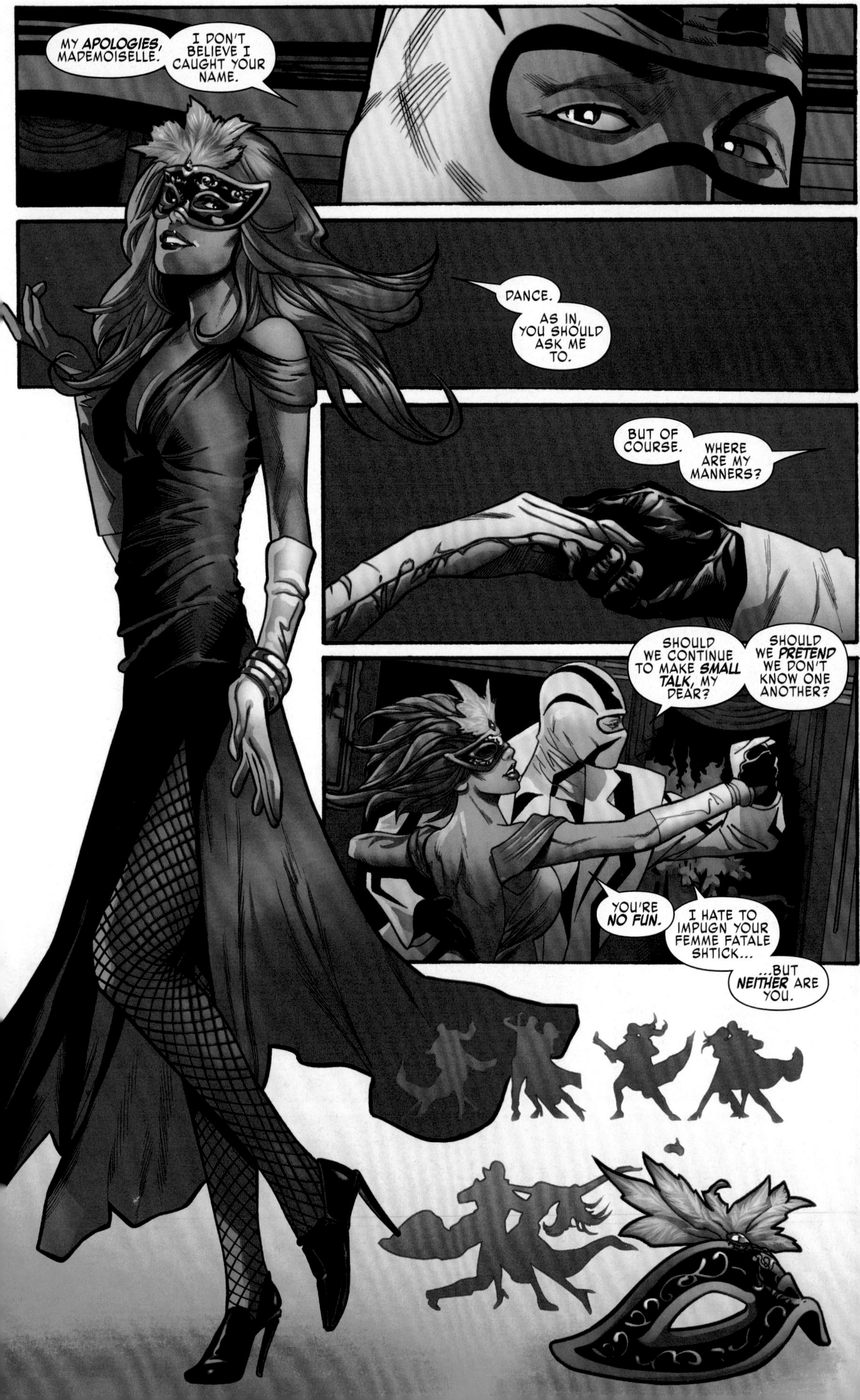
MY APOLOGIES, MADEMOISELLE.
I DON'T BELIEVE I CAUGHT YOUR NAME.
DANCE.
AS IN, YOU SHOULD ASK ME TO.
BUT OF COURSE.
WHERE ARE MY MANNERS?
SHOULD WE CONTINUE TO MAKE SMALL TALK, MY DEAR?
SHOULD WE PRETEND WE DON'T KNOW ONE ANOTHER?
YOU'RE NO FUN.
I HATE TO IMPUGN YOUR FEMME FATALE SHTICK...
...BUT NEITHER ARE YOU.

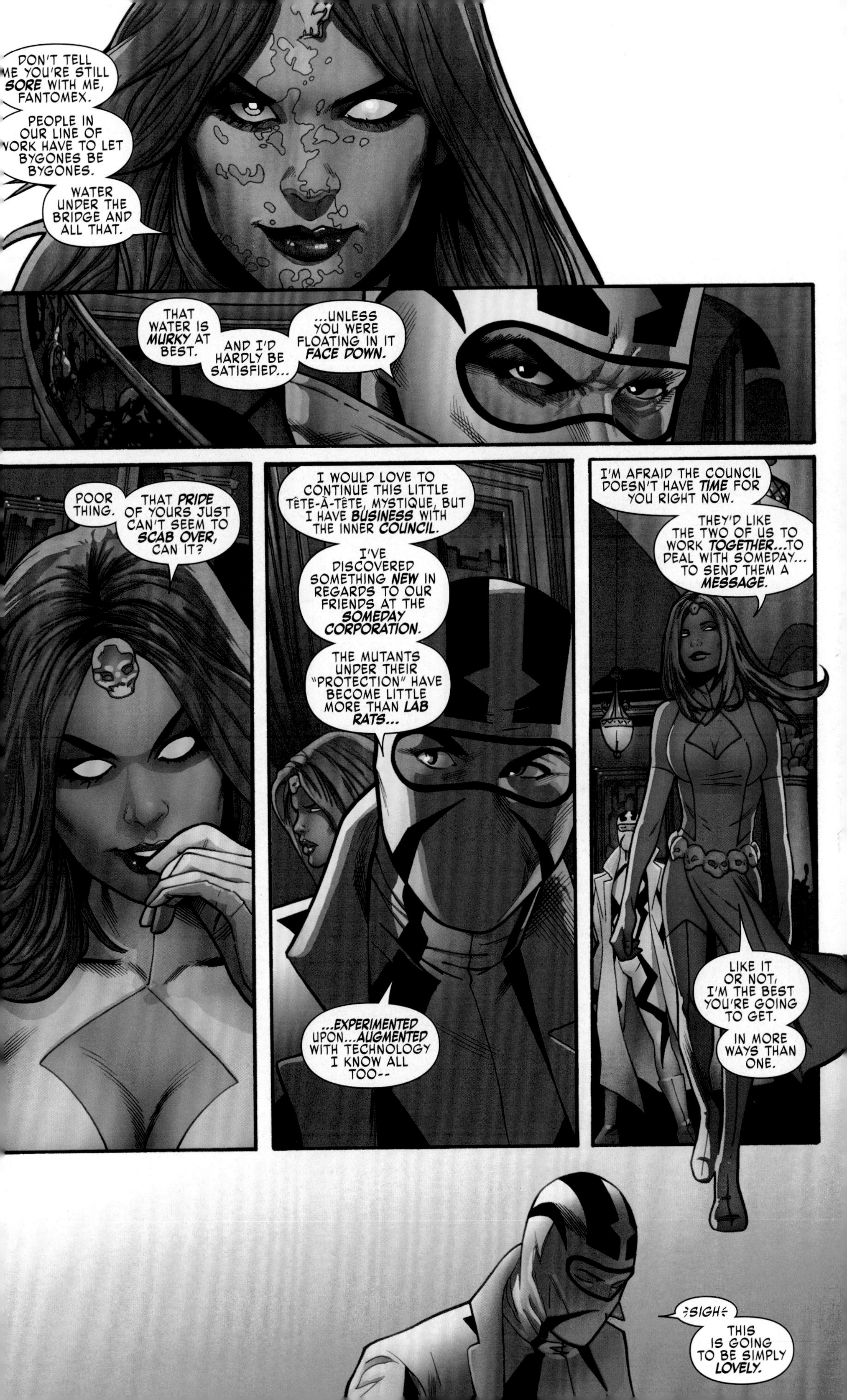
DON'T TELL ME YOU'RE STILL **SORE** WITH ME, FANTOMEX.
PEOPLE IN OUR LINE OF WORK HAVE TO LET BYGONES BE BYGONES.
WATER UNDER THE BRIDGE AND ALL THAT.
THAT WATER IS **MURKY** AT BEST.
AND I'D HARDLY BE SATISFIED...
...UNLESS YOU WERE FLOATING IN IT **FACE DOWN.**
POOR THING.
THAT **PRIDE** OF YOURS JUST CAN'T SEEM TO **SCAB OVER,** CAN IT?
I WOULD LOVE TO CONTINUE THIS LITTLE TÊTE-À-TÊTE, MYSTIQUE, BUT I HAVE **BUSINESS** WITH THE INNER **COUNCIL**.
I'VE DISCOVERED SOMETHING **NEW** IN REGARDS TO OUR FRIENDS AT THE **SOMEDAY CORPORATION**.
THE MUTANTS UNDER THEIR "PROTECTION" HAVE BECOME LITTLE MORE THAN **LAB RATS**...
...EXPERIMENTED UPON...**AUGMENTED** WITH TECHNOLOGY I KNOW ALL TOO--
I'M AFRAID THE COUNCIL DOESN'T HAVE **TIME** FOR YOU RIGHT NOW.
THEY'D LIKE THE TWO OF US TO WORK **TOGETHER**...TO DEAL WITH SOMEDAY... TO SEND THEM A **MESSAGE**.
LIKE IT OR NOT, I'M THE BEST YOU'RE GOING TO GET.
IN MORE WAYS THAN ONE.
SIGH
THIS IS GOING TO BE SIMPLY **LOVELY.**

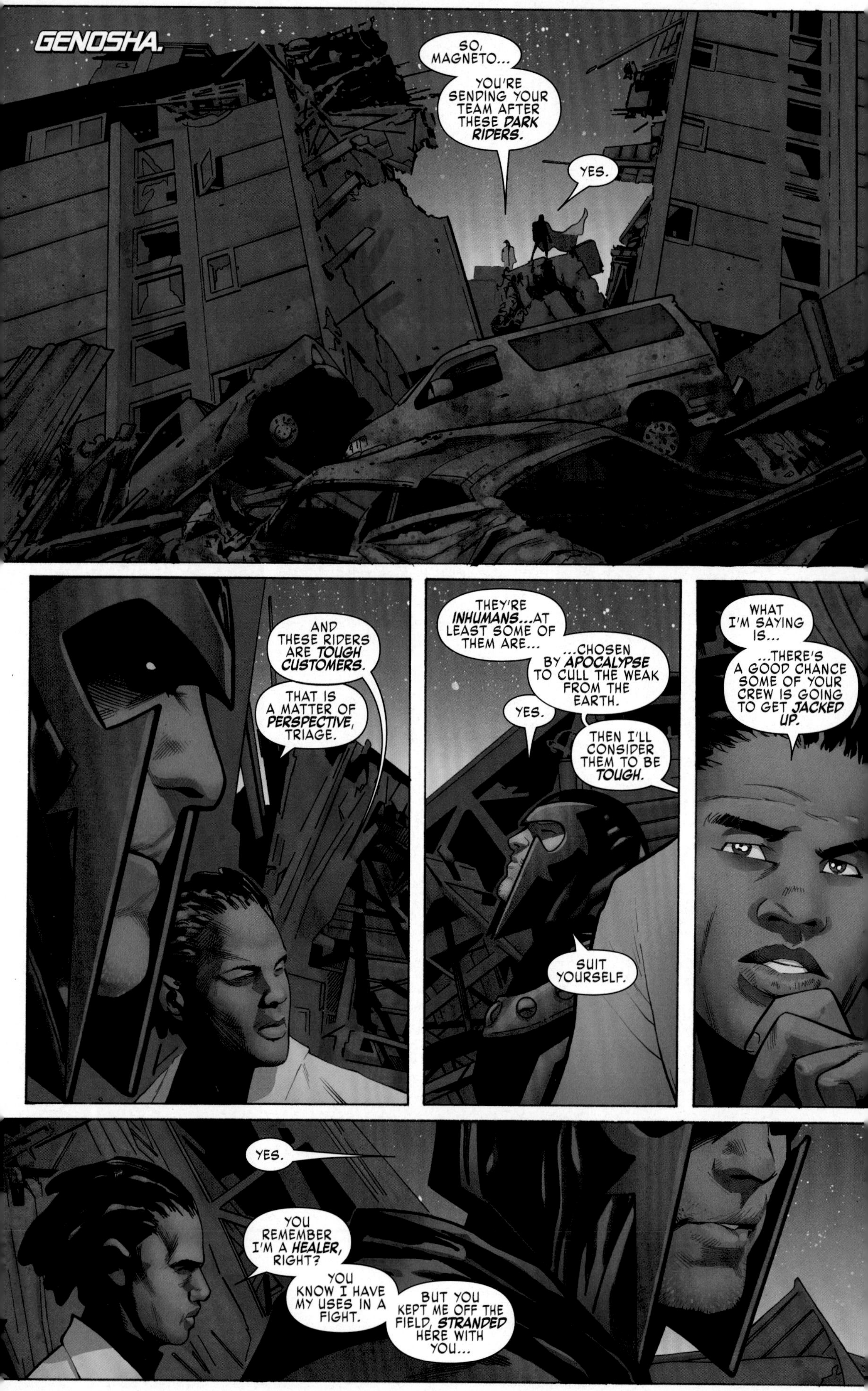
GENOSHA.
SO, MAGNETO...
YOU'RE SENDING YOUR TEAM AFTER THESE DARK RIDERS.
YES.
AND THESE RIDERS ARE TOUGH CUSTOMERS.
THAT IS A MATTER OF PERSPECTIVE, TRIAGE.
THEY'RE INHUMANS...AT LEAST SOME OF THEM ARE...
...CHOSEN BY APOCALYPSE TO CULL THE WEAK FROM THE EARTH.
YES.
THEN I'LL CONSIDER THEM TO BE TOUGH.
SUIT YOURSELF.
WHAT I'M SAYING IS...
...THERE'S A GOOD CHANCE SOME OF YOUR CREW IS GOING TO GET JACKED UP.
YES.
YOU REMEMBER I'M A HEALER, RIGHT?
YOU KNOW I HAVE MY USES IN A FIGHT.
BUT YOU KEPT ME OFF THE FIELD, STRANDED HERE WITH YOU...

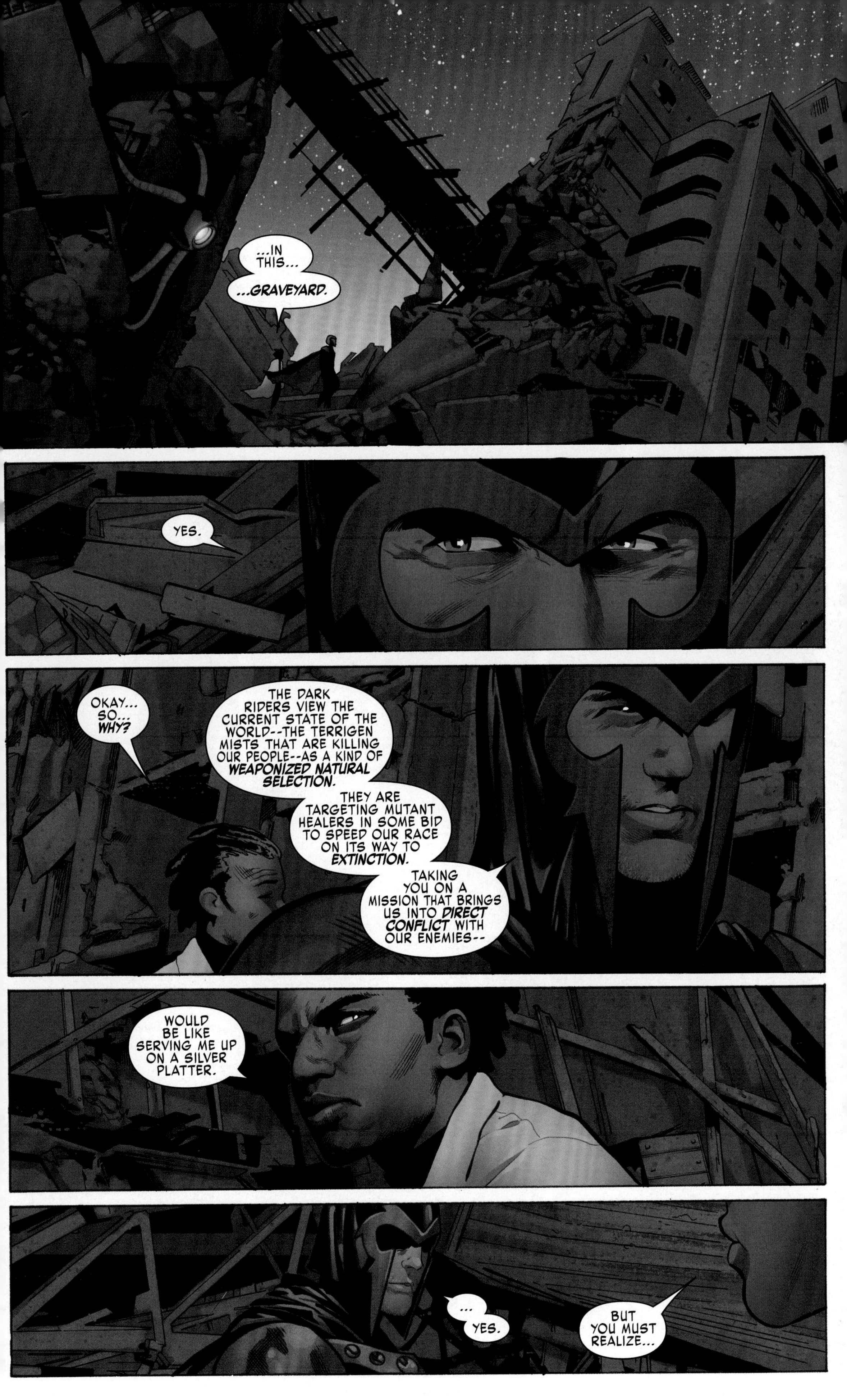

...IN THIS...
...GRAVEYARD.
YES.
OKAY... SO... WHY?
THE DARK RIDERS VIEW THE CURRENT STATE OF THE WORLD--THE TERRIGEN MISTS THAT ARE KILLING OUR PEOPLE--AS A KIND OF WEAPONIZED NATURAL SELECTION.
THEY ARE TARGETING MUTANT HEALERS IN SOME BID TO SPEED OUR RACE ON ITS WAY TO EXTINCTION.
TAKING YOU ON A MISSION THAT BRINGS US INTO DIRECT CONFLICT WITH OUR ENEMIES--
WOULD BE LIKE SERVING ME UP ON A SILVER PLATTER.
... YES.
BUT YOU MUST REALIZE...

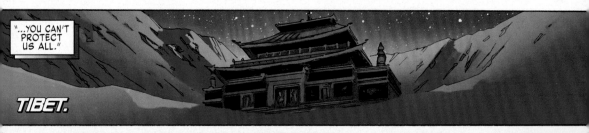

TIBET.

PLEASE. I *KNOW* YOU ARE THERE.

THERE IS NO NEED TO *HIDE.*

WHO'S *HIDING?*

THE *COMING STORM* HAS NO NEED TO SKULK.

ILL WINDS ARE BLOWING, MUTANT...

...AND YOUR KIND WILL BE *CLEANSED* FROM THE EARTH.

WHAT DO YOU SAY TO THAT?

WOULD YOU CARE FOR A CUP OF *TEA?*

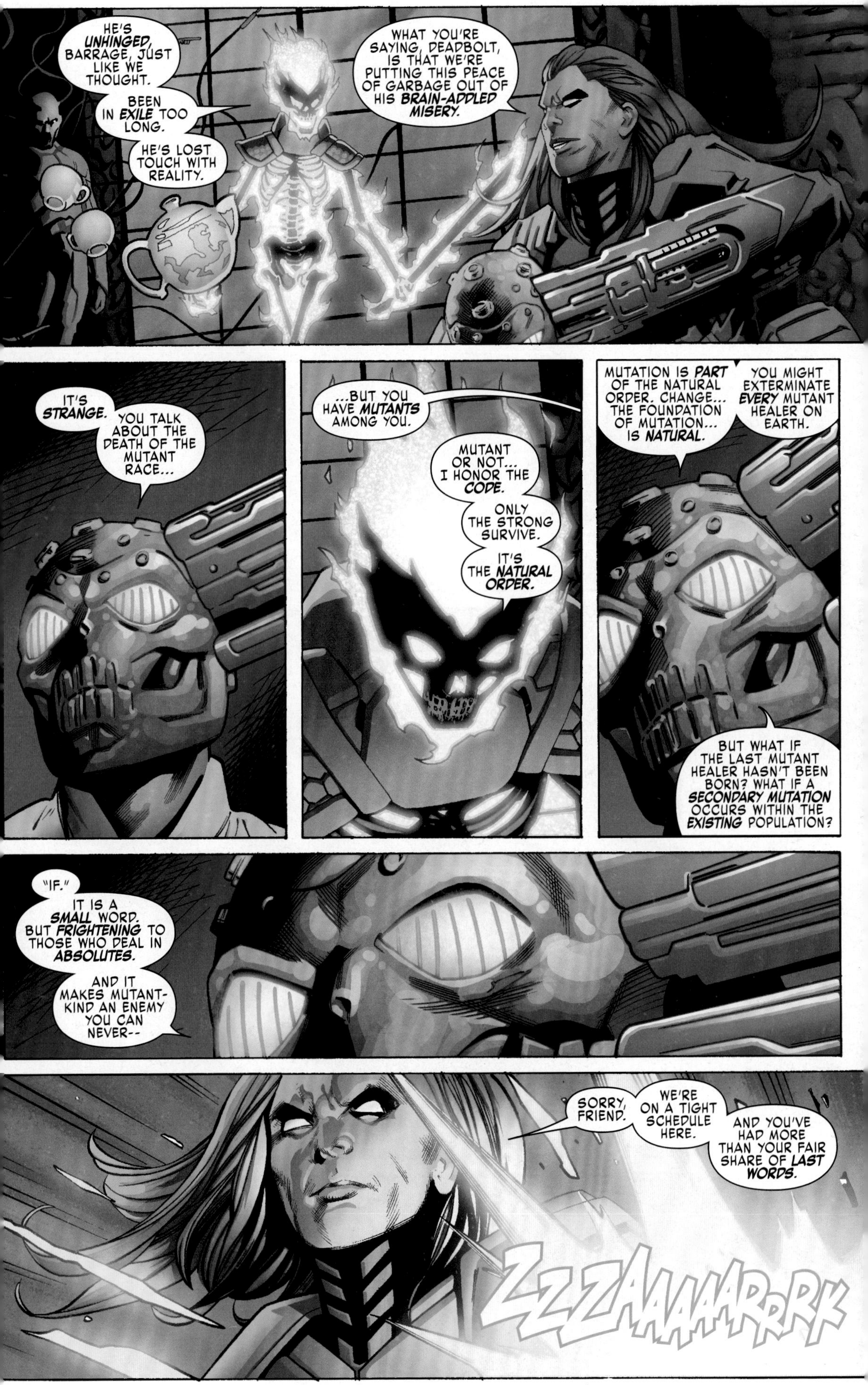
HE'S UNHINGED, BARRAGE, JUST LIKE WE THOUGHT.
BEEN IN EXILE TOO LONG.
HE'S LOST TOUCH WITH REALITY.
WHAT YOU'RE SAYING, DEADBOLT, IS THAT WE'RE PUTTING THIS PEACE OF GARBAGE OUT OF HIS BRAIN-ADDLED MISERY.
IT'S STRANGE.
YOU TALK ABOUT THE DEATH OF THE MUTANT RACE...
...BUT YOU HAVE MUTANTS AMONG YOU.
MUTANT OR NOT... I HONOR THE CODE.
ONLY THE STRONG SURVIVE.
IT'S THE NATURAL ORDER.
MUTATION IS PART OF THE NATURAL ORDER. CHANGE... THE FOUNDATION OF MUTATION... IS NATURAL.
YOU MIGHT EXTERMINATE EVERY MUTANT HEALER ON EARTH.
BUT WHAT IF THE LAST MUTANT HEALER HASN'T BEEN BORN? WHAT IF A SECONDARY MUTATION OCCURS WITHIN THE EXISTING POPULATION?
"IF."
IT IS A SMALL WORD. BUT FRIGHTENING TO THOSE WHO DEAL IN ABSOLUTES.
AND IT MAKES MUTANT-KIND AN ENEMY YOU CAN NEVER--
SORRY, FRIEND.
WE'RE ON A TIGHT SCHEDULE HERE.
AND YOU'VE HAD MORE THAN YOUR FAIR SHARE OF LAST WORDS.
ZZZAAAAARRRK

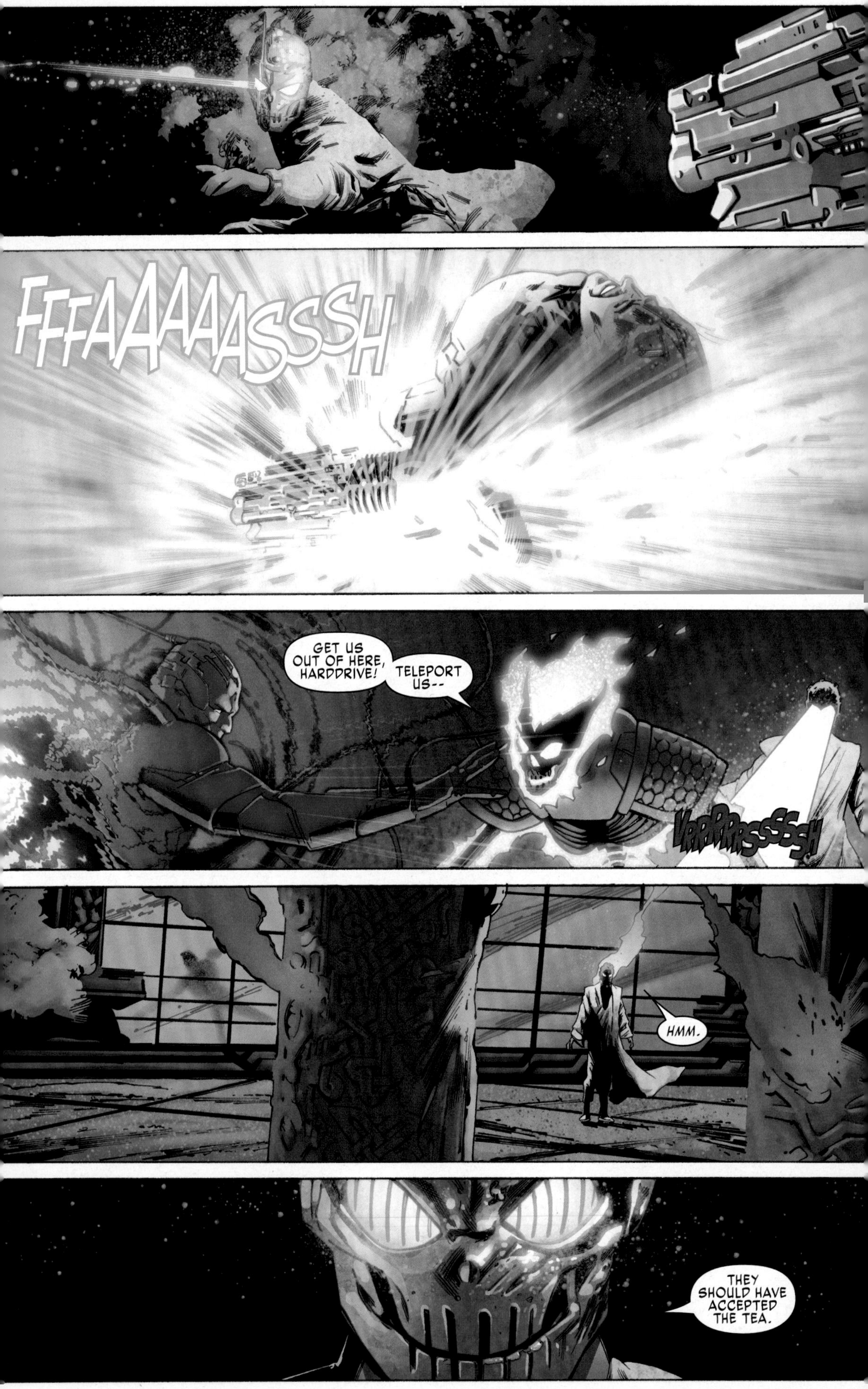
FFFAAAAASSSH
GET US OUT OF HERE, HARDDRIVE!
TELEPORT US--
VRRRRRSSSSSH!
HMM.
THEY SHOULD HAVE ACCEPTED THE TEA.

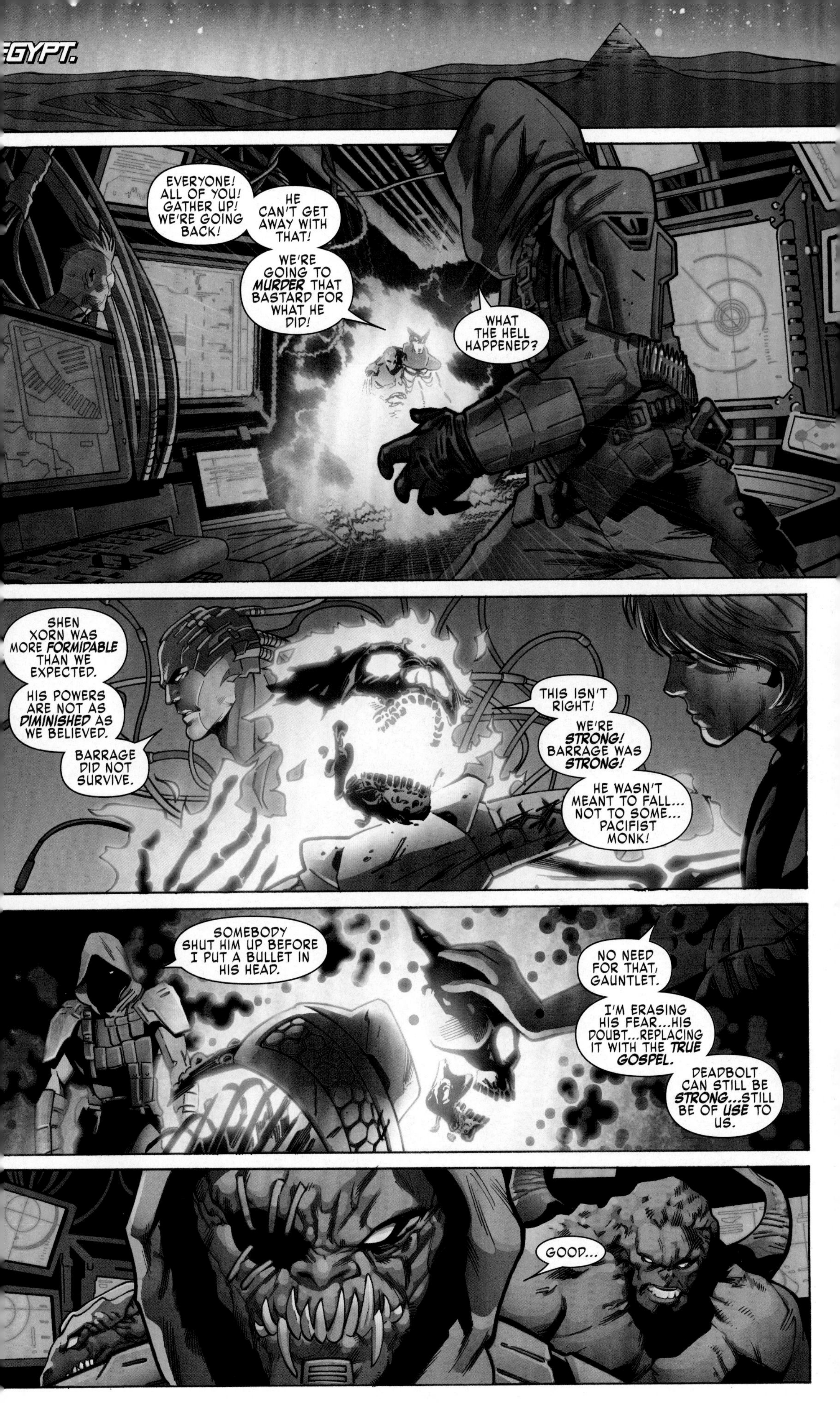
EGYPT.
EVERYONE! ALL OF YOU! GATHER UP! WE'RE GOING BACK!
HE CAN'T GET AWAY WITH THAT!
WE'RE GOING TO MURDER THAT BASTARD FOR WHAT HE DID!
WHAT THE HELL HAPPENED?
SHEN XORN WAS MORE FORMIDABLE THAN WE EXPECTED.
HIS POWERS ARE NOT AS DIMINISHED AS WE BELIEVED.
BARRAGE DID NOT SURVIVE.
THIS ISN'T RIGHT!
WE'RE STRONG! BARRAGE WAS STRONG!
HE WASN'T MEANT TO FALL... NOT TO SOME... PACIFIST MONK!
SOMEBODY SHUT HIM UP BEFORE I PUT A BULLET IN HIS HEAD.
NO NEED FOR THAT, GAUNTLET.
I'M ERASING HIS FEAR...HIS DOUBT...REPLACING IT WITH THE TRUE GOSPEL.
DEADBOLT CAN STILL BE STRONG...STILL BE OF USE TO US.
GOOD...

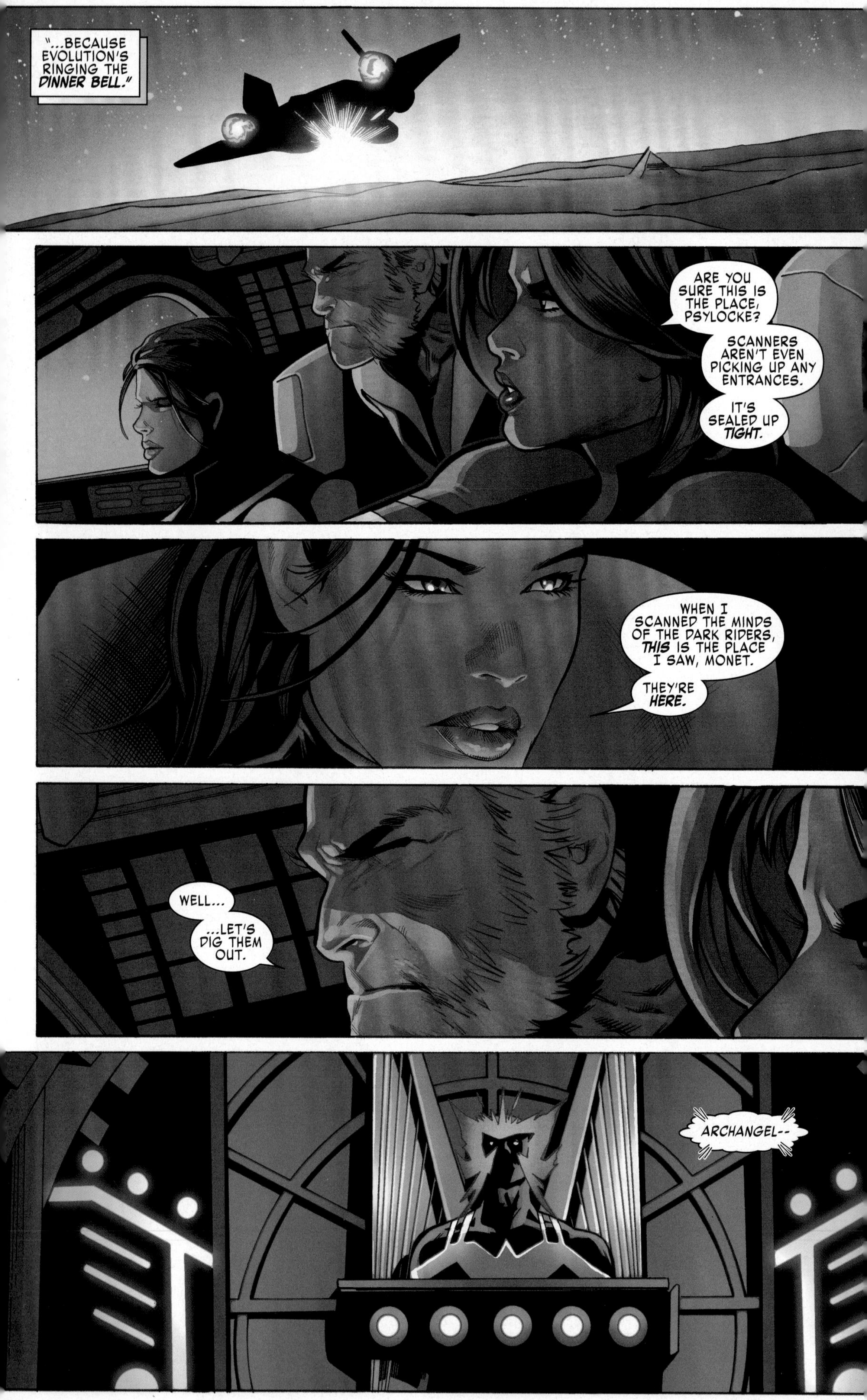

"...BECAUSE EVOLUTION'S RINGING THE DINNER BELL."
ARE YOU SURE THIS IS THE PLACE, PSYLOCKE?
SCANNERS AREN'T EVEN PICKING UP ANY ENTRANCES.
IT'S SEALED UP TIGHT.
WHEN I SCANNED THE MINDS OF THE DARK RIDERS, THIS IS THE PLACE I SAW, MONET.
THEY'RE HERE.
WELL...
...LET'S DIG THEM OUT.
ARCHANGEL--

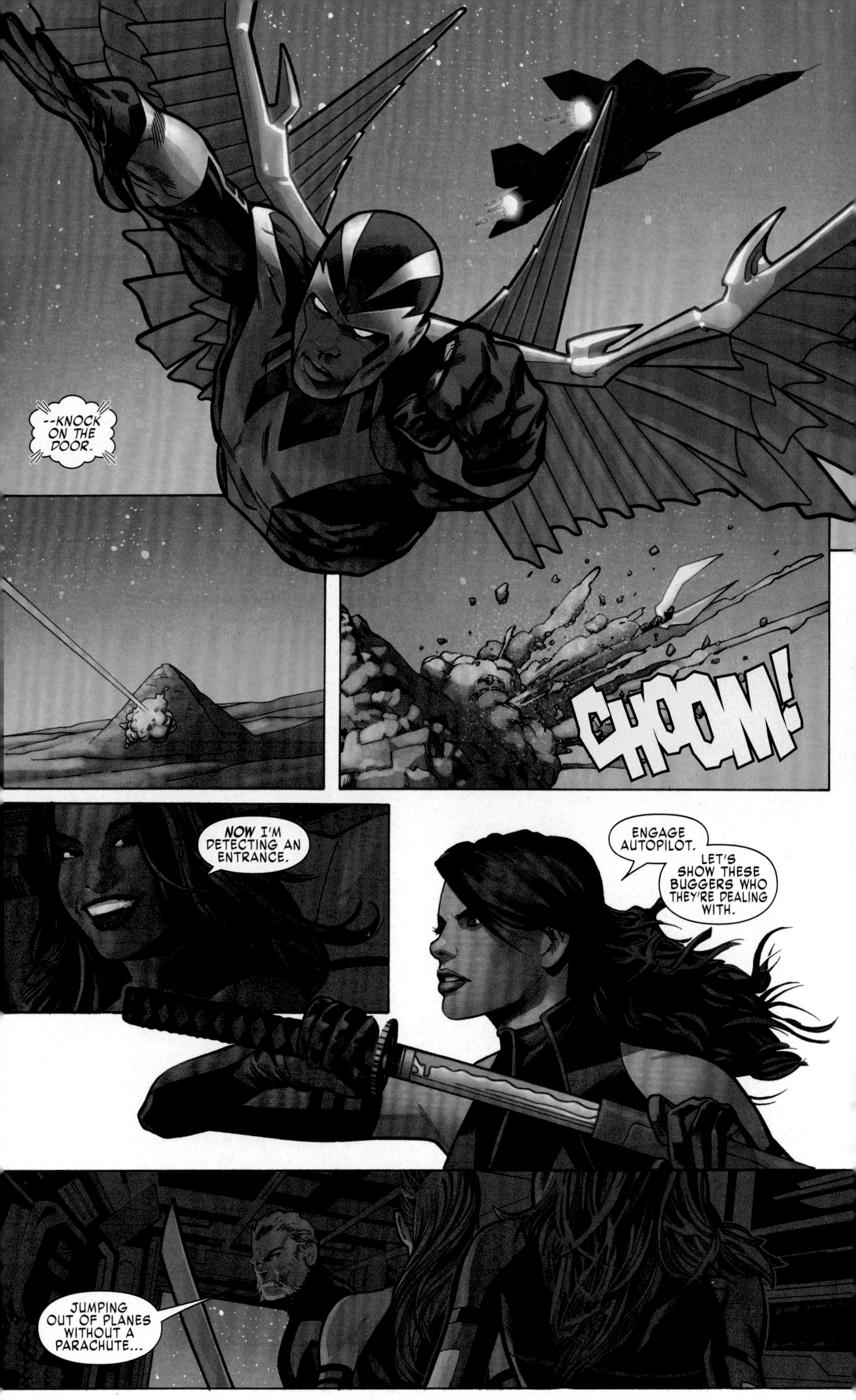
--KNOCK ON THE DOOR.
CHOOM!
NOW I'M DETECTING AN ENTRANCE.
ENGAGE AUTOPILOT.
LET'S SHOW THESE BUGGERS WHO THEY'RE DEALING WITH.
JUMPING OUT OF PLANES WITHOUT A PARACHUTE...

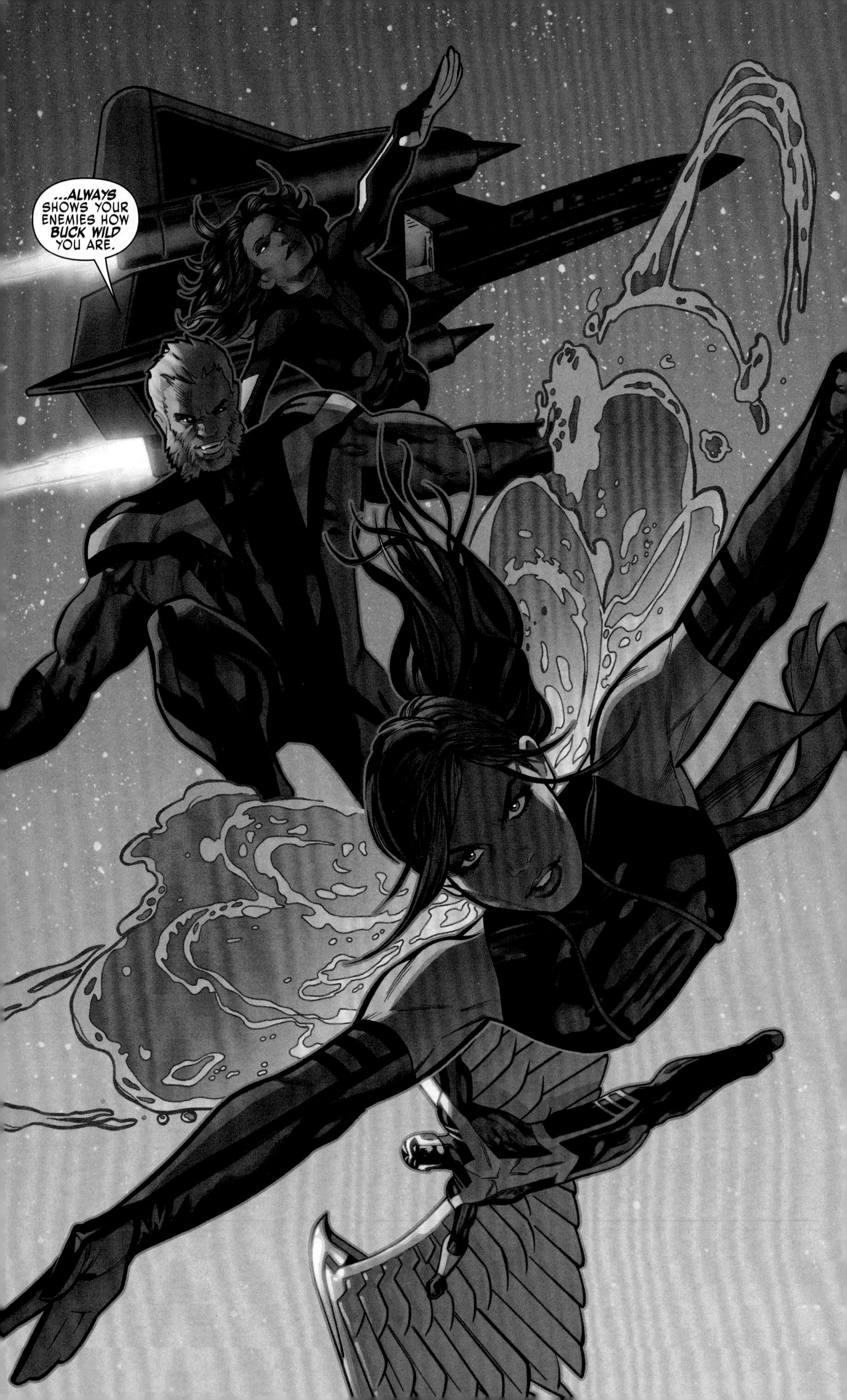
...ALWAYS SHOWS YOUR ENEMIES HOW BUCK WILD YOU ARE.

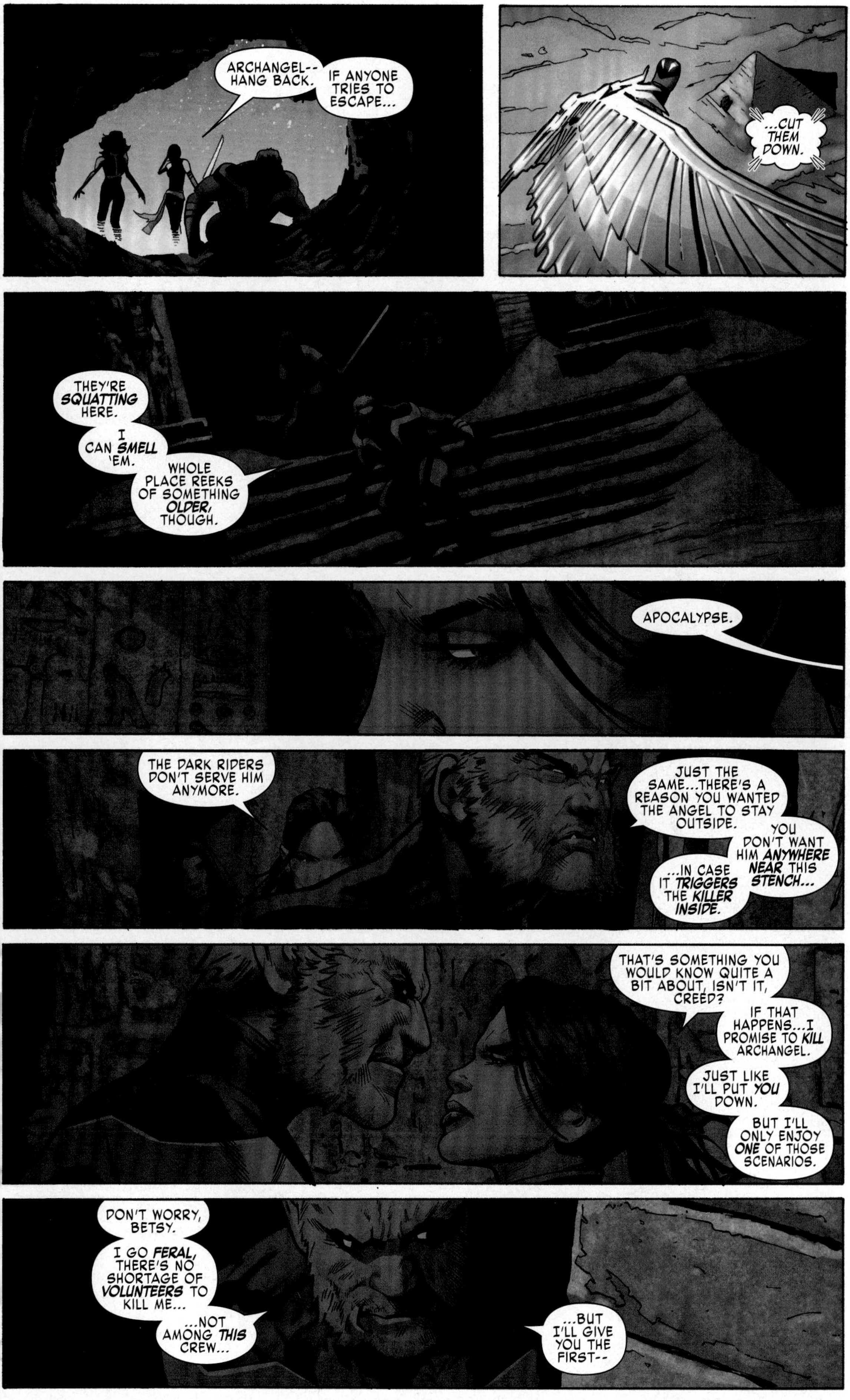
ARCHANGEL-- HANG BACK.
IF ANYONE TRIES TO ESCAPE...
...CUT THEM DOWN.
THEY'RE SQUATTING HERE.
I CAN SMELL 'EM.
WHOLE PLACE REEKS OF SOMETHING OLDER, THOUGH.
APOCALYPSE.
THE DARK RIDERS DON'T SERVE HIM ANYMORE.
JUST THE SAME...THERE'S A REASON YOU WANTED THE ANGEL TO STAY OUTSIDE.
YOU DON'T WANT HIM ANYWHERE NEAR THIS STENCH...
...IN CASE IT TRIGGERS THE KILLER INSIDE.
THAT'S SOMETHING YOU WOULD KNOW QUITE A BIT ABOUT, ISN'T IT, CREED?
IF THAT HAPPENS...I PROMISE TO KILL ARCHANGEL.
JUST LIKE I'LL PUT YOU DOWN.
BUT I'LL ONLY ENJOY ONE OF THOSE SCENARIOS.
DON'T WORRY, BETSY.
I GO FERAL, THERE'S NO SHORTAGE OF VOLUNTEERS TO KILL ME...
...NOT AMONG THIS CREW...
...BUT I'LL GIVE YOU THE FIRST--

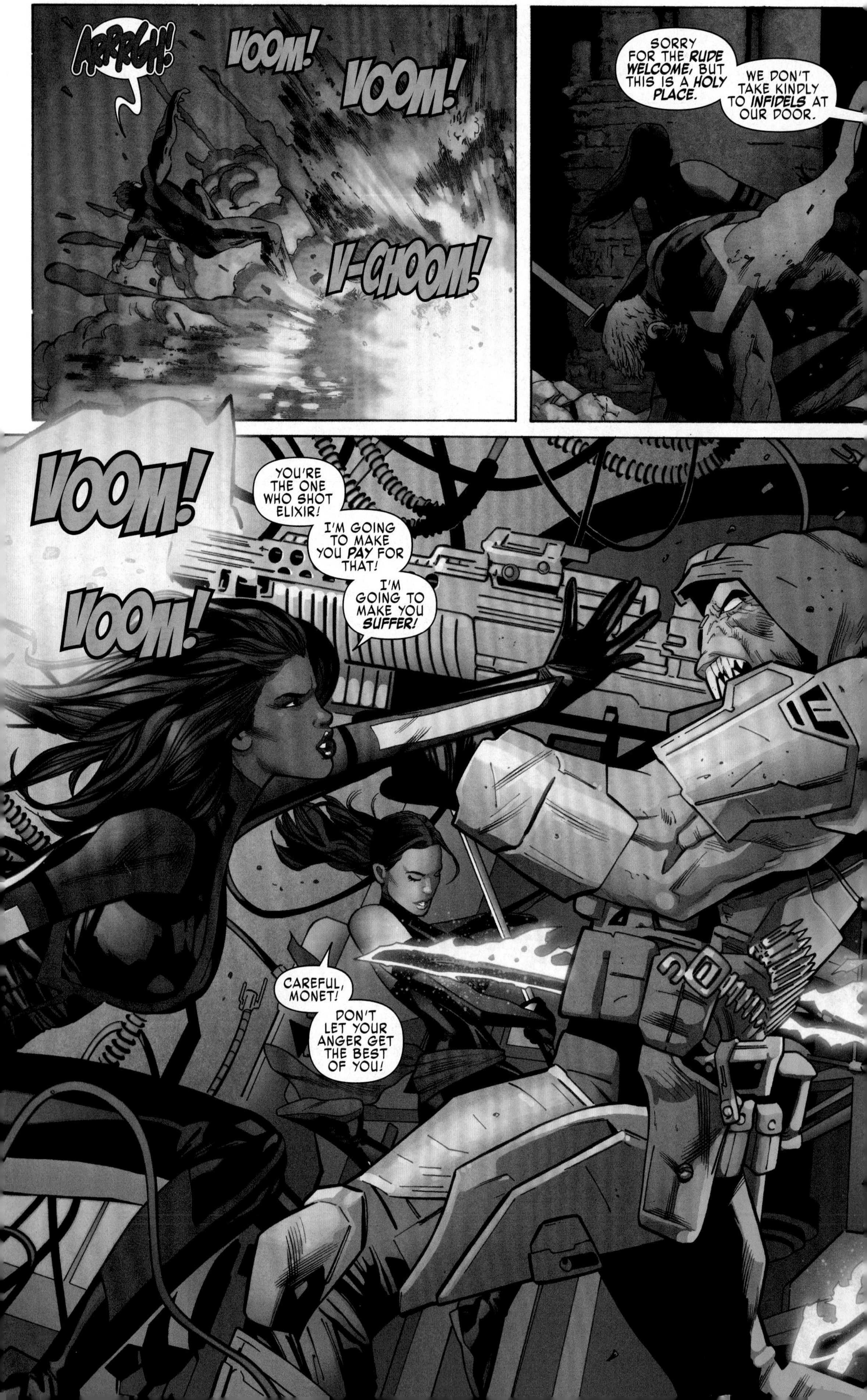
AARRGH!
VOOM!
VOOM!
V-CHOOM!
SORRY FOR THE RUDE WELCOME, BUT THIS IS A HOLY PLACE.
WE DON'T TAKE KINDLY TO INFIDELS AT OUR DOOR.
VOOM!
VOOM!
YOU'RE THE ONE WHO SHOT ELIXIR!
I'M GOING TO MAKE YOU PAY FOR THAT!
I'M GOING TO MAKE YOU SUFFER!
CAREFUL, MONET!
DON'T LET YOUR ANGER GET THE BEST OF YOU!

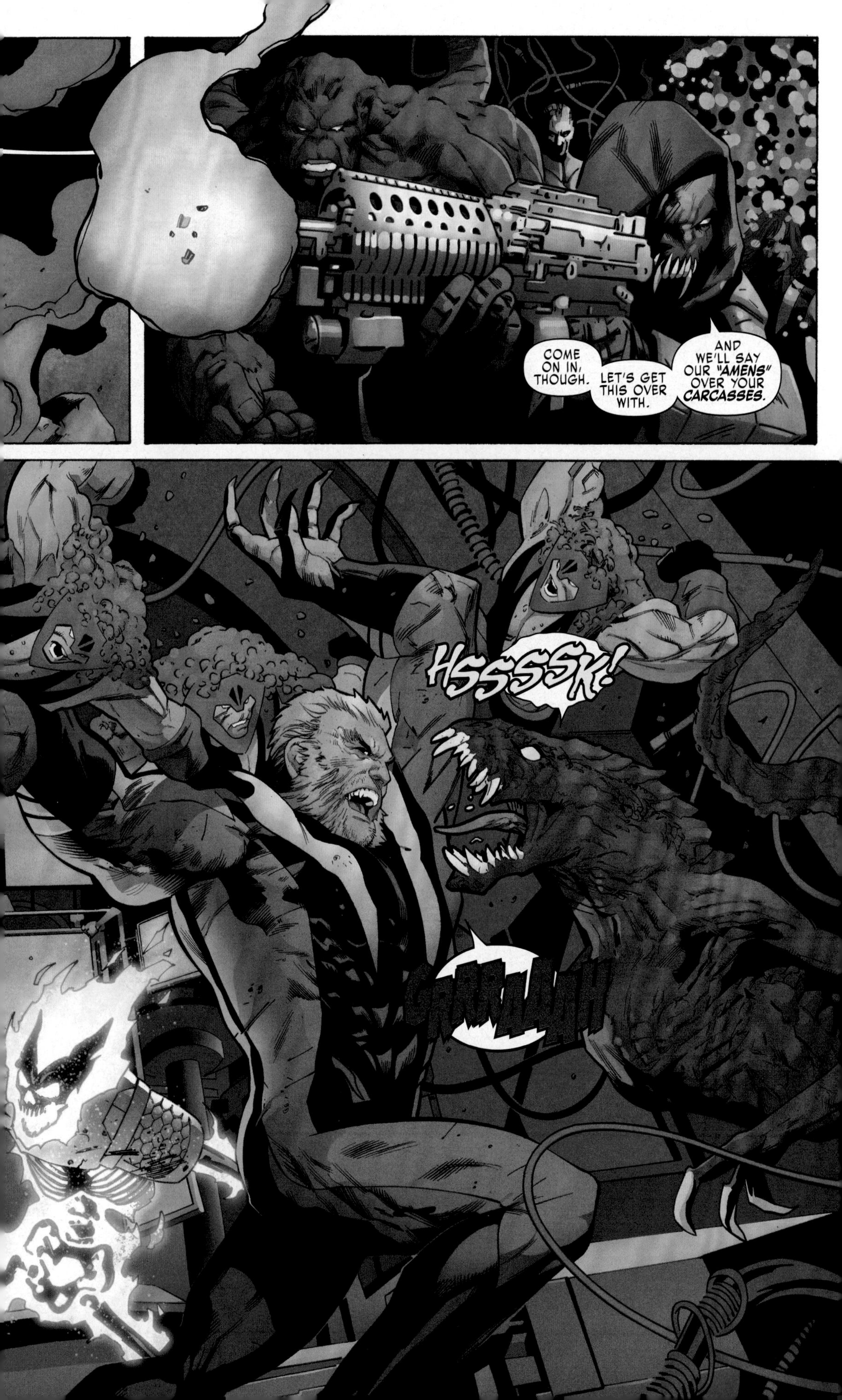

COME ON IN, THOUGH.
LET'S GET THIS OVER WITH.
AND WE'LL SAY OUR "AMENS" OVER YOUR CARCASSES.
HSSSSK!
GRRRAAAHH

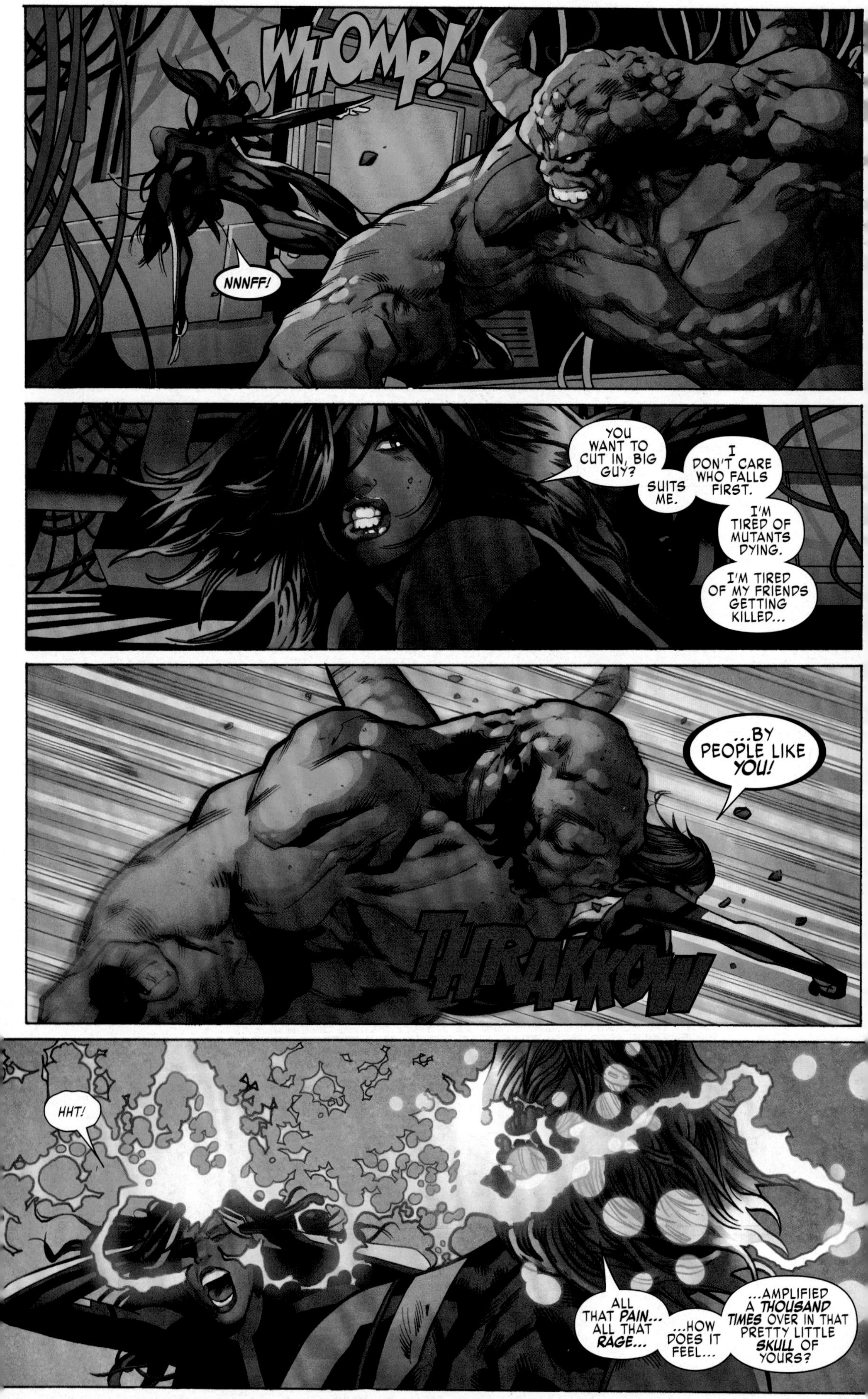
WHOMP!
NNNFF!
YOU WANT TO CUT IN, BIG GUY?
SUITS ME.
I DON'T CARE WHO FALLS FIRST.
I'M TIRED OF MUTANTS DYING.
I'M TIRED OF MY FRIENDS GETTING KILLED...
...BY PEOPLE LIKE YOU!
THRAKKOW
HHT!
ALL THAT PAIN... ALL THAT RAGE...
...HOW DOES IT FEEL...
...AMPLIFIED A THOUSAND TIMES OVER IN THAT PRETTY LITTLE SKULL OF YOURS?

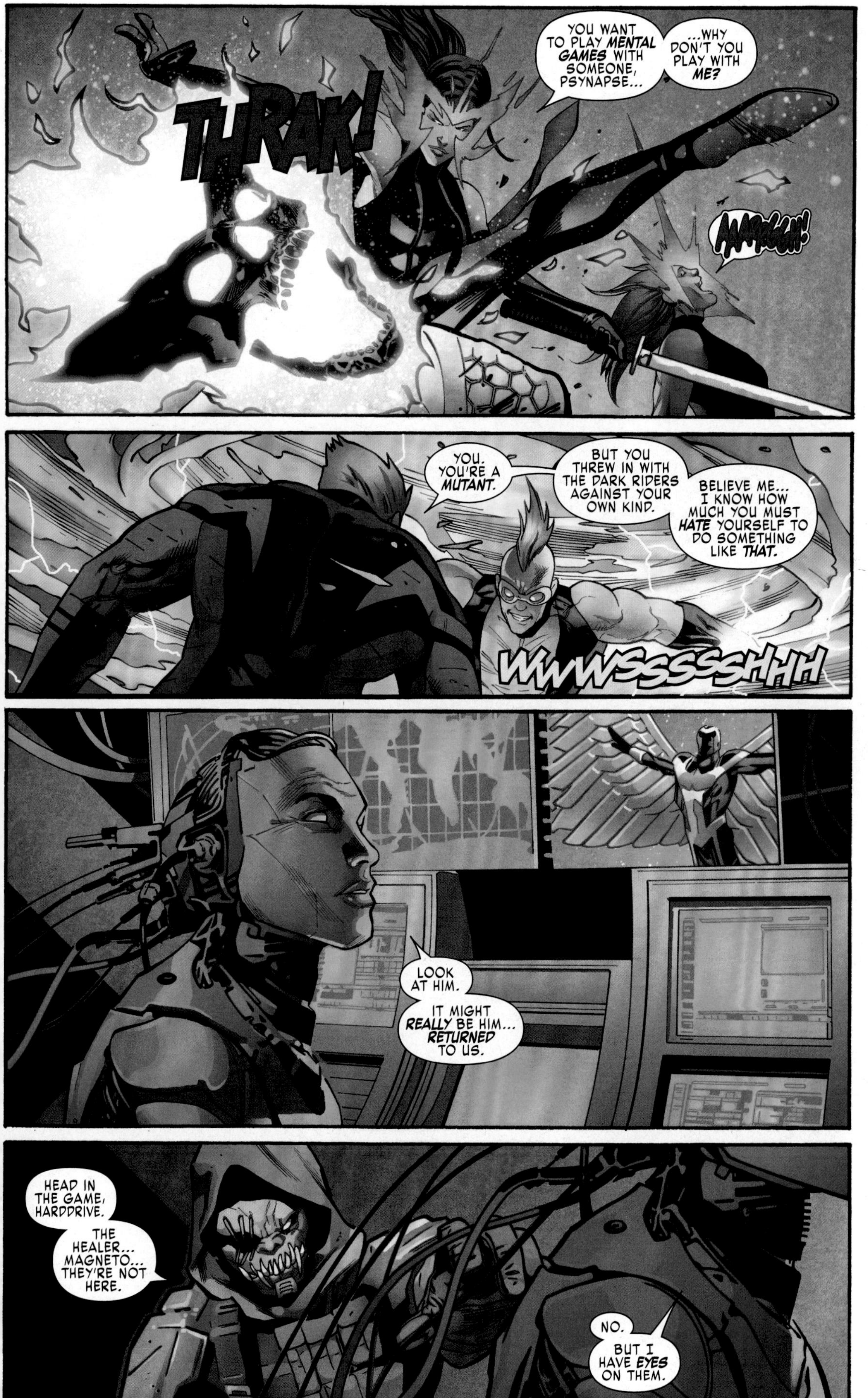
THRAK!
YOU WANT TO PLAY MENTAL GAMES WITH SOMEONE, PSYNAPSE...
...WHY DON'T YOU PLAY WITH ME?
AAARGGH!
YOU. YOU'RE A MUTANT.
BUT YOU THREW IN WITH THE DARK RIDERS AGAINST YOUR OWN KIND.
BELIEVE ME... I KNOW HOW MUCH YOU MUST HATE YOURSELF TO DO SOMETHING LIKE THAT.
WWWWSSSSSHHH
LOOK AT HIM.
IT MIGHT REALLY BE HIM... RETURNED TO US.
HEAD IN THE GAME, HARDDRIVE.
THE HEALER... MAGNETO... THEY'RE NOT HERE.
NO.
BUT I HAVE EYES ON THEM.

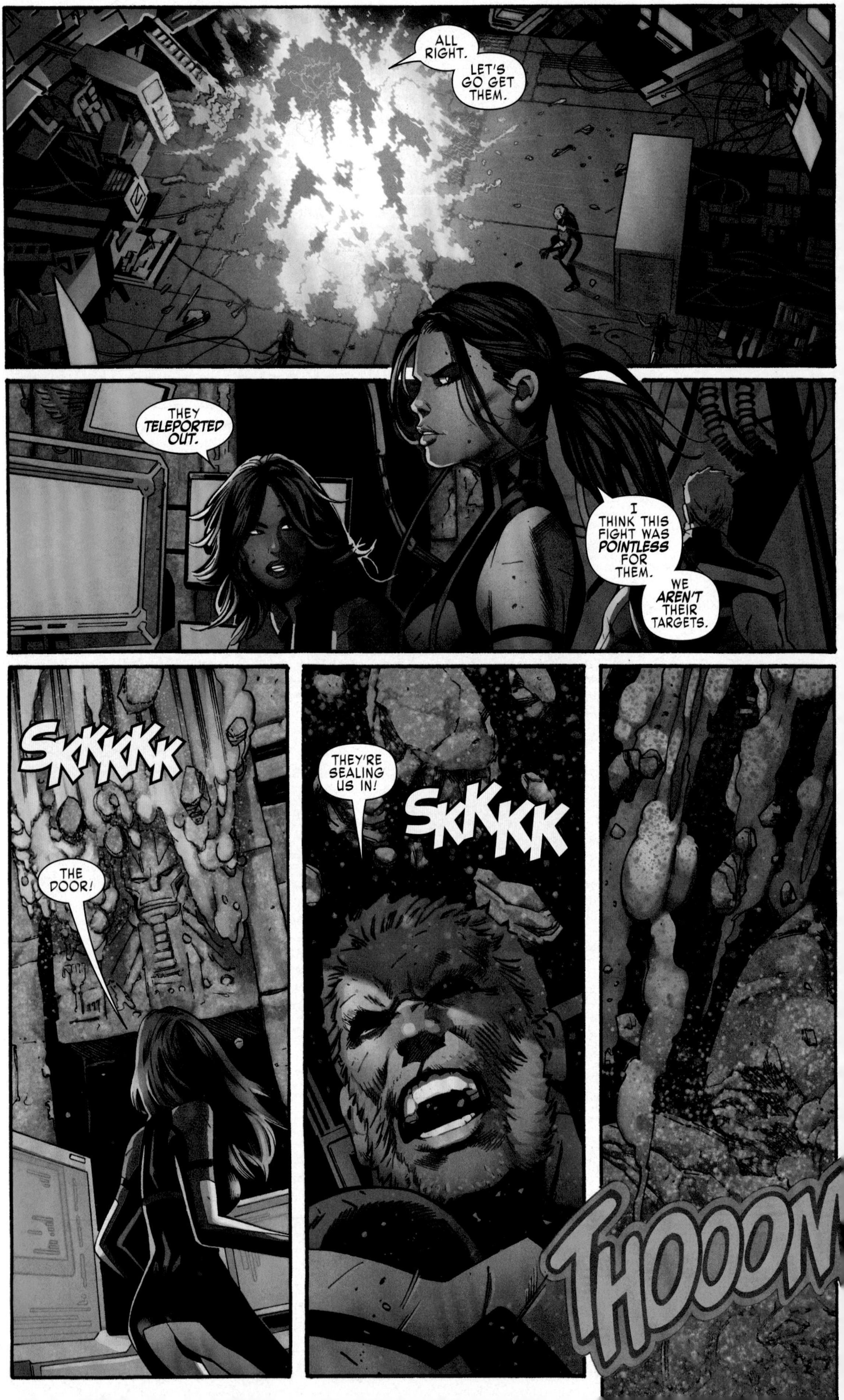
ALL RIGHT.
LET'S GO GET THEM.
THEY TELEPORTED OUT.
I THINK THIS FIGHT WAS POINTLESS FOR THEM.
WE AREN'T THEIR TARGETS.
SKKKKK
THE DOOR!
THEY'RE SEALING US IN!
SKKKK

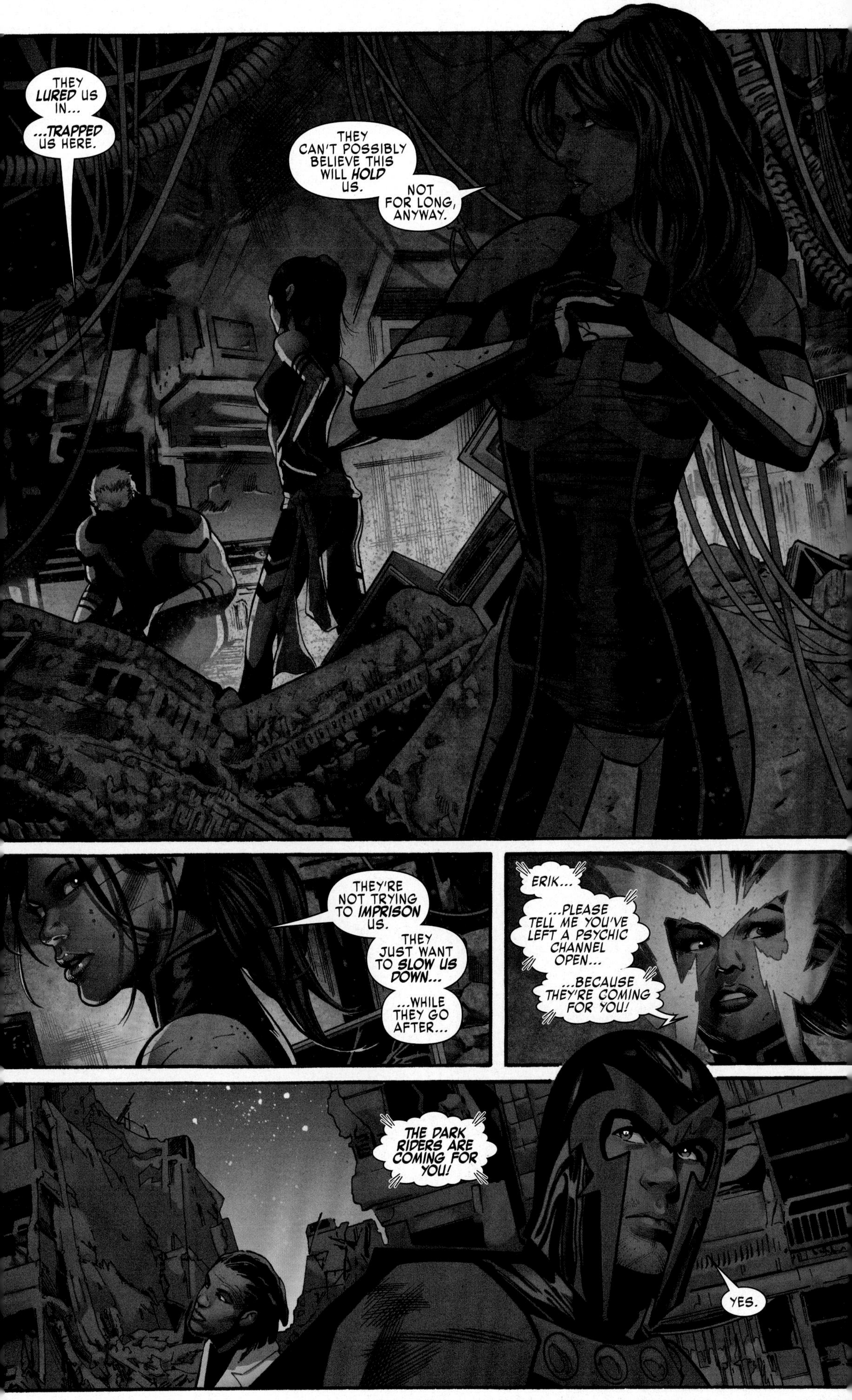
THEY LURED US IN...
...TRAPPED US HERE.
THEY CAN'T POSSIBLY BELIEVE THIS WILL HOLD US.
NOT FOR LONG, ANYWAY.
THEY'RE NOT TRYING TO IMPRISON US.
THEY JUST WANT TO SLOW US DOWN...
...WHILE THEY GO AFTER...
ERIK...
...PLEASE TELL ME YOU'VE LEFT A PSYCHIC CHANNEL OPEN...
...BECAUSE THEY'RE COMING FOR YOU!
THE DARK RIDERS ARE COMING FOR YOU!
YES.

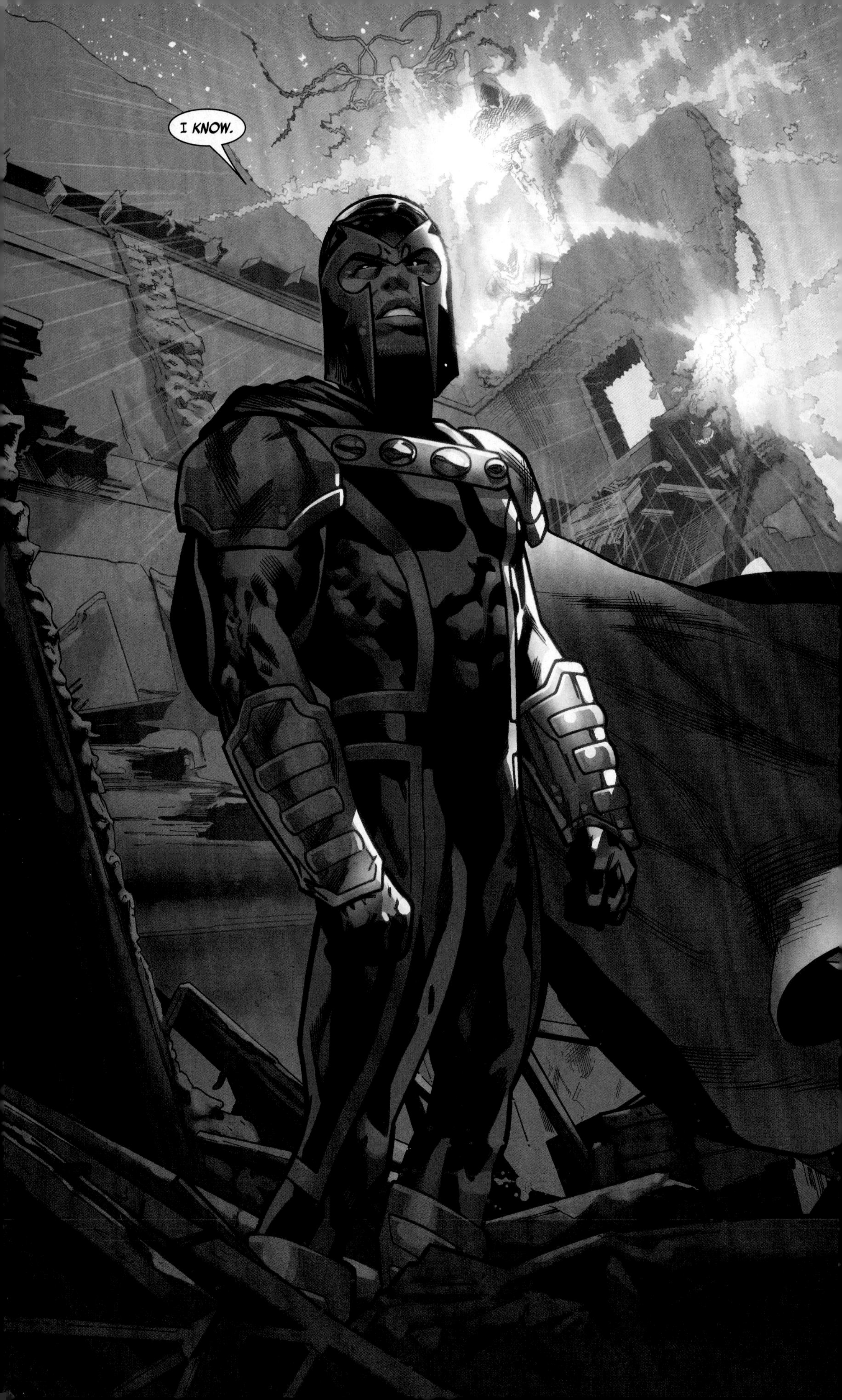
I KNOW.

#2 VARIANT BY
KRIS ANKA

#3 VARIANT BY
GREG LAND & NOLAN WOODARD

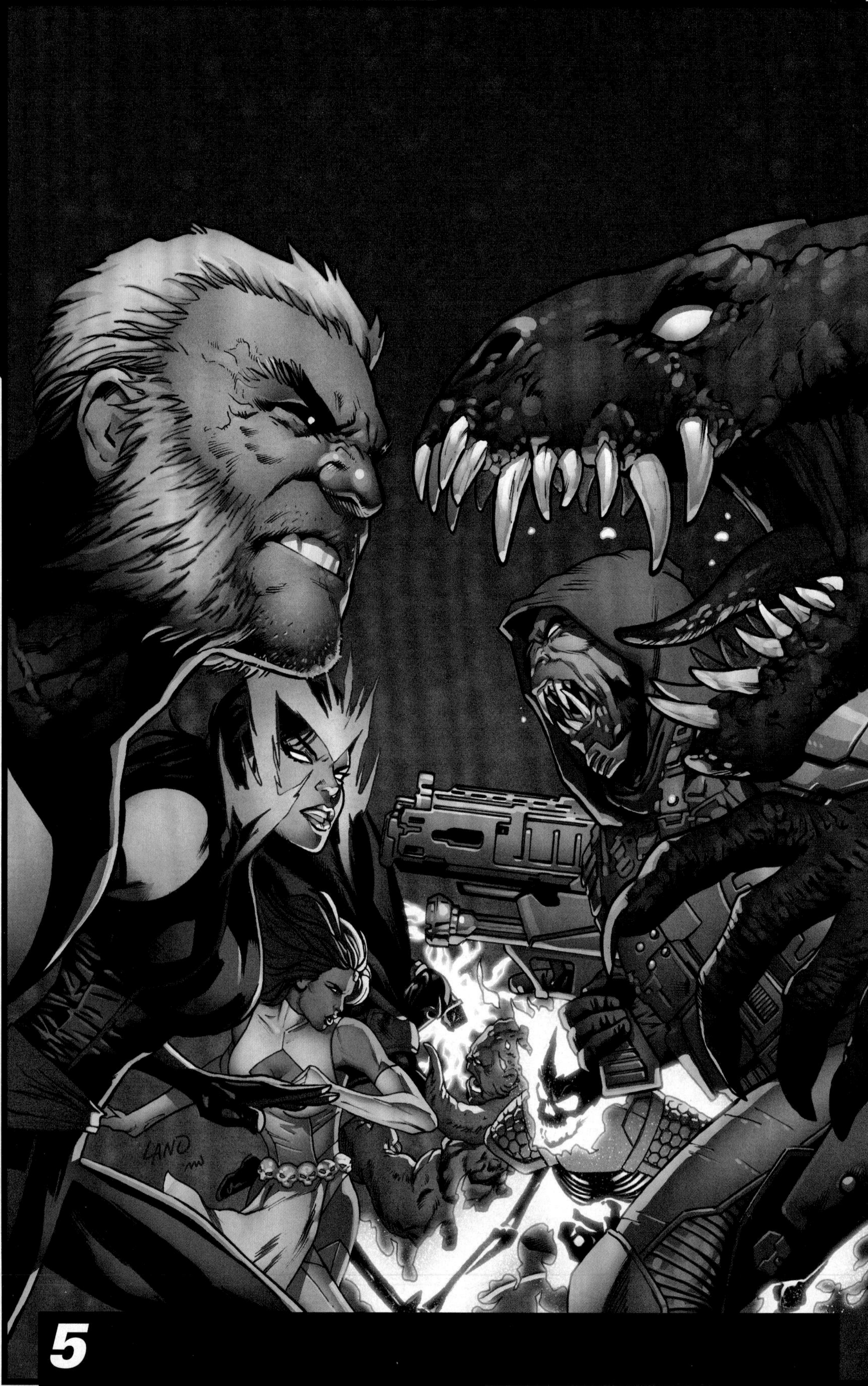
LAND
5

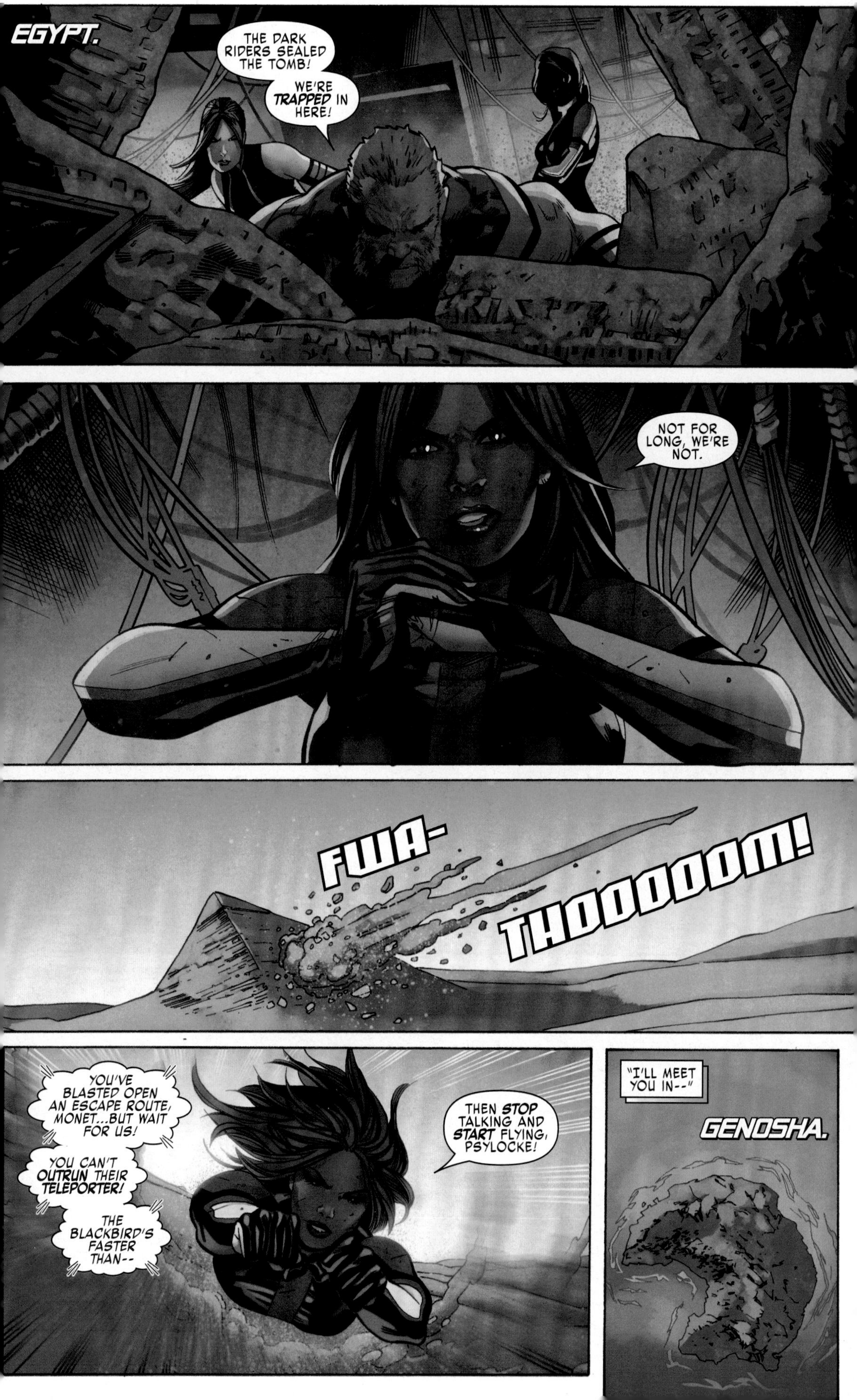

EGYPT.
THE DARK RIDERS SEALED THE TOMB!
WE'RE TRAPPED IN HERE!
NOT FOR LONG, WE'RE NOT.
FWA-THOOOOOOM!
YOU'VE BLASTED OPEN AN ESCAPE ROUTE, MONET...BUT WAIT FOR US!
YOU CAN'T OUTRUN THEIR TELEPORTER!
THE BLACKBIRD'S FASTER THAN--
THEN STOP TALKING AND START FLYING, PSYLOCKE!
"I'LL MEET YOU IN--"
GENOSHA.

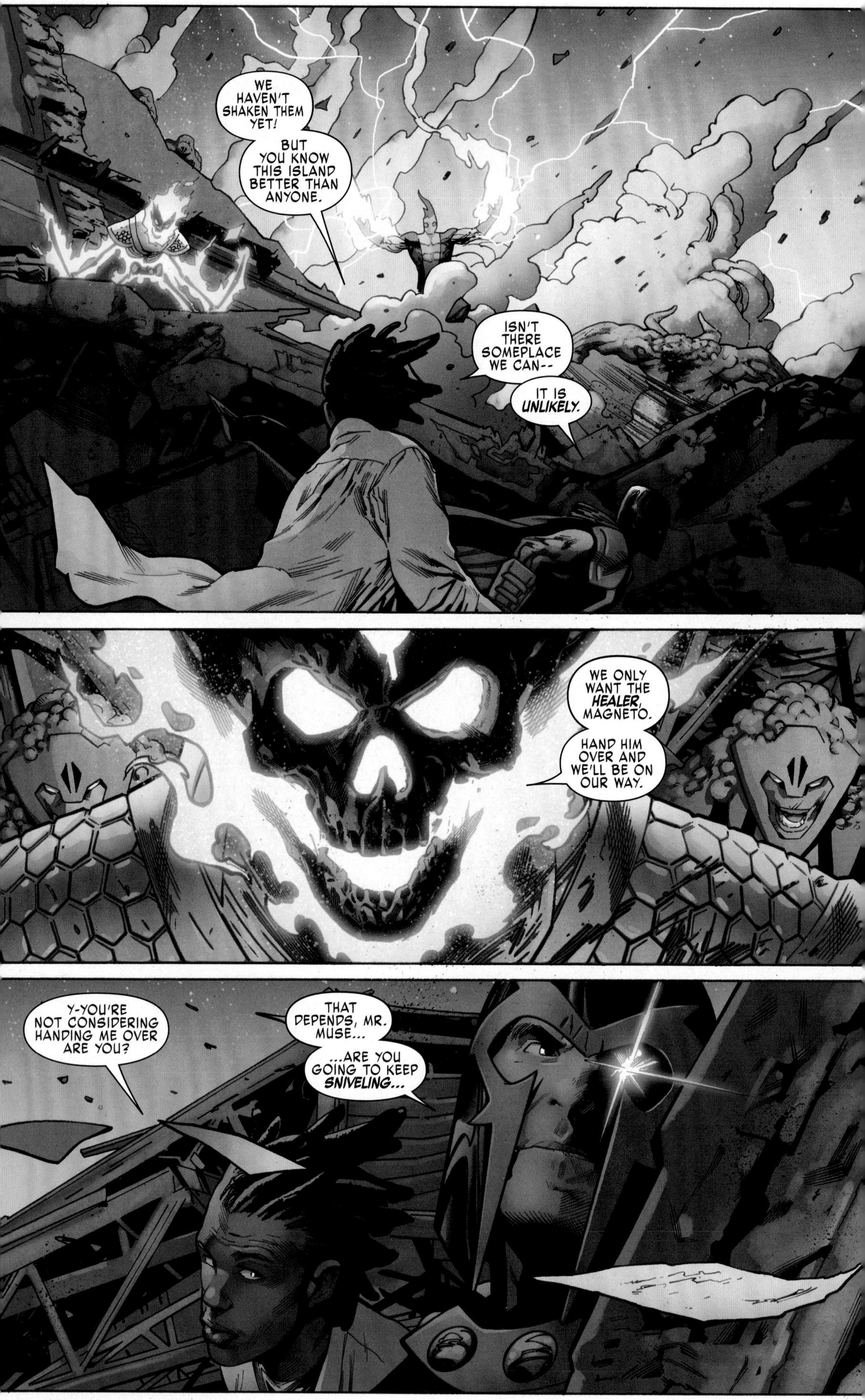
WE HAVEN'T SHAKEN THEM YET!
BUT YOU KNOW THIS ISLAND BETTER THAN ANYONE.
ISN'T THERE SOMEPLACE WE CAN--
IT IS UNLIKELY.
WE ONLY WANT THE HEALER, MAGNETO.
HAND HIM OVER AND WE'LL BE ON OUR WAY.
Y-YOU'RE NOT CONSIDERING HANDING ME OVER ARE YOU?
THAT DEPENDS, MR. MUSE...
...ARE YOU GOING TO KEEP SNIVELING...

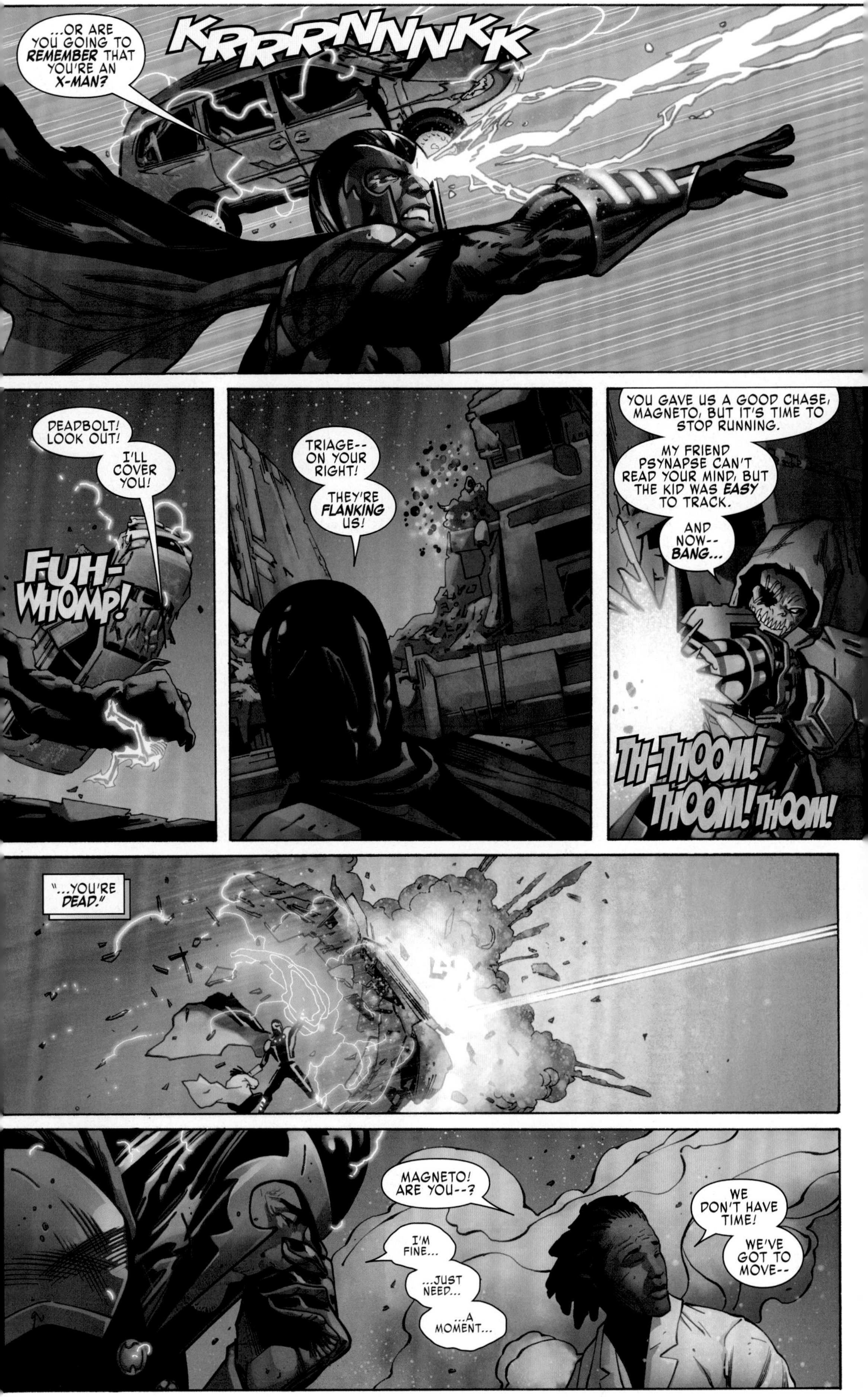
...OR ARE YOU GOING TO *REMEMBER* THAT YOU'RE AN *X-MAN?*
KRRRNNNKK
DEADBOLT! LOOK OUT!
I'LL COVER YOU!
FUH-WHOMP!
TRIAGE-- ON YOUR RIGHT!
THEY'RE *FLANKING* US!
YOU GAVE US A GOOD CHASE, MAGNETO, BUT IT'S TIME TO STOP RUNNING.
MY FRIEND PSYNAPSE CAN'T READ YOUR MIND, BUT THE KID WAS *EASY* TO TRACK.
AND NOW-- *BANG...*
TH-THOOM! THOOM! THOOM!
"...YOU'RE *DEAD.*"
MAGNETO! ARE YOU--?
I'M FINE...
...JUST NEED...
...A MOMENT...
WE DON'T HAVE TIME!
WE'VE GOT TO MOVE--

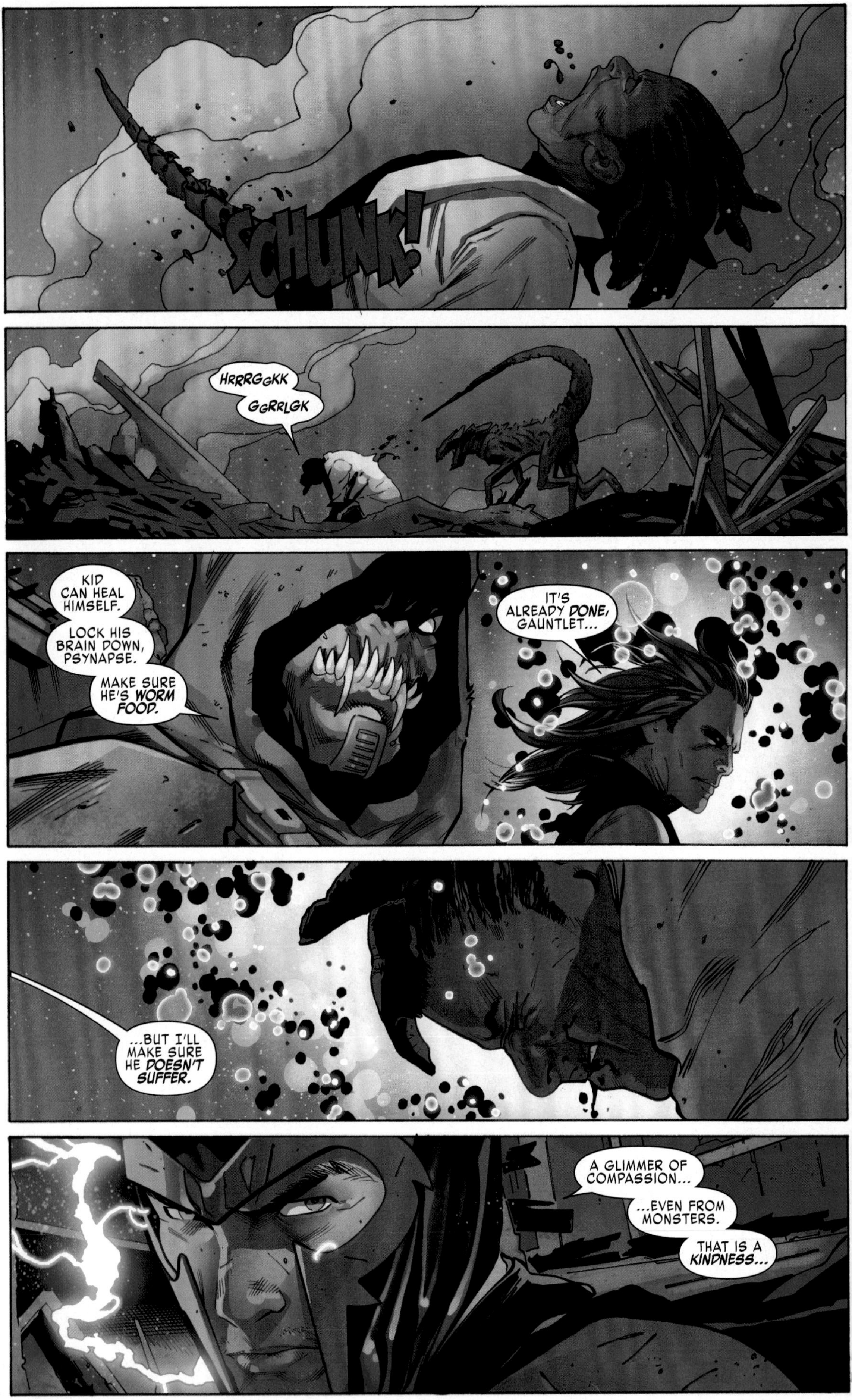
SCHUNK!
HRRRGGKK
GGRRLGK
KID CAN HEAL HIMSELF.
LOCK HIS BRAIN DOWN, PSYNAPSE.
MAKE SURE HE'S WORM FOOD.
IT'S ALREADY DONE, GAUNTLET...
...BUT I'LL MAKE SURE HE DOESN'T SUFFER.
A GLIMMER OF COMPASSION...
...EVEN FROM MONSTERS.
THAT IS A KINDNESS...

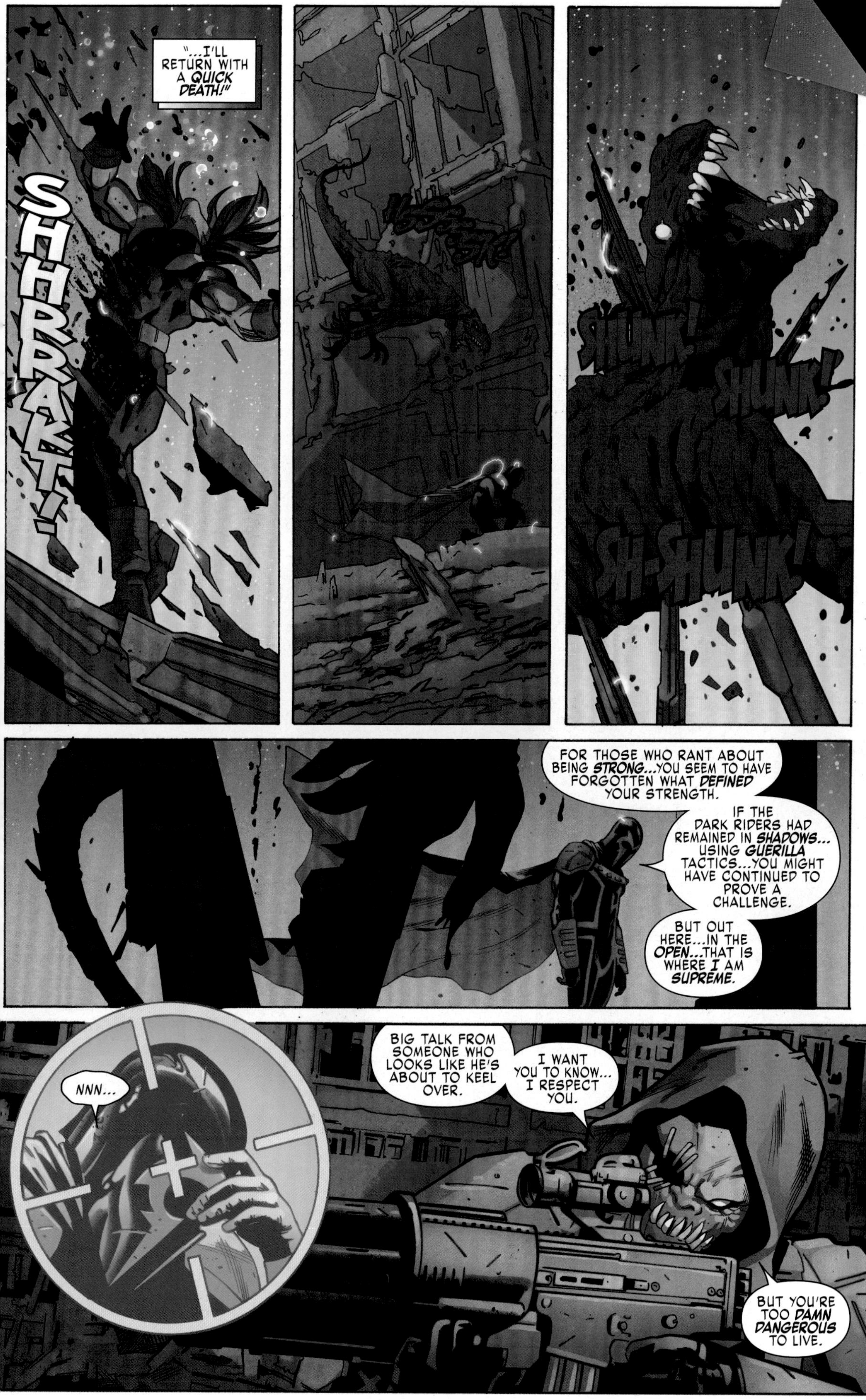

"...I'LL RETURN WITH A QUICK DEATH!"
SHHRAKT!
SHUNK!
SHUNK!
SH-SHUNK!
FOR THOSE WHO RANT ABOUT BEING STRONG...YOU SEEM TO HAVE FORGOTTEN WHAT DEFINED YOUR STRENGTH.
IF THE DARK RIDERS HAD REMAINED IN SHADOWS... USING GUERILLA TACTICS...YOU MIGHT HAVE CONTINUED TO PROVE A CHALLENGE.
BUT OUT HERE...IN THE OPEN...THAT IS WHERE I AM SUPREME.
NNN...
BIG TALK FROM SOMEONE WHO LOOKS LIKE HE'S ABOUT TO KEEL OVER.
I WANT YOU TO KNOW... I RESPECT YOU.
BUT YOU'RE TOO DAMN DANGEROUS TO LIVE.

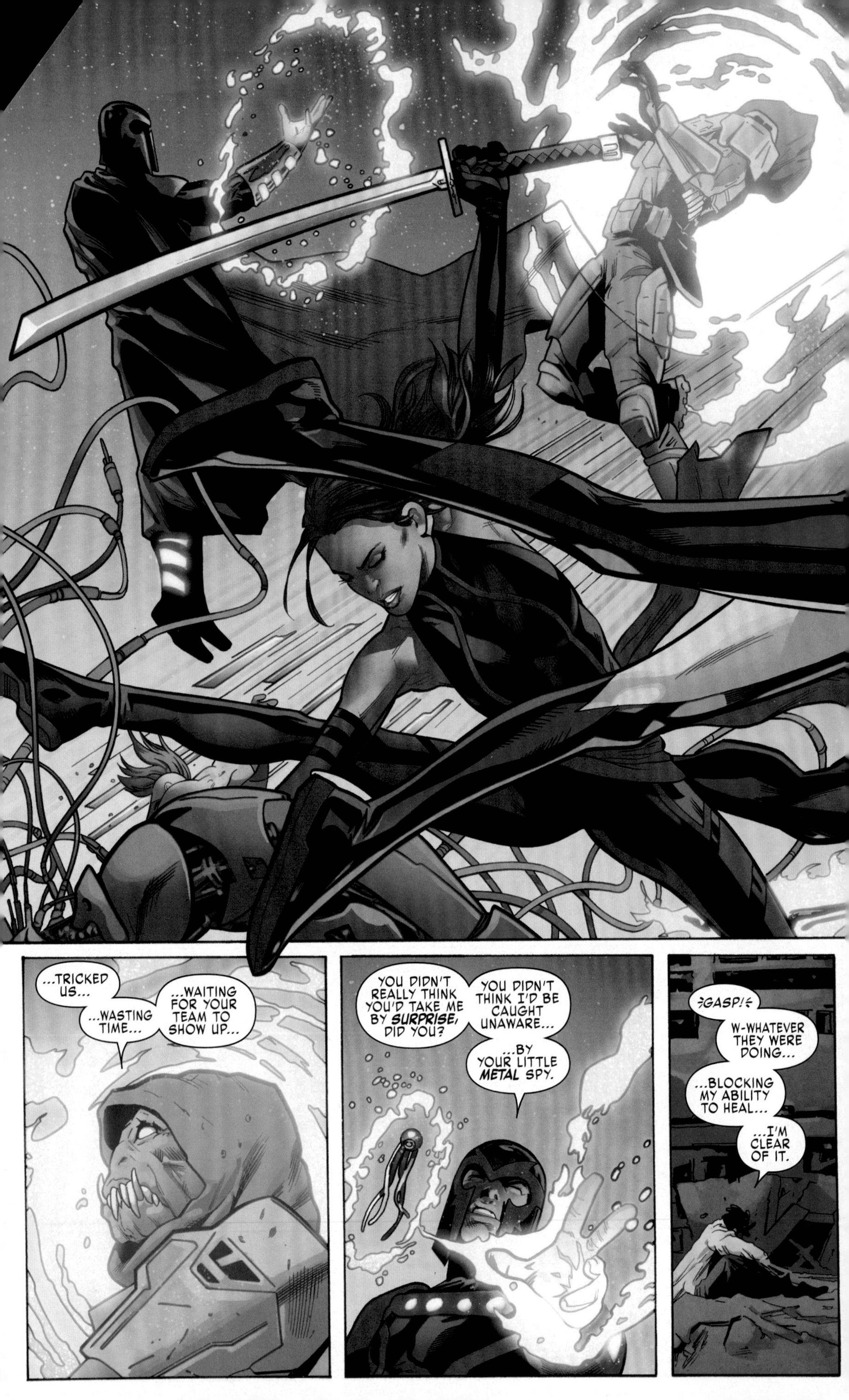

...TRICKED US...
...WASTING TIME...
...WAITING FOR YOUR TEAM TO SHOW UP...
YOU DIDN'T REALLY THINK YOU'D TAKE ME BY SURPRISE, DID YOU?
YOU DIDN'T THINK I'D BE CAUGHT UNAWARE...
...BY YOUR LITTLE METAL SPY.
GASP!
W-WHATEVER THEY WERE DOING...
...BLOCKING MY ABILITY TO HEAL...
...I'M CLEAR OF IT.

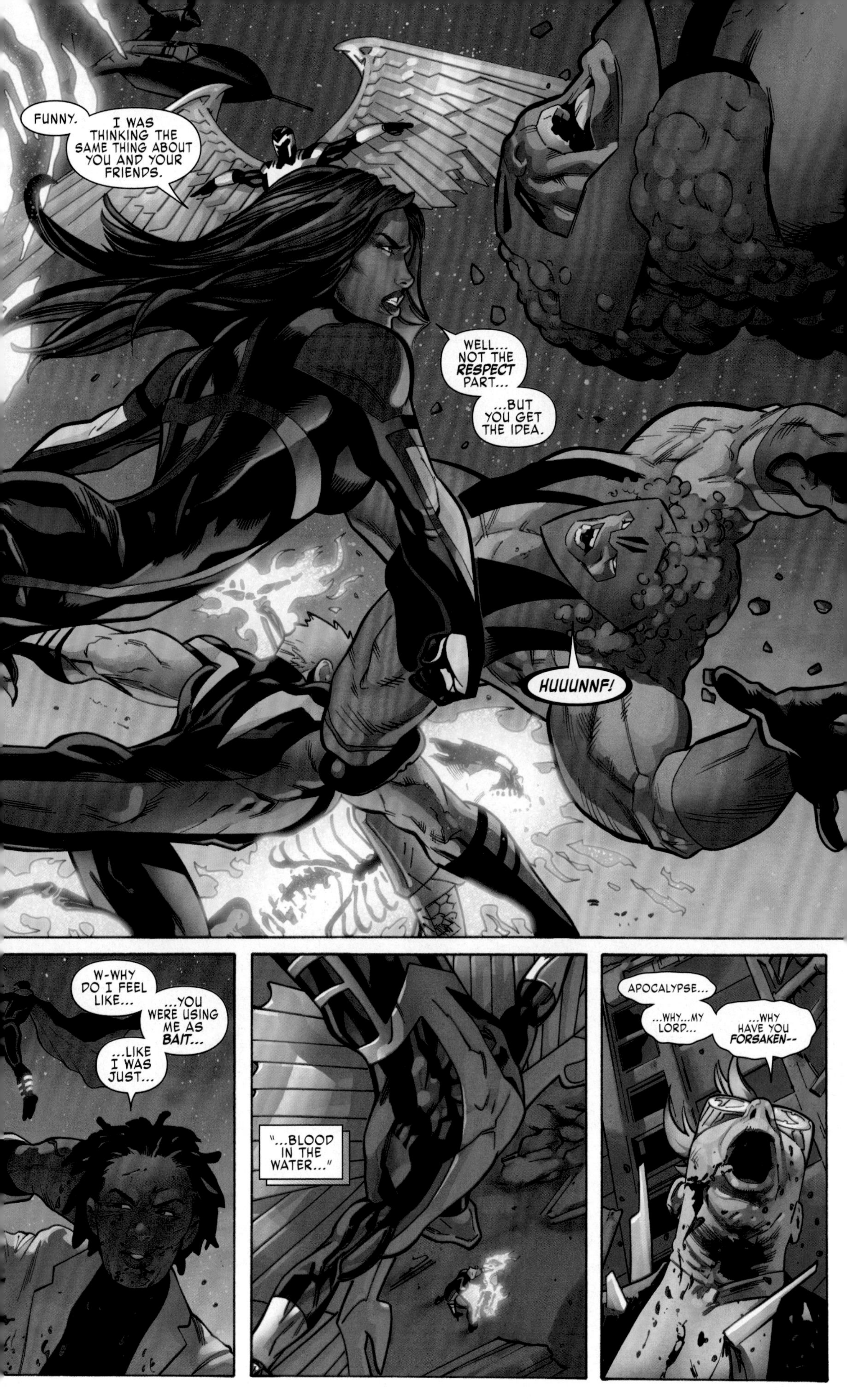
FUNNY.
I WAS THINKING THE SAME THING ABOUT YOU AND YOUR FRIENDS.
WELL... NOT THE RESPECT PART...
...BUT YOU GET THE IDEA.
HUUUNNF!
W-WHY DO I FEEL LIKE...
...YOU WERE USING ME AS BAIT...
...LIKE I WAS JUST...
"...BLOOD IN THE WATER..."
APOCALYPSE...
...WHY...MY LORD...
...WHY HAVE YOU FORSAKEN--

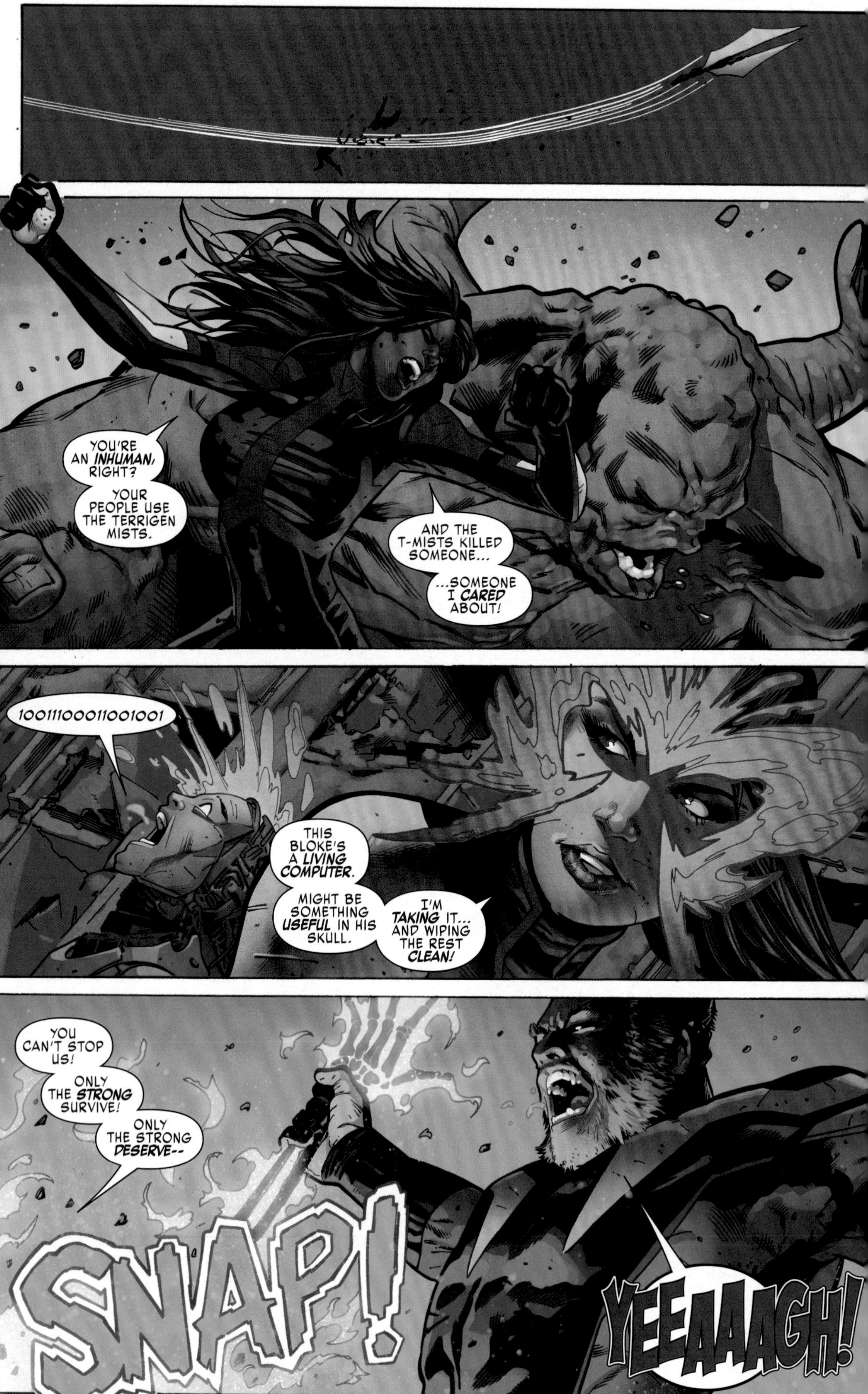
YOU'RE AN INHUMAN, RIGHT?
YOUR PEOPLE USE THE TERRIGEN MISTS.
AND THE T-MISTS KILLED SOMEONE...
...SOMEONE I CARED ABOUT!
1001110001100100l
THIS BLOKE'S A LIVING COMPUTER.
MIGHT BE SOMETHING USEFUL IN HIS SKULL.
I'M TAKING IT... AND WIPING THE REST CLEAN!
YOU CAN'T STOP US!
ONLY THE STRONG SURVIVE!
ONLY THE STRONG DESERVE--
SNAP!
YEEAAAGH!

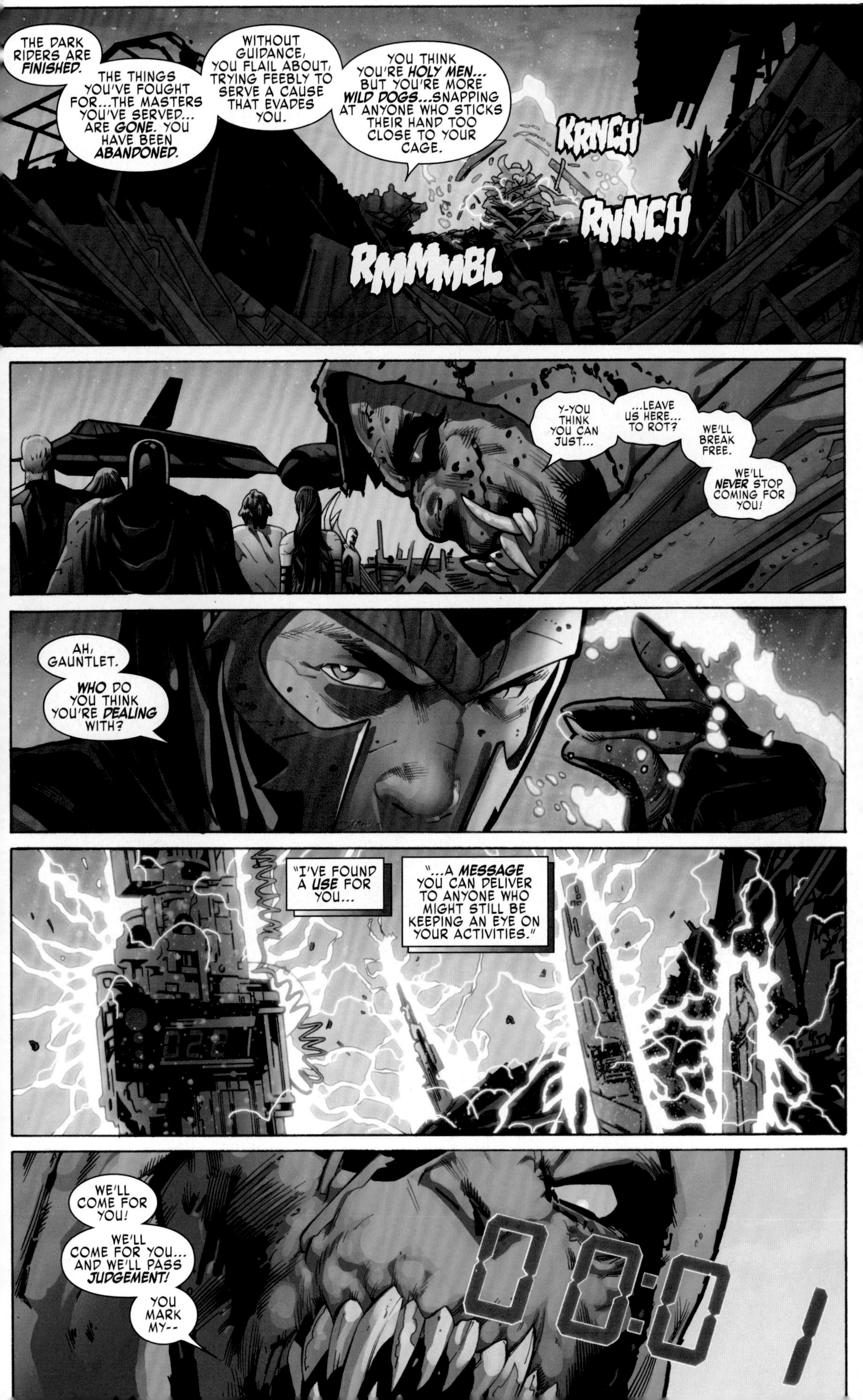
THE DARK RIDERS ARE *FINISHED*.
THE THINGS YOU'VE FOUGHT FOR...THE MASTERS YOU'VE SERVED... ARE *GONE*. YOU HAVE BEEN *ABANDONED*.
WITHOUT GUIDANCE, YOU FLAIL ABOUT, TRYING FEEBLY TO SERVE A CAUSE THAT EVADES YOU.
YOU THINK YOU'RE *HOLY MEN...* BUT YOU'RE MORE *WILD DOGS...*SNAPPING AT ANYONE WHO STICKS THEIR HAND TOO CLOSE TO YOUR CAGE.
KRNCH
RNNCH
RMMMBL
Y-YOU THINK YOU CAN JUST...
...LEAVE US HERE... TO ROT?
WE'LL BREAK FREE.
WE'LL *NEVER* STOP COMING FOR YOU!
AH, GAUNTLET.
WHO DO YOU THINK YOU'RE *DEALING* WITH?
"I'VE FOUND A *USE* FOR YOU...
"...A *MESSAGE* YOU CAN DELIVER TO ANYONE WHO MIGHT STILL BE KEEPING AN EYE ON YOUR ACTIVITIES."
WE'LL COME FOR YOU!
WE'LL COME FOR YOU... AND WE'LL PASS *JUDGEMENT!*
YOU MARK MY--
00:01

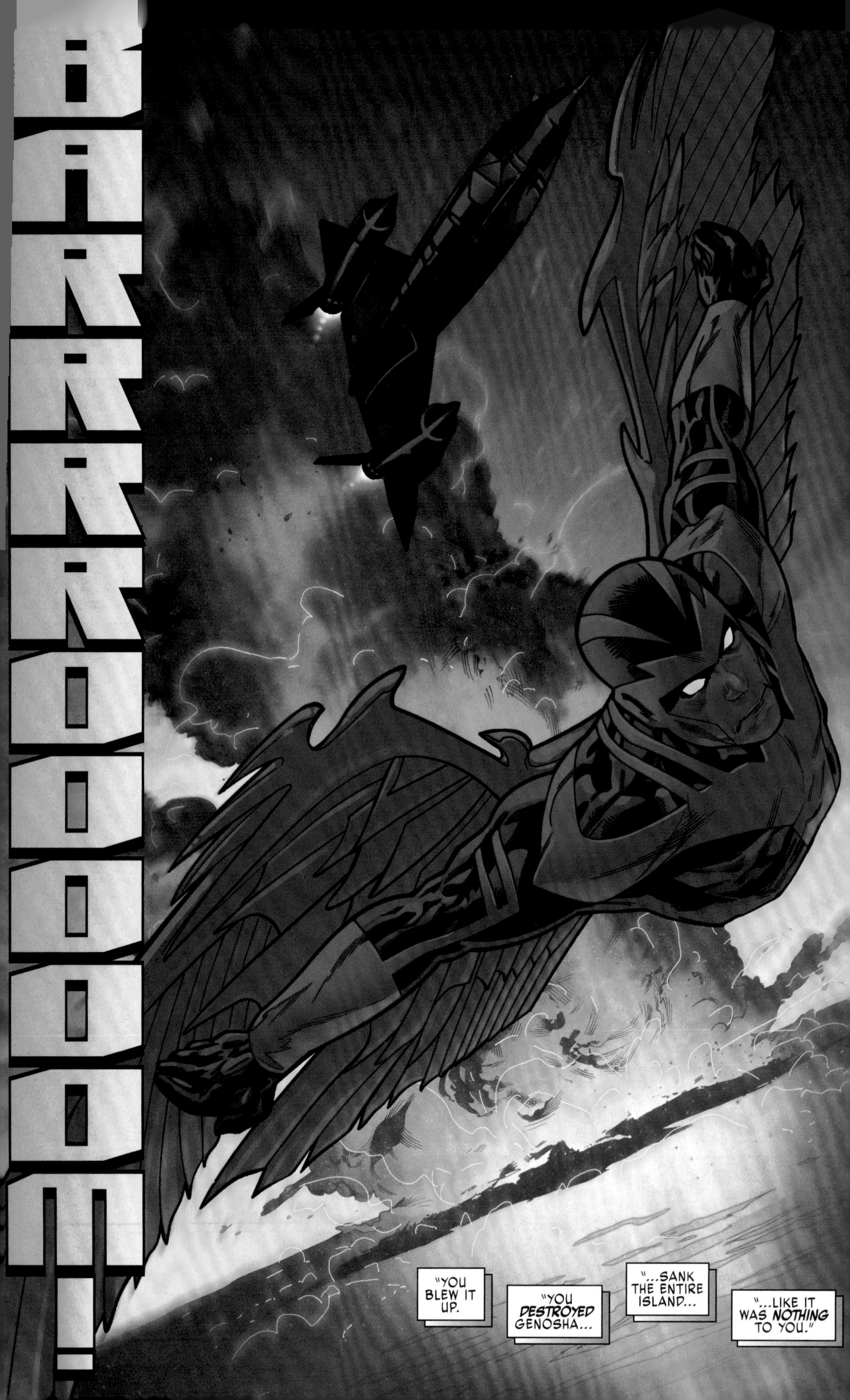
BARRROOOM!
"YOU BLEW IT UP.
"YOU *DESTROYED* GENOSHA...
"...SANK THE ENTIRE ISLAND...
"...LIKE IT WAS *NOTHING* TO YOU."

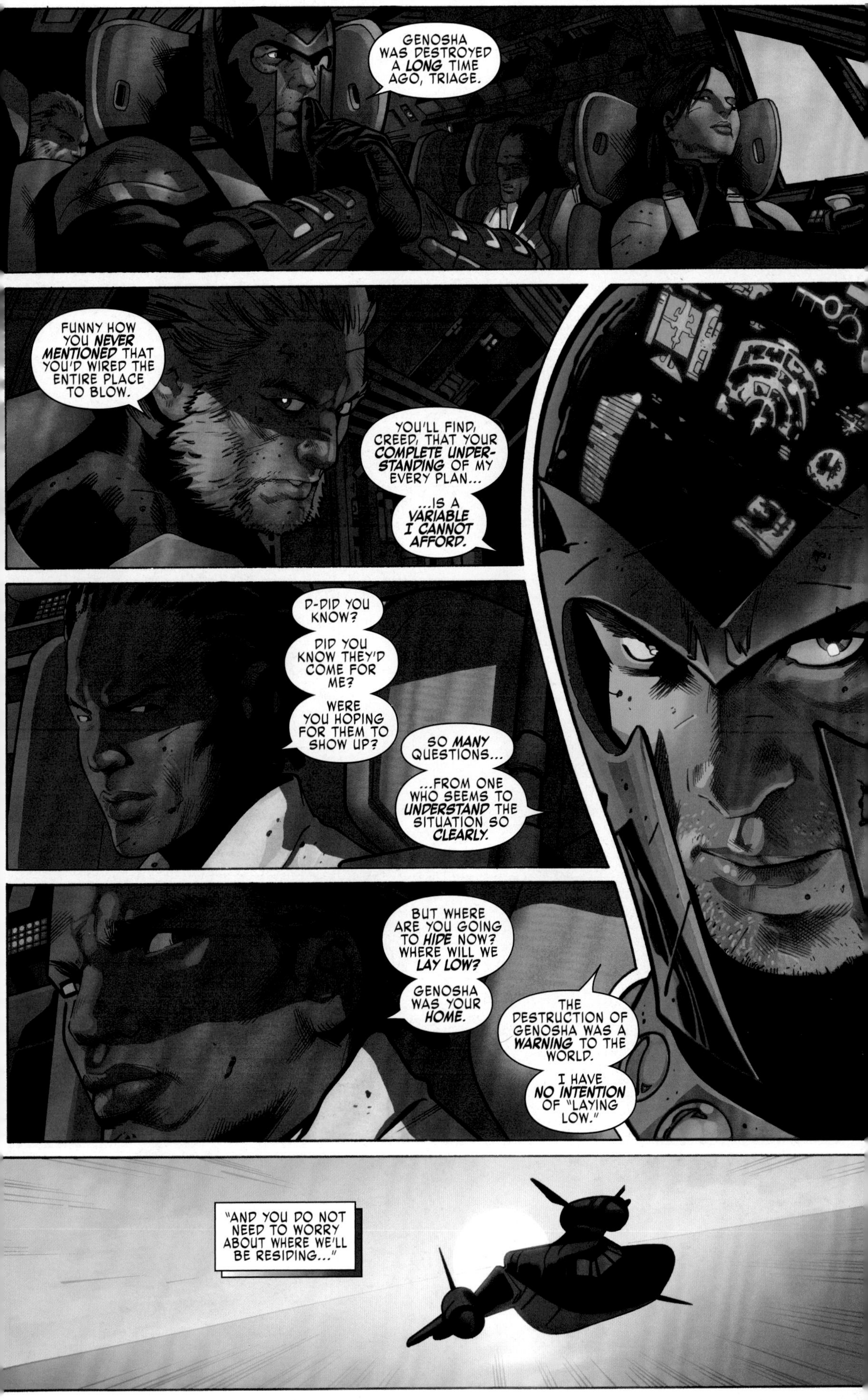
GENOSHA WAS DESTROYED A LONG TIME AGO, TRIAGE.
FUNNY HOW YOU NEVER MENTIONED THAT YOU'D WIRED THE ENTIRE PLACE TO BLOW.
YOU'LL FIND, CREED, THAT YOUR COMPLETE UNDER-STANDING OF MY EVERY PLAN...
...IS A VARIABLE I CANNOT AFFORD.
D-DID YOU KNOW?
DID YOU KNOW THEY'D COME FOR ME?
WERE YOU HOPING FOR THEM TO SHOW UP?
SO MANY QUESTIONS...
...FROM ONE WHO SEEMS TO UNDERSTAND THE SITUATION SO CLEARLY.
BUT WHERE ARE YOU GOING TO HIDE NOW? WHERE WILL WE LAY LOW?
GENOSHA WAS YOUR HOME.
THE DESTRUCTION OF GENOSHA WAS A WARNING TO THE WORLD.
I HAVE NO INTENTION OF "LAYING LOW."
"AND YOU DO NOT NEED TO WORRY ABOUT WHERE WE'LL BE RESIDING..."

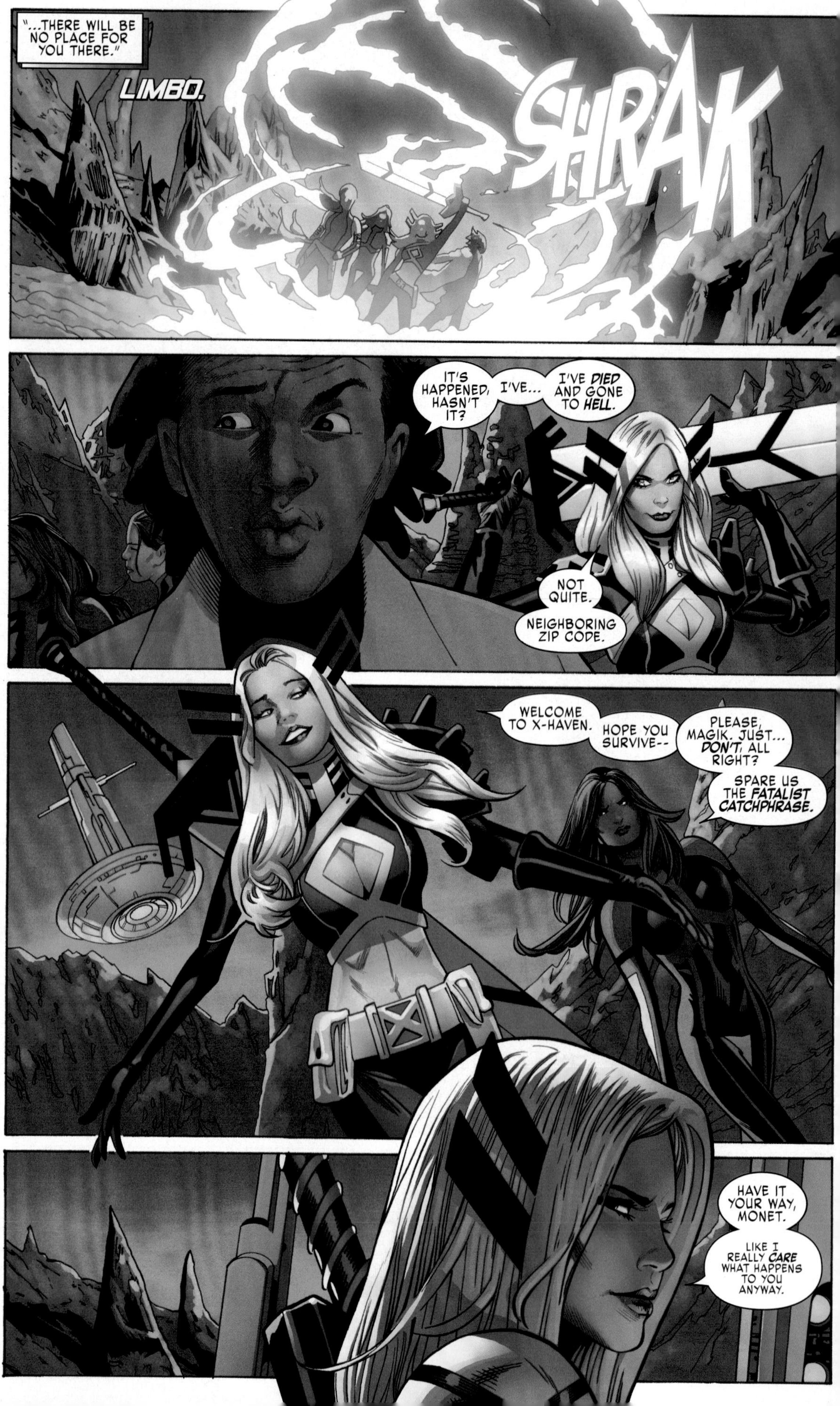
"...THERE WILL BE NO PLACE FOR YOU THERE."
LIMBO.
SHRAK
IT'S HAPPENED, HASN'T IT?
I'VE...
I'VE DIED AND GONE TO HELL.
NOT QUITE.
NEIGHBORING ZIP CODE.
WELCOME TO X-HAVEN.
HOPE YOU SURVIVE--
PLEASE, MAGIK. JUST... DON'T, ALL RIGHT?
SPARE US THE FATALIST CATCHPHRASE.
HAVE IT YOUR WAY, MONET.
LIKE I REALLY CARE WHAT HAPPENS TO YOU ANYWAY.

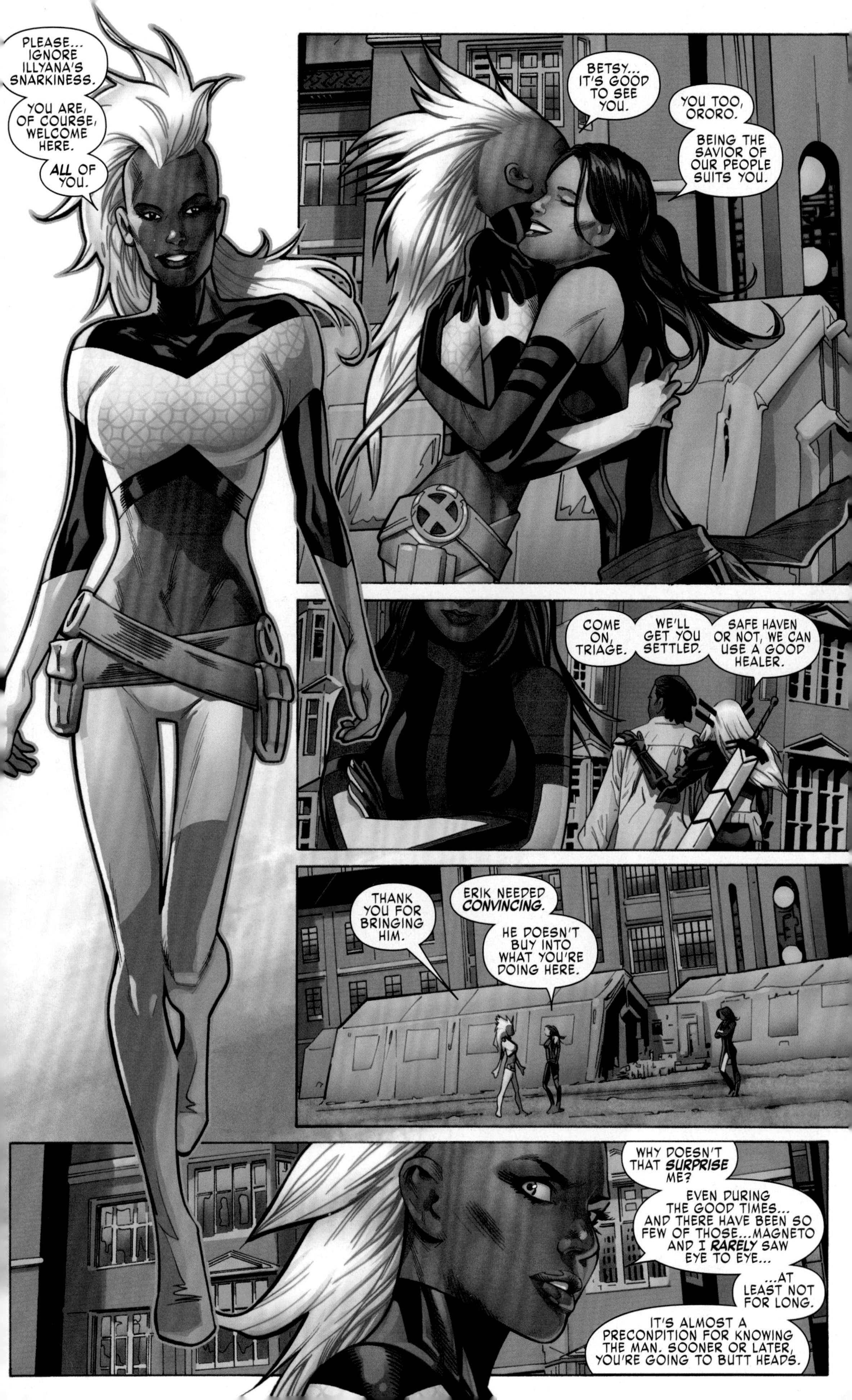
PLEASE... IGNORE ILLYANA'S SNARKINESS.
YOU ARE, OF COURSE, WELCOME HERE.
ALL OF YOU.
BETSY... IT'S GOOD TO SEE YOU.
YOU TOO, ORORO.
BEING THE SAVIOR OF OUR PEOPLE SUITS YOU.
COME ON, TRIAGE.
WE'LL GET YOU SETTLED.
SAFE HAVEN OR NOT, WE CAN USE A GOOD HEALER.
THANK YOU FOR BRINGING HIM.
ERIK NEEDED CONVINCING.
HE DOESN'T BUY INTO WHAT YOU'RE DOING HERE.
WHY DOESN'T THAT SURPRISE ME?
EVEN DURING THE GOOD TIMES... AND THERE HAVE BEEN SO FEW OF THOSE...MAGNETO AND I RARELY SAW EYE TO EYE...
...AT LEAST NOT FOR LONG.
IT'S ALMOST A PRECONDITION FOR KNOWING THE MAN. SOONER OR LATER, YOU'RE GOING TO BUTT HEADS.

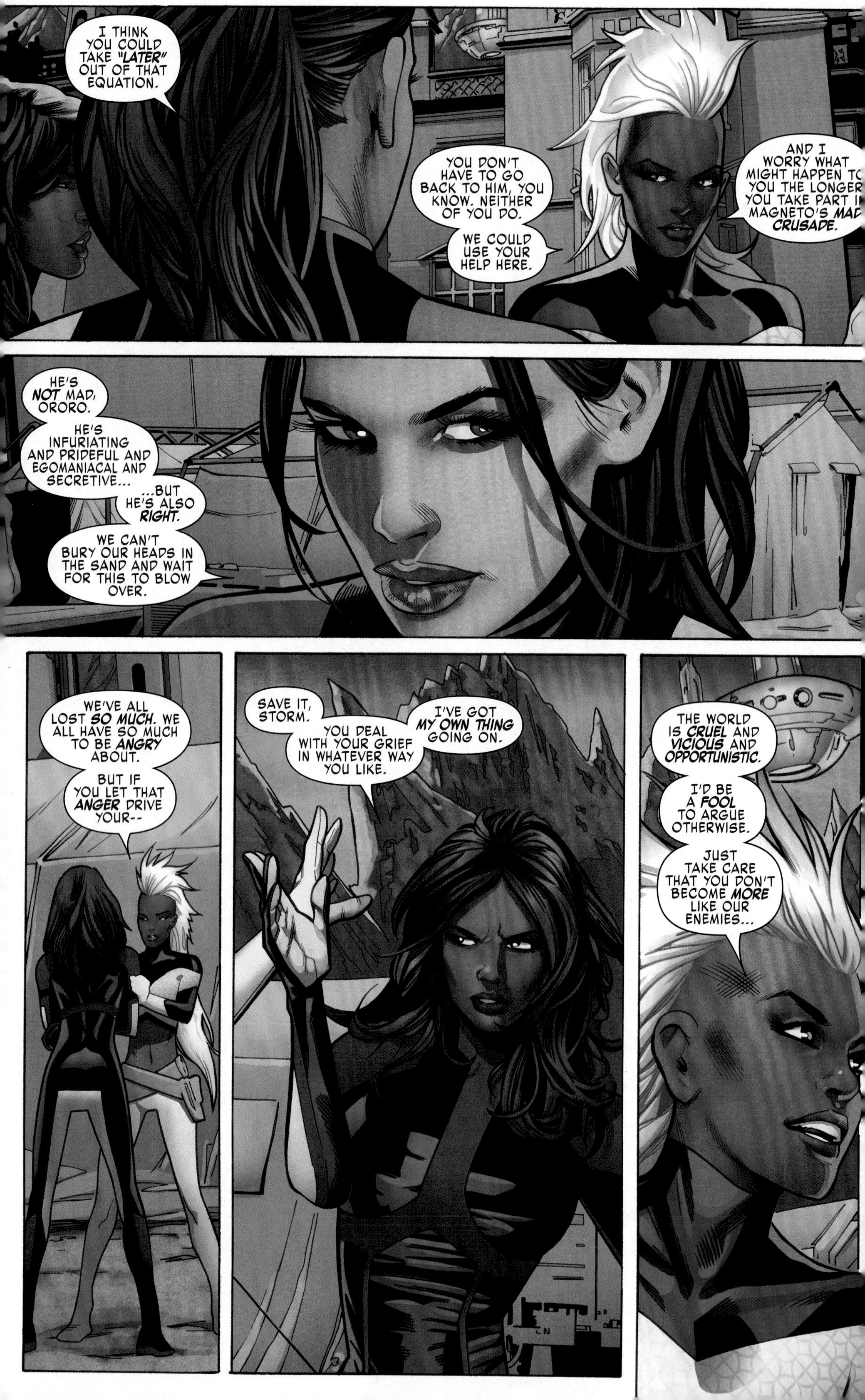
I THINK YOU COULD TAKE "LATER" OUT OF THAT EQUATION.
YOU DON'T HAVE TO GO BACK TO HIM, YOU KNOW. NEITHER OF YOU DO.
WE COULD USE YOUR HELP HERE.
AND I WORRY WHAT MIGHT HAPPEN TO YOU THE LONGER YOU TAKE PART IN MAGNETO'S MAD CRUSADE.
HE'S NOT MAD, ORORO.
HE'S INFURIATING AND PRIDEFUL AND EGOMANIACAL AND SECRETIVE...
...BUT HE'S ALSO RIGHT.
WE CAN'T BURY OUR HEADS IN THE SAND AND WAIT FOR THIS TO BLOW OVER.
WE'VE ALL LOST SO MUCH. WE ALL HAVE SO MUCH TO BE ANGRY ABOUT.
BUT IF YOU LET THAT ANGER DRIVE YOUR--
SAVE IT, STORM.
YOU DEAL WITH YOUR GRIEF IN WHATEVER WAY YOU LIKE.
I'VE GOT MY OWN THING GOING ON.
THE WORLD IS CRUEL AND VICIOUS AND OPPORTUNISTIC.
I'D BE A FOOL TO ARGUE OTHERWISE.
JUST TAKE CARE THAT YOU DON'T BECOME MORE LIKE OUR ENEMIES...

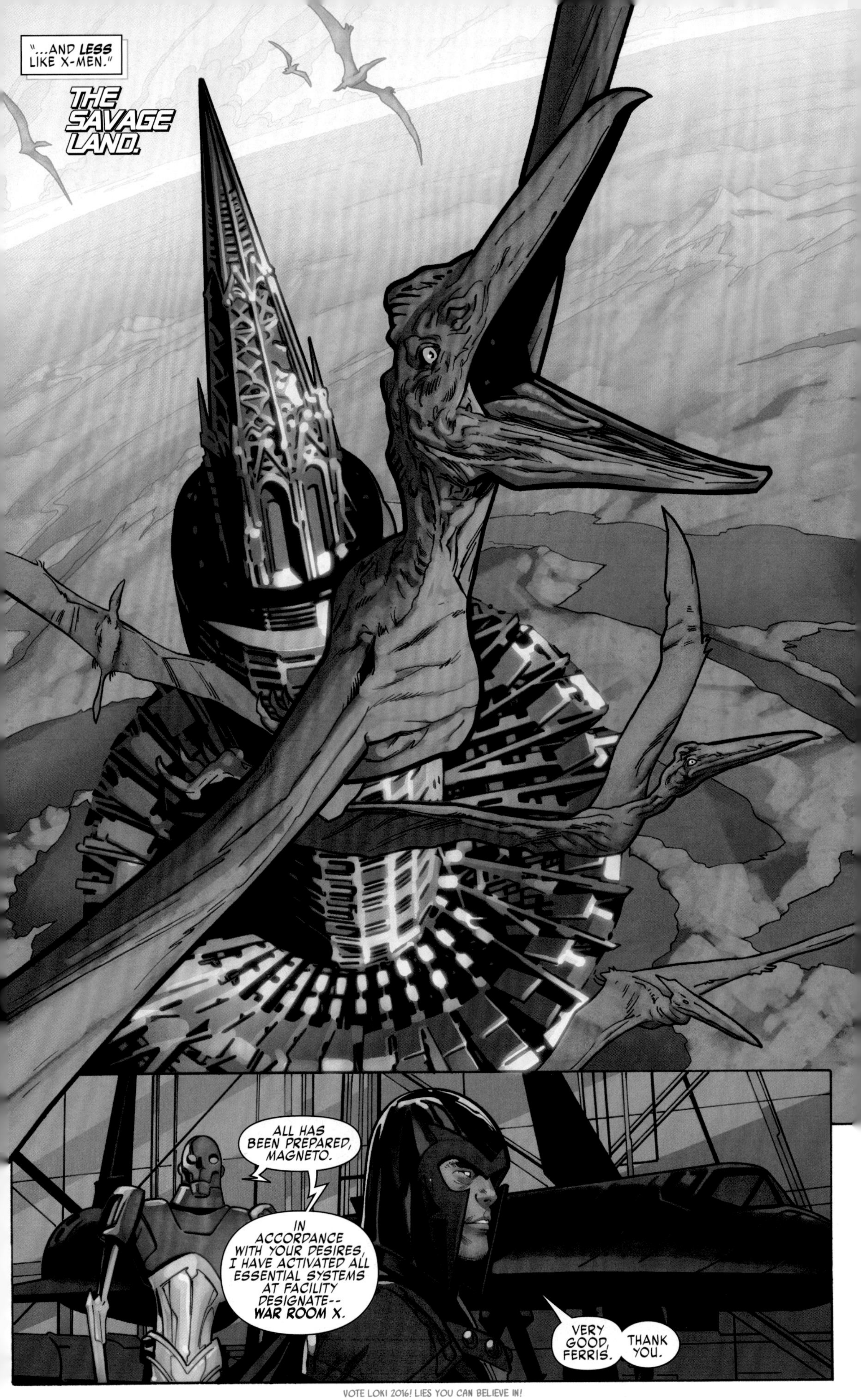
"...AND LESS LIKE X-MEN."
THE SAVAGE LAND.
ALL HAS BEEN PREPARED, MAGNETO.
IN ACCORDANCE WITH YOUR DESIRES, I HAVE ACTIVATED ALL ESSENTIAL SYSTEMS AT FACILITY DESIGNATE-- WAR ROOM X.
VERY GOOD, FERRIS.
THANK YOU.

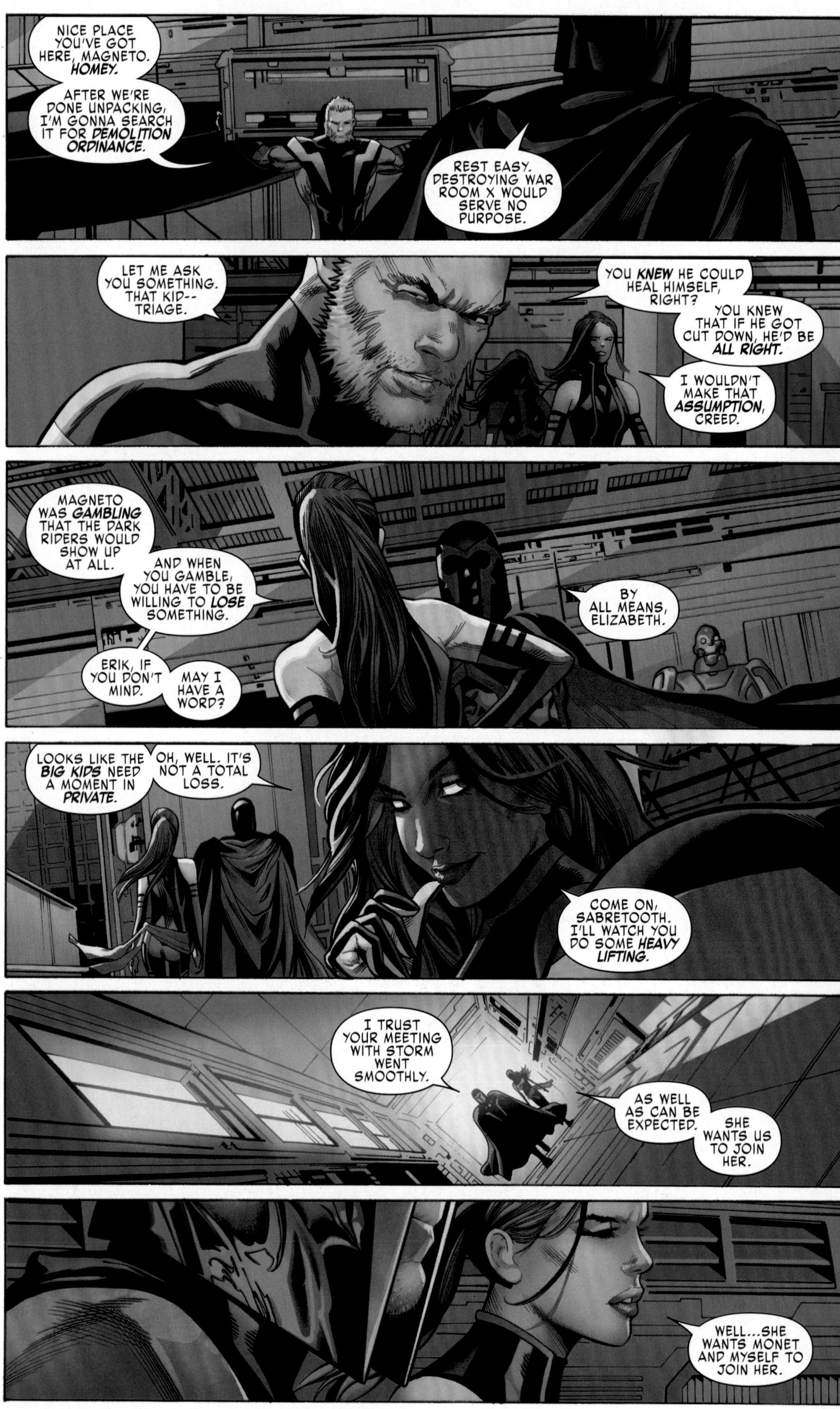
NICE PLACE YOU'VE GOT HERE, MAGNETO. HOMEY.
AFTER WE'RE DONE UNPACKING, I'M GONNA SEARCH IT FOR DEMOLITION ORDINANCE.
REST EASY. DESTROYING WAR ROOM X WOULD SERVE NO PURPOSE.
LET ME ASK YOU SOMETHING. THAT KID--TRIAGE.
YOU KNEW HE COULD HEAL HIMSELF, RIGHT?
YOU KNEW THAT IF HE GOT CUT DOWN, HE'D BE ALL RIGHT.
I WOULDN'T MAKE THAT ASSUMPTION, CREED.
MAGNETO WAS GAMBLING THAT THE DARK RIDERS WOULD SHOW UP AT ALL.
AND WHEN YOU GAMBLE, YOU HAVE TO BE WILLING TO LOSE SOMETHING.
ERIK, IF YOU DON'T MIND.
MAY I HAVE A WORD?
BY ALL MEANS, ELIZABETH.
LOOKS LIKE THE BIG KIDS NEED A MOMENT IN PRIVATE.
OH, WELL. IT'S NOT A TOTAL LOSS.
COME ON, SABRETOOTH. I'LL WATCH YOU DO SOME HEAVY LIFTING.
I TRUST YOUR MEETING WITH STORM WENT SMOOTHLY.
AS WELL AS CAN BE EXPECTED.
SHE WANTS US TO JOIN HER.
WELL...SHE WANTS MONET AND MYSELF TO JOIN HER.

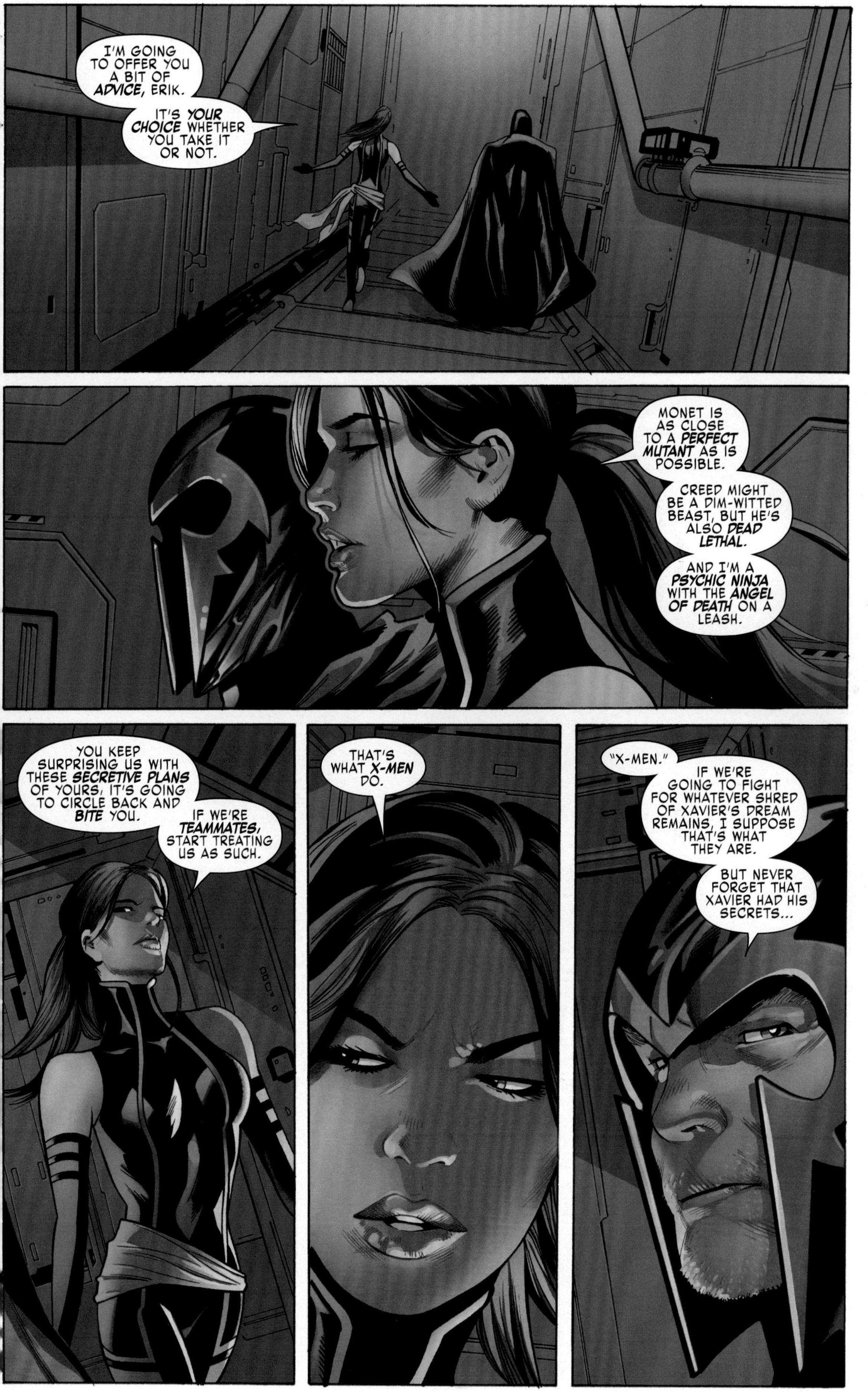

I'M GOING TO OFFER YOU A BIT OF ADVICE, ERIK.
IT'S YOUR CHOICE WHETHER YOU TAKE IT OR NOT.
MONET IS AS CLOSE TO A PERFECT MUTANT AS IS POSSIBLE.
CREED MIGHT BE A DIM-WITTED BEAST, BUT HE'S ALSO DEAD LETHAL.
AND I'M A PSYCHIC NINJA WITH THE ANGEL OF DEATH ON A LEASH.
YOU KEEP SURPRISING US WITH THESE SECRETIVE PLANS OF YOURS, IT'S GOING TO CIRCLE BACK AND BITE YOU.
IF WE'RE TEAMMATES, START TREATING US AS SUCH.
THAT'S WHAT X-MEN DO.
"X-MEN."
IF WE'RE GOING TO FIGHT FOR WHATEVER SHRED OF XAVIER'S DREAM REMAINS, I SUPPOSE THAT'S WHAT THEY ARE.
BUT NEVER FORGET THAT XAVIER HAD HIS SECRETS...

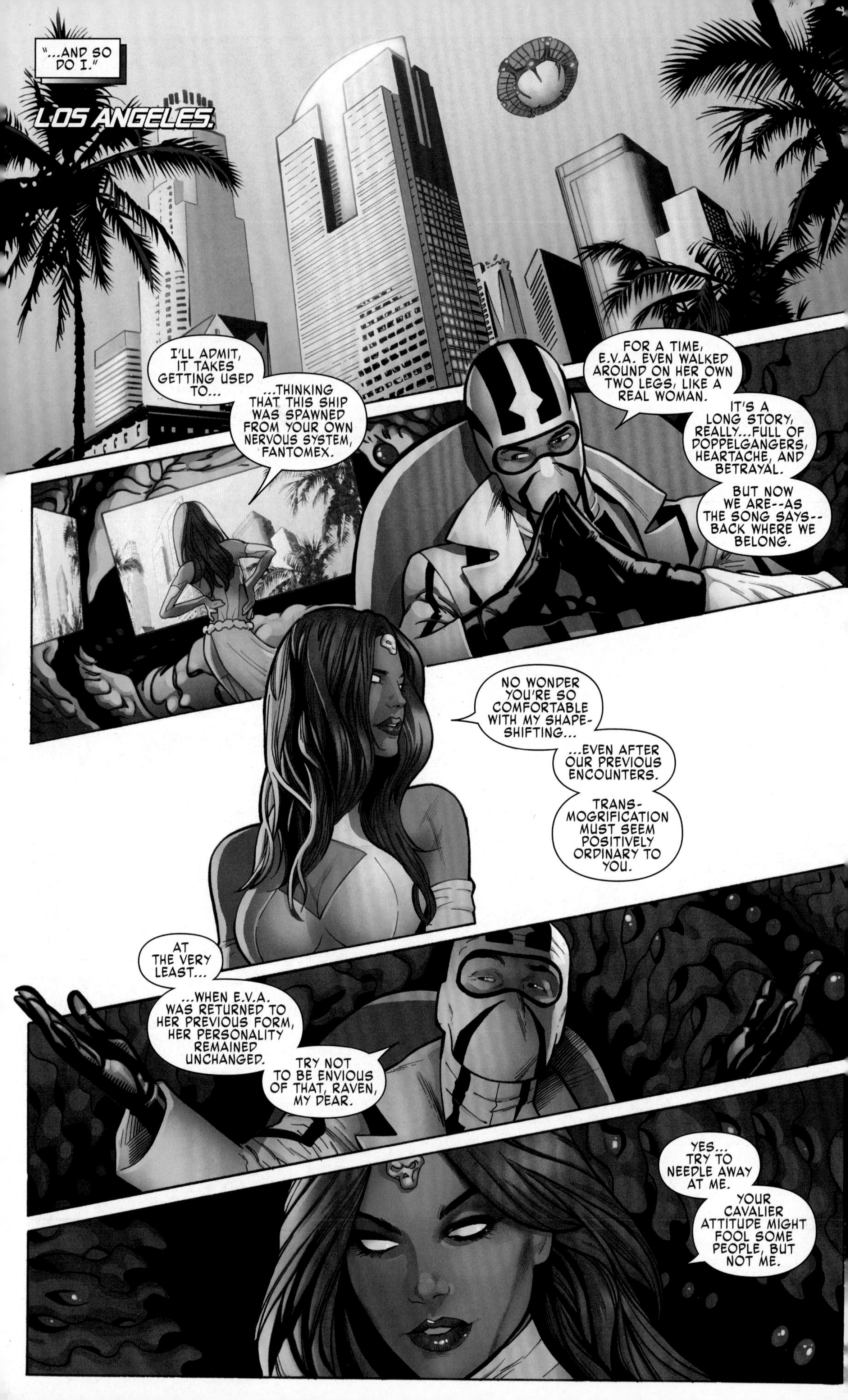
"...AND SO DO I."
LOS ANGELES.
I'LL ADMIT, IT TAKES GETTING USED TO...
...THINKING THAT THIS SHIP WAS SPAWNED FROM YOUR OWN NERVOUS SYSTEM, FANTOMEX.
FOR A TIME, E.V.A. EVEN WALKED AROUND ON HER OWN TWO LEGS, LIKE A REAL WOMAN.
IT'S A LONG STORY, REALLY...FULL OF DOPPELGANGERS, HEARTACHE, AND BETRAYAL.
BUT NOW WE ARE--AS THE SONG SAYS--BACK WHERE WE BELONG.
NO WONDER YOU'RE SO COMFORTABLE WITH MY SHAPE-SHIFTING...
...EVEN AFTER OUR PREVIOUS ENCOUNTERS.
TRANS-MOGRIFICATION MUST SEEM POSITIVELY ORDINARY TO YOU.
AT THE VERY LEAST...
...WHEN E.V.A. WAS RETURNED TO HER PREVIOUS FORM, HER PERSONALITY REMAINED UNCHANGED.
TRY NOT TO BE ENVIOUS OF THAT, RAVEN, MY DEAR.
YES... TRY TO NEEDLE AWAY AT ME.
YOUR CAVALIER ATTITUDE MIGHT FOOL SOME PEOPLE, BUT NOT ME.

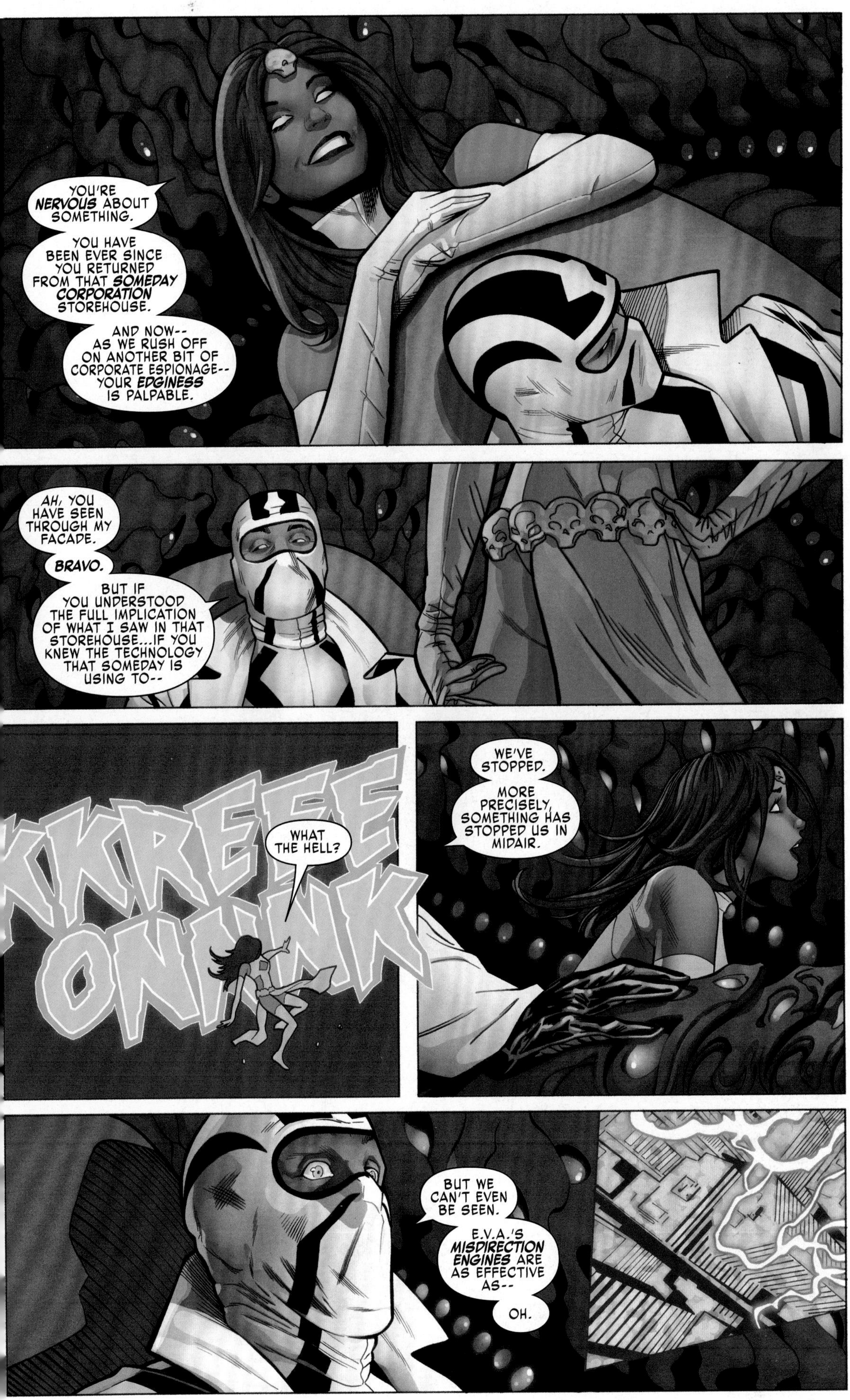
YOU'RE NERVOUS ABOUT SOMETHING.
YOU HAVE BEEN EVER SINCE YOU RETURNED FROM THAT SOMEDAY CORPORATION STOREHOUSE.
AND NOW-- AS WE RUSH OFF ON ANOTHER BIT OF CORPORATE ESPIONAGE-- YOUR EDGINESS IS PALPABLE.
AH, YOU HAVE SEEN THROUGH MY FACADE.
BRAVO.
BUT IF YOU UNDERSTOOD THE FULL IMPLICATION OF WHAT I SAW IN THAT STOREHOUSE...IF YOU KNEW THE TECHNOLOGY THAT SOMEDAY IS USING TO--
KREEE ONNNK
WHAT THE HELL?
WE'VE STOPPED.
MORE PRECISELY, SOMETHING HAS STOPPED US IN MIDAIR.
BUT WE CAN'T EVEN BE SEEN.
E.V.A.'S MISDIRECTION ENGINES ARE AS EFFECTIVE AS--
OH.

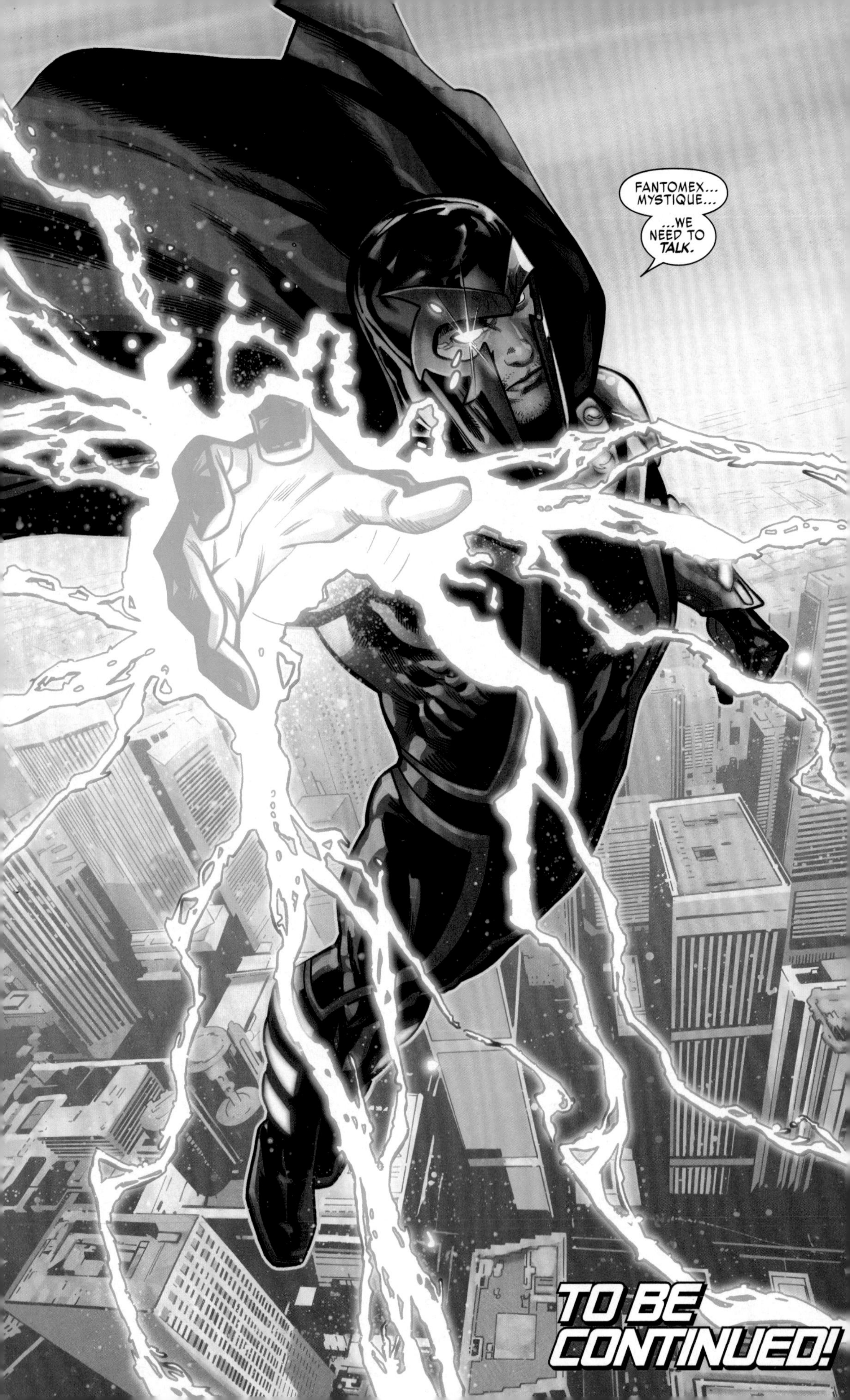
FANTOMEX... MYSTIQUE...
...WE NEED TO TALK.
TO BE CONTINUED!